MW00578424

INDIGO
BAR HARBOR

ACADIA NATIONAL PARK
THE COMPLETE GUIDE

7th Edition

ISBN: 978-1-940754-54-3

Written, Photographed & Illustrated
by James Kaiser

This book would not have been possible without the help of many generous people.

Special thanks to Christie Anastasia, Wanda Moran, Ginny Reams, Brooke Childrey, and the entire staff at Acadia National Park, professors Bill Carpenter and Helen Hess at COA, Mindy Viechnicki at Allied Whale, Rebecca Cole-Will at the Abbe Museum, and Erika Latty at Unity College. Special thanks also to Andrea Rincon, Rick Crowe, Whitney Crowe, Kevin Crowe, every other Crowe, Steve Foley, Cathy McDonald, Dan Shubert, Scott Petticord, Abby Johnston, Matt Tracy, Alyssa and Seth, Josia and Maria, and Lacey Sinclair. And a very special thanks to my family & friends, who have always supported me—even when they shouldn't have.

All information in this guide has been exhaustively researched, but names, phone numbers, and other details do change. If you encounter a change or mistake while using this guide, please send an email to changes@jameskaiser.com. Your input will help improve future editions of this guide. Special thanks to eagle-eyed readers Joseph Snider, Mark Goldstein, Pat Bonnell, Mary Katheryne Zagora, Beth Turney, Thomas Davie, Mel Coker, and Daniel Willeford who found typos/errors in past editions!

Printed in Malaysia

ACADIA NATIONAL PARK

THE COMPLETE GUIDE

7th Edition

Bestselling Acadia Guidebook

2003-2022

A portion of this book's profits will be donated to Friends of Acadia, the nonprofit partner of Acadia National Park. Learn more about Friends of Acadia at

friendsofacadia.org

JAMES KAISER

CONGRATULATIONS!

IF YOU'VE PURCHASED this book, you're going to Acadia National Park and Mount Desert Island. Perhaps you're already here. If so, you're in one of America's most remarkable places—a stunning island where glacially sculpted mountains tower above the sea. An island so beautiful nearly half of it has been permanently protected as a national park. A place where you can hike in the morning, go sea kayaking in the afternoon, and sit down to a gourmet meal at night.

So who am I and why should you listen to me? My name is James Kaiser, and I was born and raised near Mount Desert Island. I spent my childhood summers hiking and biking in Acadia and my college summers working in Bar Harbor. Although my work as a travel writer has carried me away from home, I return as often as possible. It's my favorite place in the world. I know the park, I know the towns, I know the locals—I know the secrets! And I'm going to share my decades of experience with you.

You could easily spend a month exploring Mount Desert Island and not run out of things to do. But if you're like most people, you've only got a few days. Make those few days count! With a limited amount of time, you've got to plan your trip wisely. This book puts the best of Mount Desert Island and Acadia National Park at your fingertips, helping you maximize your time for an unforgettable vacation. Whether you're here to hike, here to sight-see, or just here to eat and hang out, *Acadia: The Complete Guide* is the only guide you'll need.

Now let me show you the best of Mount Desert Island and Acadia National Park!

CONTENTS

Acadia National Park p.129

Nearly half of Mount Desert Island has been protected as Acadia National Park. The Park Loop Road twists through the heart of Acadia, passing world-class hiking trails and carriage roads. Acadia also includes Schoodic Peninsula on the mainland and half of Isle au Haut, a small, rugged island 15 miles southwest.

Island Towns p.207

From tourist towns to fishing villages, there's something for everyone on Mount Desert Island. The island's eastern side is home to Bar Harbor, the island's unofficial capital, and the exclusive summer colonies of Northeast Harbor and Seal Harbor. The island's western side, home to Southwest Harbor and Bass Harbor, is more traditional and easy-going.

Offshore Islands p.283

Over a dozen small islands lie offshore Mount Desert Island, several of which are accessible by ferry. Day tripping to small islands is a great adventure. Physically separated from the mainland, these islands are home to some of the most rugged and remote communities in America.

ACADIA TOP 5

TOP 5 SIGHTS

Cadillac Mountain, 172
Bass Harbor Lighthouse, 260
Jordan Pond House, 160
Sand Beach, 146
Bar Island, 214

TOP 5 ADVENTURES

Hiking, 15
Biking, 19
Sea Kayaking, 17
Rock Climbing, 21
Scenic Flights, 219

TOP 5 HIKES

The Precipice, 178
Beehive, 176
Penobscot Mountain, 186
Acadia Mountain, 190
Sargent Mountain, 188

TOP 5 PLACES TO SWIM

Echo Lake Beach, 251
Echo Lake Ledges, 251
Long Pond, 247
Seal Harbor Beach, 227
Sand Beach, 146

TOP 5 RESTAURANTS

Burning Tree, 221
Red Sky, 253
Salt and Steel, 221
Cafe This Way, 221
XYZ, 253

TOP 5 PLACES FOR LOBSTER

Thurston's, 259
Beal's, 253
Trenton Bridge, 209
C-Ray, 209
Islesford Dock, 286

TOP 5 BOAT TRIPS

Diver Ed, 24
Bar Harbor Whale Watch, 24
R.L. Gott, 25
Acadia Lobster Cruise, 25
Alice E., 25

TOP 5 RAINY DAY ACTIVITIES

Mount Desert Oceanarium, 207
Abbe Museum, 217
Dorr Museum, 217
Criterion Theater, 220
Reel Pizza, 220

INTRODUCTION

TWO-THIRDS OF the way up the craggy coast of Maine lies Mount Desert Island, home to granite mountains, picture-perfect harbors, and Acadia National Park. Mount Desert Island is the crown jewel of coastal New England—the only place on the East Coast where mountains meet the sea. Those mountains, rounded and smoothed by Ice Age glaciers, form one of the most distinctive profiles in the world. From sea they look like a string of giant ice cream scoops rising out of the water. Cadillac Mountain, the island's tallest peak, is 1,530 feet above sea level—the highest point on the Eastern Seaboard.

Nestled between the island's two dozen peaks are forests, lakes, meadows, marshes, and Somes Sound, a narrow inlet that nearly slices the island in two. Roughly half of Mount Desert Island is protected as Acadia National Park. At just 46,000 acres, Acadia is one of America's smallest national parks, but it's also one of the most popular, luring four million visitors a year. Acadia's most famous attraction is the 27-mile Park Loop Road, which runs along the island's rugged eastern shore before turning into the forest, passing two pristine lakes, and twisting to the top of Cadillac Mountain.

Acadia also boasts 125 miles of fabulous hiking trails and 45 miles of carriage roads for biking or horseback riding. In addition to land on Mount Desert Island, the park also includes Schoodic Peninsula on the mainland and half of Isle au Haut, a remote island 14 miles southwest of Mount Desert Island.

Half a dozen towns dot the shores of Mount Desert Island. Some, like Bar Harbor, revolve around tourism. Others, like Bass Harbor, carry on as quiet fishing villages, much as they always have. There are also wealthy summer towns like Seal Harbor and Northeast Harbor, and historic villages like Somesville, the island's oldest town. Several offshore islands are accessible by ferry, making them great for day tripping.

For thousands of years, Mount Desert Island was the seasonal home of Wabanaki tribes. European settlers arrived in the late 1700s, followed by artists and tourists in the mid-1800s. Within a few decades, Bar Harbor had become one of America's most exclusive summer resorts. By the 1930s, however, the island's glamour had faded, and in 1947 a massive fire burned many of Bar Harbor's once-grand mansions. Following the fire, the island rebuilt and reestablished itself as a major tourist destination.

Physically beautiful, ecologically diverse, culturally unique—Mount Desert Island and Acadia National Park are among America's most fascinating places.

Penobscot Mountain

HIKING

ACADIA NATIONAL PARK is a hiking paradise. There are roughly 125 miles of trails, ranging from gentle strolls to sheer ascents up nearly vertical cliffs. Hikers can summit over a dozen magnificent peaks, enjoying the most dramatic scenery on the Eastern Seaboard.

If Acadia's trails were nothing but dirt paths, they'd still be amazing. But here on Mount Desert Island—home to wealthy, civic-minded summer residents—the hiking trails have been spiffed up beyond belief. Many feature exquisitely crafted stone steps guiding hikers up steep terrain. Nearly all trails are well marked and easy to follow, with blue blazes and historic Bates cairns pointing the way. This is rich man's hiking, open to the public. If you visit Acadia without going on at least one hike, you should return to the mainland ashamed.

Acadia National Park rates hikes as Easy, Moderate, Strenuous, or Ladder. ("Ladder" means strenuous with some climbing on iron ladders or rungs). This book provides maps and trail info for ten terrific hikes (p.176). My favorite summit hikes are The Precipice (p.178), Penobscot Mtn. (p.186), Pemetic Mtn. (p.184), and Acadia Mtn. (p.190). My favorite easy hikes are the Ocean Trail (p.146), Cadillac Mountain Summit (p.172), Jordan Pond east shore (p.160), and Ship Harbor (p.259). If your thirst for hiking exceeds that of the average visitor, pick up a copy of Tom St. Germain's *A Walk In The Park*.

Hikers can take advantage of the free Island Explorer Shuttle (p.30), which removes parking hassles and opens up fabulous hiking possibilities. In the pre-Island Explorer days, hikers had to loop back to wherever they parked. Now you can start at one trailhead, finish someplace different, and ride the Island Explorer back, taking full advantage of Acadia's extensive trail network.

Note: overnight backpacking is not allowed in Acadia National Park. Bicycles and horses are not allowed on any hiking trails, and dogs must be kept on a leash no greater than six feet in length at all times.

Bates Cairns

Many of Acadia's trails are marked by distinctive rock piles called Bates cairns, named for Waldron Bates, who mapped Acadia's trails in the late 1800s. Bates cairns are unique to Acadia. Two base stones support a lintel (platform) topped by a pointer rock that indicates the trail's direction. Please respect these historic markers by not tampering with them in any way.

Porcupine Islands

SEA KAYAKING

THE COAST OF Maine is famous for sea kayaking, and everything that sea kayakers love about Maine—beautiful islands, calm bays, pristine water, abundant wildlife—are found near Mount Desert Island. Not surprisingly, sea kayaking is one of Acadia's top adventures.

The most popular paddles are Frenchman Bay (just offshore Bar Harbor), western Mount Desert Island (calm water, great wildlife, beautiful sunsets), and Somes Sound (a dramatic fjard nestled between mountains).

Be aware that Maine sea kayaking presents unique challenges. Frigid water, craggy shorelines, lobster boats, dense fog, unpredictable weather, 12-foot tides, and swift currents are just some of the hazards you might encounter. With a trained guide, you're in good hands. Without a trained guide, you can get in trouble fast. If you're new to paddling, don't go it alone.

Some of Maine's best sea kayaking guides work on Mount Desert Island, so everyone—even beginners—can get out on the water. The following outfitters are highly recommended.

COASTAL KAYAKING TOURS

This Bar Harbor outfit specializes in tours of Frenchman Bay, including the gorgeous Porcupine Islands. Half- and full-day tours are offered, plus sunset paddles, family tours, and multi-day island camping trips. (Bar Harbor, 207-288-9605, acadiafun.com)

NATIONAL PARK SEA KAYAKING

Although based in Bar Harbor, National Park Sea Kayaking specializes in paddles on the western shores of Mount Desert Island, which is quieter and less developed than Frenchman Bay. Half-day tours and sunset paddles. (Bar Harbor, 207-288-0342, acadiakayak.com)

MAINE STATE SEA KAYAK

Based in Southwest Harbor, Maine State Sea Kayak offers tours on western Mount Desert Island, plus Somes Sound and the Cranberry Islands. Half-day tours and sunset paddles. (Southwest Harbor, 207-244-9500, mainestateseakayak.com)

Carriage Roads

BIKING

ACADIA BOASTS ONE of the most genteel biking experiences in any national park: a 45-mile network of meticulously landscaped carriage roads. Originally designed for horse-drawn carriages, these broken-stone roads were built by John D. Rockefeller Jr. on his private estate. Rockefeller later donated his beloved carriage roads to the park, and today bicyclists, horse-drawn carriage riders, and horseback riders all enjoy these exquisite roads.

The carriage road system, which stretches from Bar Harbor to Seal Harbor, explores the heart of Acadia National Park. You'll pass pristine lakes and ponds, meander through beautiful forests, and cross dramatic stone bridges. At times, riding the carriage roads feels like entering a fairy tale. In autumn, when fiery foliage lights up the trees, there's arguably no better way to enjoy the park. Biking the carriage roads is one of Acadia's top experiences.

Most carriage roads follow a gentle grade, but there are a few hilly sections that offer good workouts. The best places to enter the carriage roads near Bar Harbor are Eagle Lake and Duck Brook Bridge. The Island Explorer's free Bicycle Express shuttle runs between the Bar Harbor Village Green and Eagle Lake. Farther south, you can enter the carriage roads at Bubble Pond, Jordan Pond House, Brown Mountain Gatehouse, or Parkman Mountain Parking Area. For detailed information about Acadia's carriage roads, see page 197.

Acadia does not allow off-road biking or biking on any hiking trail. There are some spectacular paved roads open to bikes, most notably the Park Loop Road and Cadillac Summit Road. But these popular roads are often congested. Another, less crowded option is Sargent Drive (p.237), which passes along the beautiful eastern shore of Somes Sound. The island's least congested paved roads are found on western Mount Desert Island, particularly Route 102A and Route 102 between Bass Harbor and Pretty Marsh.

There are also some great biking destinations beyond Mount Desert Island. The six-mile Schoodic Loop Road (p.263) offers beautiful coastal scenery with significantly less traffic than the Park Loop Road. Another interesting option is Swan's Island (p.295), a 7,000-acre island accessible by ferry from Bass Harbor. Swan's Island has over a dozen miles of paved roads that pass working harbors and quaint fishing villages—with virtually no traffic.

Wherever you choose to explore, bicycle rentals are available in Bar Harbor (p.219), Seal Harbor (p.227), and Southwest Harbor (p.252).

Otter Cliffs

ROCK CLIMBING

ACADIA'S BOLD MOUNTAINS and stunning coastal scenery make it one of the East Coast's most spectacular rock climbing destinations. There are plenty of great climbs from Georgia to Maine, but only in Acadia can you scale cliffs directly above the Atlantic Ocean. Spend an afternoon climbing above crashing waves while lobster boats motor past offshore, and you'll understand why so many rock climbers dream about visiting Acadia.

If you've never gone rock climbing before, Acadia National Park is a great place to learn. There are plenty of great beginner routes, and two Bar Harbor climbing schools offer private lessons and guided climbs. One-on-one lessons run about $175 half-day, $300 full-day. Group rates are much cheaper. Experienced rock climbers should pick up a copy of *Acadia: A Climber's Guide* by Jeff Butterfield or *Rock Climbs of Acadia* by Grant Simmons.

Acadia's most popular rock climbing destination is Otter Cliffs (p.152). Rising straight out of the ocean, these vertical cliffs offer stunning views along the Park Loop Road. Otter Cliffs is often crowded, but there are plenty of other, less famous climbs with stunning views. South Wall, a multi-pitch route on Champlain Mountain, rises hundreds of feet above Frenchman Bay. There are also terrific climbs on Great Head, near Sand Beach, and South Bubble, which rises above the northern end of Jordan Pond.

Rock Climbing Outfitters

ACADIA MOUNTAIN GUIDES

Based out of Alpenglow Adventure Sports in Bar Harbor, AMG offers everything from beginner to expert classes—even winter ice climbing! (207-288-8186, acadiamountainguides.com)

ATLANTIC CLIMBING SCHOOL

Atlantic Climbing School offers a full range of guided climbs, including specialty introductory classes for women and families. (207-288-2521, climbacadia.com)

Sailing on the *Alice*. E

SAILING & BOAT TOURS

THE ISLAND-STREWN coast of Maine is one of America's premier boating destinations, and the waters around Mount Desert Island offer some of the best boating in Maine. Fortunately, you don't need to own a boat or possess any maritime skills to spend some time on the water. Over a dozen boat tours depart from Mount Desert Island, featuring everything from mellow day sails to whale watching on jet-powered catamarans.

I adore boats, and I've never been on a boat tour I didn't enjoy. Most tours are worth it simply for the incredible offshore views of Mount Desert Island. That said, some boat tours are definitely better than others. I've listed my favorites on the following pages. If none of these tours strikes your fancy, there are plenty of additional tours that depart from Bar Harbor (p.218), Northeast Harbor (p.233), and Southwest Harbor (p.252).

The most popular boat tours are on motorboats, which cover more distance in less time than sailboats. Motorboat tours include whale watching, nature tours, lobstering demonstrations, deep sea fishing, lighthouse tours, and day trips to small offshore islands.

Sailboat tours, by contrast, tend to focus more on the experience and the scenery. If you just want to spend a relaxing day on the water, sailboats are the way to go. The question is: big or small? Small sailboats offer a more intimate experience where you'll definitely get to know your captain and fellow passengers. Big sailboats, by contrast, offer a smoother ride, a better value, and the unique experience of watching trained crew hoist massive sails—a rare sight today, but an important part of Maine life a century ago. The big drawback of big sailboats is the impersonal feel of sailing with dozens of other passengers.

If you're more interested in hands-on boating, head to Southwest Harbor, the unofficial boating capital of Mount Desert Island. In Southwest Harbor you can charter private boats or—if your pockets are deep enough—buy them. Also worth mentioning is the Wooden Boat School (thewoodenboatschool.com), a delightful sailing and boat-building school located west of Mount Desert Island in the small town of Brooklin, on the mainland.

ACADIA'S BEST BOAT TOURS

Diver Ed

I can't recommend Diver Ed's "Dive-In Theater" cruise highly enough! The supremely entertaining Diver Ed (Downeast Maine's Jacques Cousteau) and his knowledgeable wife "Captain Evil" show off Maine's fascinating underwater world from the 51-foot *Starfish Enterprise.* After putting on a dry suit, Ed jumps overboard with an HD video camera and seeks out strange and fascinating creatures on the seafloor. Live images are shown on a giant screen onboard, revealing crabs, starfish, lobsters and other ocean critters in their natural habitat. Ed then resurfaces with a bag full of sea creatures for a highly entertaining show-and-tell. If you're visiting with kids, this will probably be the highlight of their trip. (207-288-3483, divered.com)

Bar Harbor Whale Watch

The nutrient-rich Gulf of Maine is home to humpback, finback, right, and minke whales, and the waters off Mount Desert Island are some of the best places to see them. If you'd like to catch a glimpse of these majestic mammals, book a trip on the *Friendship V.* This jet-powered, 112-foot aluminum catamaran whisks passengers 25–30 miles offshore in search of whales and other sea creatures, including porpoises, seals, and seabirds. On clear days you'll also enjoy beautiful views. I personally like trips that combine whale watching with a cruise to Petit Manan Island, home to puffins and Maine's second tallest lighthouse (p.111). The *Friendship V* works with Allied Whale (p.79), so whale watching trips are enjoyable *and* help a great cause. Note: zipping around offshore can get chilly, even on hot summer days, so be sure to bring jackets, hats, and warm clothes. It's also a good idea to pack binoculars (or rent them onboard). (207-288-2386, barharborwhales.com)

Alice E.

Friendship sloops were the original Maine lobster boat, and the 42-foot *Alice E.*, built in 1899, is the oldest known Friendship sloop still sailing today. Her affable captain, Karl Brunner, had this historic vessel exquisitely restored, and today she sails from Southwest Harbor on two- and three-hour cruises around Somes Sound or the Cranberry Isles, two of the region's most scenic waterways. Private charters available. (207-266-5210, sailacadia.com)

R.L. Gott

Captain Eli Strauss grew up on Blue Hill Bay, and his narrated cruises aboard the 40-foot *R.L. Gott* offer a rich, local perspective. As you cruise past the gorgeous islands south of Bass Harbor, you'll look for marine wildlife, learn about the region's history, and watch Captain Strauss haul lobster traps. Two tours are available: a 3.5-hour lunch cruise that includes a stop on Frenchboro Island (p.293) and a two-hour afternoon trip focused on wildlife. (207-244-5785, bassharborcruises.com)

Acadia Lobster Cruise

"The only thing better than lobster fresh off the boat ... is lobster fresh ON the boat!" That's the motto of Jason Clark, who was born and raised on Mount Desert Island and learned to lobster from his father. Today Jason takes visitors on his 1966 wooden lobster boat *Seven Bells*, which departs Southwest Harbor. After hauling traps, Jason cooks a traditional Maine lobster feast onboard, which you'll enjoy surrounded by Acadia's stunning scenery. Lunch and sunset trips are available. (acadialobstercruise.com, 207-370-7663)

Astronomy in Acadia

Today nearly two-thirds of Americans live where they can't see the Milky Way due to light pollution (artificial light). But in Acadia National Park, home to some of the darkest night skies on the East Coast, the Milky Way still blazes across the heavens at night. To help keep Acadia's skies dark, the park and local communities have installed special light fixtures to reduce light pollution. If you're not looking at the stars in Acadia, you're missing half the show. Don't know much about astronomy? Check out the ranger program "Stars Over Sand Beach." Or visit in September during the Acadia Night Sky Festival (acadianightskyfestival.org), a multi-day event that features workshops, live presentations, and lots of telescopes aimed at the stars.

Long before modern astronomy, native tribes developed rich mythologies to explain the cosmos. The Wabanaki believe the Milky Way is filled with the souls of ancient ancestors, and the northern lights are the work of a spirit who plays games with light. The Big Dipper is a bear (four stars of the cup) chased by three birds (the handle). The first handle star is a robin, which the bear kills when he approaches the horizon in autumn. The robin's blood washes over the trees, coloring them red, and stains the robin's red breast.

Mount Desert Island BASICS

Getting to Mount Desert Island

You don't need a boat to get to Mount Desert Island—which is only an island by about 50 feet at low tide. The Trenton Bridge connects the island to the mainland via Route 1A. How you get to the Trenton Bridge is up to you.

BY CAR

Driving is the most popular way to visit Mount Desert Island. From southern Maine there are two options: the fast route and the scenic route. The fast route follows I-95 north to Bangor, heads east on I-395 to Route 1A, then follows Route 1A to Mount Desert Island (about a 3-hour drive from Portland). The scenic route starts in Portland and follows Route 1 up the coast, passing Rockland, Camden, and other beautiful coastal towns along the way. In Ellsworth Route 1 connects with Route 1A, which goes to Mount Desert Island. The scenic route takes about 5–6 hours from Portland (not counting weekend traffic).

BY PLANE

The Hancock County Bar Harbor Airport (BHB, bhbairport.com) is located in the town of Trenton on the mainland, 12 miles from downtown Bar Harbor. Cape Air (capeair.com) offers regular flights between Boston and Bar Harbor. The Island Explorer Shuttle (p.30) offers free shuttles between the Bar Harbor Airport and downtown Bar Harbor. Taxis and rental cars are also available. The next closest airports are Bangor International Airport in Bangor, Maine (1.5-hour drive from MDI) and Portland International Jetport in Portland, Maine (3-hour drive from MDI).

BY BUS

Greyhound and Concord Coach offer daily service to Bangor. Downeast Transportation (207-667-5796, downeasttrans.org) offers routes connecting Bangor, Ellsworth, Trenton, and Bar Harbor. The Bar Harbor Shuttle (207-479-5911, barharborshuttle.net) also offers service from Bangor to Bar Harbor (advance reservations required).

BY BOAT

Over 150 cruise ships call to port in Bar Harbor each year. Most arrive in September and October on fall foliage cruises.

Mount Desert Island At a Glance

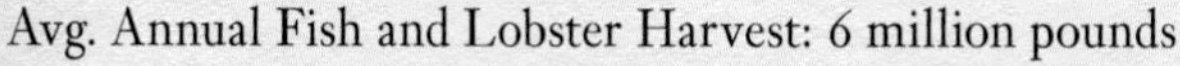

Area: 108 square miles
Length: 16 miles
Width: 10 miles
Mountain Peaks: 26
Lakes and Ponds: 28
Average Tides: 8–12 feet
Population: 10,500
Year-round Residents: 5,000
Summer Residents: 2,100
Avg. Annual Rainfall: 48 inches
Avg. Annual Snowfall: 61 inches
Avg. Annual Fish and Lobster Harvest: 6 million pounds
Total Assessed Value of Private Property on MDI: $4.6 billion
Latitude: 44.3° N, Longitude: 68.3° W
If you headed due east from MDI, you'd hit Bordeaux, France; Bologna, Italy; the Gobi Desert, China; and Mongolia.
If you headed due south from MDI, you'd hit Caracas, Venezuela; La Paz, Bolivia; and Mendoza, Argentina.

Pronouncing Mount "Desert" Island

Is it "Desert" (as in the Sahara) or "Dessert" (as in ice cream)? Strangely, Mainers say both, and the name's linguist roots offer little clarification. The island was named in 1604 by the French explorer Samuel Champlain, who dubbed it *L'Isle des Monts-déserts* ("Island of Barren Mountains"). The "desert" camp claims they are justified by the "barren" description. The granite peaks, they argue, are barren like a desert. Meanwhile, the "dessert" camp claims the French pronunciation of *desert* sounds more like "dessert." In addition, Champlain wrote the peaks were "deserted" which sounds more like "dessert." Where do I stand? I grew up saying "dessert," which I learned from my mother, a seventh-generation Mainer. And far be it for me to argue with Mom.

Getting Around Mount Desert Island

BY CAR

There are only a handful of major roads on Mount Desert Island, so it's hard to get lost. Unfortunately, parking can be a hassle across much of the island, particularly along Park Loop Road. When parking in Acadia National Park, all four tires must be on the pavement in a designated spot—otherwise you risk a ticket. A much better option is the free Island Explorer.

ISLAND EXPLORER SHUTTLE

These free propane-powered buses are the best way to get around Acadia and Mount Desert Island. The Island Explorer runs multiple routes linking hotels and campgrounds with popular destinations. An additional route circles Schoodic Peninsula on the mainland. Shuttles run from late June through mid-October, with scaled-back service after Labor Day. Island Explorer maps are available at visitor centers and the Island Explorer Web site (exploreacadia.com). Unless you're headed somewhere the Island Explorer doesn't go, riding these free shuttles is generally easier and more convenient than driving. Not only will you save time and money, you'll help reduce pollution and congestion.

TAXI & TOUR COMPANIES

Recommended taxi services, which also offer private tours, include **At Your Service** (207-288-9222) and **Bar Harbor Coastal Cab** (207-288-1222).

Acadia Entrance Passes

Entrance passes are required anywhere in Acadia National Park. This applies to parked cars (which must display an entrance pass) as well as bicyclists and pedestrians. Weekly and annual park passes are available at Hulls Cove Visitor Center, Sand Beach Entrance Station, Thompson Island Visitor Center, and park campgrounds. You can also buy entrance passes online at yourpassnow.com.

Acadia Permits

As visitation to Acadia exploded in the 2010s, vehicle congestion became a major issue in the park. In 2020, Acadia National Park began experimenting with timed-entry vehicle permits for some the park's most popular roads, including Ocean Drive and Cadillac Summit Road. As of this writing, vehicle permits are required on Cadillac Summit Road from late May to late October. Permits are available on recreation.gov. Thirty percent of timed-entry vehicle permits become available three months in advance. The remaining 70 percent become available two days in advance at 10am. Acadia's vehicle permit system is a work in progress. Check Acadia's website and recreation.gov for the most up-to-date information.

Hotels & Lodging

There are dozens of places to stay on Mount Desert Island, and listing them here would take dozens of pages. Rather than waste all that paper (when all you need is one room), I've posted all lodging information at jameskaiser.com.

The vast majority of lodging is found in Bar Harbor, but Northeast Harbor and Southwest Harbor also have some great options. No matter where you end up, the island is relatively small, so you're never too far from anything. If island hotels are beyond your price range, check out some of the off-island options in Trenton or Ellsworth.

Camping

Acadia National Park has four campgrounds, all of which require advance reservations (available on recreation.gov). There are roughly a dozen private campgrounds just outside the park. Visit jameskaiser.com for additional camping info.

BLACKWOODS CAMPGROUND

Acadia's most popular campground has 281 campsites on the eastern side of Mount Desert Island. Located in the woods five miles south of Bar Harbor, Blackwoods Campground is a 10-minute walk from the ocean. Open May through mid-October. Cost: $30 per night.

SEAWALL CAMPGROUND

This 202-site campground is located near the southwestern tip of Mount Desert Island. Some people love the quiet, remote location; others find it a bit too far from the island's famous attractions. Open late May through mid-October. Cost: $30 per night drive-in sites, $22 per night walk-in sites.

SCHOODIC WOODS CAMPGROUND

Acadia's newest campground (opened in 2015) has 94 campsites near Schoodic Peninsula, about three miles southeast of Winter Harbor. There are 8.5 miles of bike paths near the campground, plus hiking trails that connect to Schoodic Head. Cost: $22 walk-in tent sites, $30 drive-up tent/small RV, $36 RV with electric-only sites, $40 RV with electric and water. Open late May through mid-October.

DUCK HARBOR CAMPGROUND

Located on remote Isle au Haut, 15 miles southwest of Mount Desert Island, Duck Harbor Campground is my favorite campground in Acadia. It offers a fabulous combination of peace, quiet, and natural beauty. There are five primitive campsites, each with a three-sided, lean-to shelter. Duck Harbor Campground is open mid-May to mid-October. Cost: $20.

Weather & When to Go

"If you don't like the weather in Maine, wait a minute. It'll change." It's a long-standing cliché, but it also happens to be true. The weather in Maine, especially along the coast, is *highly* unpredictable. It varies from day to day, month to month, and year to year. There's simply no rhyme or reason to it—as any local weatherman will attest.

My favorite source of forecasts and weather info is the National Weather Service (weather.gov). But in my experience, even its forecasts are only partially reliable. Most are based on regional forecasts, and there's tremendous variability within the region. In my highly non-scientific study of local forecasts, I've found that 24-hour reports are right about 70% of the time, 48-hour reports are right about 50% of the time, and 36-hour reports are right about 30% of the time. Any report over 36 hours is pretty much useless.

That said, when the weather is good in Acadia, it's incredible—sunny, warm, with a cool ocean breeze. And even when it's bad—foggy, rainy, snowy—the coast has a beautiful mystique. Also keep in mind that, in terms of annual precipitation, coastal Maine is ranked second in America only to the Pacific Northwest. It can rain any time of the year on short notice, so pack accordingly.

SPRING

Spring (aka "mud season") definitely has its pros and cons. Melting ice and snow keep things soggy in early spring, but by late spring the island often dries out and temperatures can be divine. Spring is also bug season. Biting bugs are most active between mid-May and mid-June, when running water provides optimum breeding conditions. But bug numbers vary considerably depending on how rainy it has been (p.42). Spring is also when local businesses come out of their long winter hibernation. Hotels and shops start opening in April, and by Memorial Day most of the island is open for business. Peak tourist season doesn't arrive until Fourth of July, at which point everything is open.

SUMMER

Sunny summer days bring perfect temperatures to Mount Desert Island: high 70s with a cool ocean breeze. But summer can also bring thick fog that blankets the island for hours—or sometimes days. Sunny or not, July is when things get busy on Mount Desert Island—booked hotels, waiting lists at restaurants, crowded parking lots. (This is all relative, of course. By Maine standards it's crazy, but New Yorkers will probably appreciate the peace and quiet.) August is even busier than July, with families trying to cram in one last vacation before school starts and Mainers trying to enjoy one last blast of warm temperatures. Just when things seem like they can't get any crazier, Labor Day hits and peak season ends.

FALL

Fall is one of the best times to visit Mount Desert Island. The weather is crisp, the crowds are reduced, and the foliage is spectacular. Weather in early September is generally excellent, but temperatures start dropping by the end of the month. Fall is also the busiest season for cruise ships, which dock in Bar Harbor and disgorge thousands of passengers onto the town's narrow streets. But there's usually a lull in visitation in mid-September between peak summer season and "leaf peeping" season. Fall foliage generally peaks around October 13–22, but dates vary from year to year. (Check mainefoliage.com for current conditions.) By late October, temperatures start dropping, tourists start departing en masse, and locals start hunkering down. By early November, many storefront windows in Bar Harbor are covered in plywood, and the island enters its long winter hibernation.

WINTER

Winter is a cold, desolate season on Mount Desert Island—which is exactly why some people love it. New England has some of the longest winters in the United States, although the ocean does warm things up a bit on the coast. Average snowfall on Mount Desert Island is around 60 inches, but snow tends to melt quickly. When the snow sticks, Acadia's carriage roads are fantastic for cross country skiing, and snowmobiling is allowed on the Park Loop Road. Although most private businesses are closed in winter, a few hardy restaurants and hotels stay open year-round.

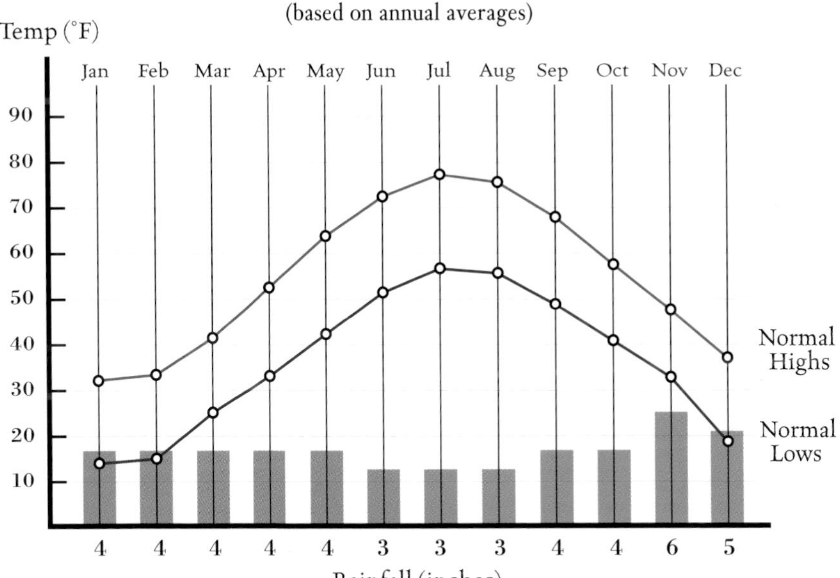

ACADIA WEATHER

Weather in coastal Maine is, in a word, unpredictable. Although summers on the coast are generally sunny, conditions can quickly change. What started out as a sunny day can end in rain, fog, or (in very rare cases) snow! It turns out that weather patterns in Maine—and all of New England for that matter—are more variable and more extreme than almost any other place in the United States. As Mark Twain once said, "I reverently believe that the Maker who made us all makes everything in New England but the weather. I don't know who makes that, but I think it must be some raw apprentices in the weather-clerk's factory."

Maine is located at roughly 45° N latitude, exactly halfway between the Equator and the North Pole. This puts Maine in the middle battleground between the hot, humid air of the tropics and the cold, dry air of the Arctic. Storms in these middle latitudes follow fairly predictable paths called storm tracks, and almost all storm tracks in the United States have the potential to pass through Maine.

In addition to regular storms, Maine must also contend with hurricane season, which runs from June through November. Most hurricanes make landfall in the Southeast and dissipate long before reaching Maine. Hurricanes that do make it here generally arrive in August, September, or October. Most are Category 2 or less by the time they arrive.

Temperatures in Maine vary dramatically throughout the year, but temperatures along the coast are moderated by the ocean. During the dog days of summer, when inland Maine is hot and humid, the Gulf of Maine's cold water keeps temperatures mild. And in the dead of winter, when inland Maine suffers sub-zero temperatures, the ocean's relative warmth boosts temperatures along the coast.

Long-term weather trends in Maine are also influenced by a weather system known as the North Atlantic Oscillation (NAO). The NAO results from the interaction between a semi-permanent low pressure system over Iceland (the Icelandic Low) and a semi-permanent high pressure system over Bermuda (the Bermuda High). The interactions between these two systems have the power to alter storm tracks across the North Atlantic. When pressure differences between the two systems is high, the NAO is in positive mode, resulting in relatively milder temperatures and decreased storm activity in Maine. When the pressure difference between the Icelandic Low and the Bermuda High is low, the NAO is in negative mode, which often brings cold temperatures and increased storm activity to Maine. NAO modes are long-term trends that can last for decades. The present NAO mode has been mostly positive since the late 1970s.

Reading the Wind

Maine weather is unpredictable, but you can still get a sense of what lies ahead by doing what sailors have done for hundreds of years: reading the wind.

Winds from the west generally bring sunny days. Winds blowing from the southwest bring warm, dry air. Winds blowing from the northwest bring cool, dry air that sweeps away moisture, often resulting in crystal-clear visibility.

Eastern winds are far less desirable. Southeasterly winds can bring overcast days with the possibility of drizzle and fog. And if wind starts blowing from the northeast ... batten down the hatches—a dreaded nor'easter could be on the way.

Although most common in winter, nor'easters can occur any time of year. They form when cold, arctic air from Canada collides with warm, tropical air moving up the East Coast. The collision creates a counterclockwise spinning cyclone, similar to a hurricane. As the cyclone moves offshore, winds arrive from the northeast—hence the term "nor'easter." When nor'easters form offshore, they can bring gale force winds, extreme surf, and massive amounts of rain, sleet, or snow. Remember *The Perfect Storm*? That was an offshore nor'easter. Onshore nor'easters are far less catastrophic, behaving much more like regular storms.

"Nor'easter" or "No-theaster"?

Today everyone calls them nor'easters. But old salts claim the original word, spoken by true Mainers, was "no-theaster." Back then, the distinction was critical in life-or-death situations, because "nor'east" might be mistaken for "nor'west," especially when wind, waves, and Maine accents were taken into account.

MAINE WINDS

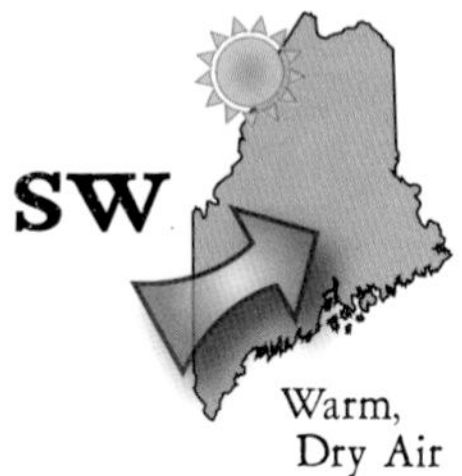

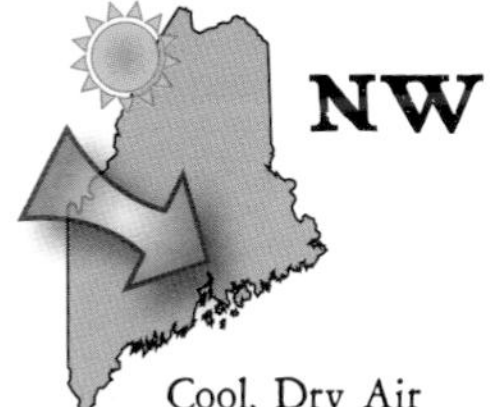

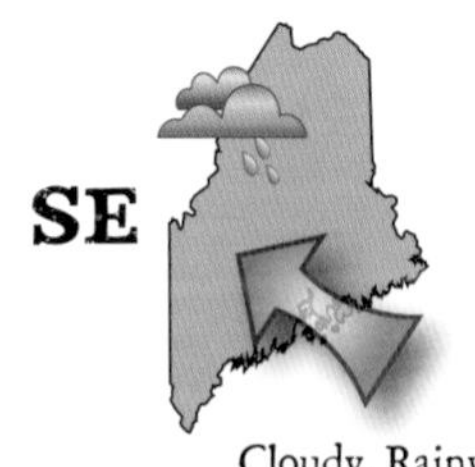

Coastal Fog

Fog is a fact of life in Downeast Maine, which typically sees 55 or more foggy days each year. (Locals sometimes refer to August as "Fogust.") Fog is essentially a cloud that forms at ground level when moist air cools to the dew point. Along the coast there are two common types of fog: evaporation fog and advection fog. Evaporation fog, also known as "sea smoke," forms in winter when frigid air flows over the ocean. As ocean water evaporates into the frigid air, the air saturates and condenses. Sea smoke is light and thin and generally burns off by late morning. Advection fog, on the other hand, forms when warm and cold air interact. This happens in summer when cool, moist air from the ocean blows over heated land. It also happens offshore when warm, moist air from the Gulf Stream comes into contact with cold air in the Gulf of Maine. This is the classic "pea-soup" fog that blows in from the ocean and can linger along the coast for days.

"You'll find fogs all the world over, but the Gulf Stream fog beats 'em all. It will heave in sight sooner, stay longer, and become thicker, and go away quicker than any fog I ever met in all my voyaging."

Maine Sailor
Harper's Magazine, 1872

One Perfect Day on Mount Desert Island

- Sunrise (p.40)
- Breakfast at Cafe This Way (p.221) or Two Cats (p.222)
- Midmorning walk on the Bar Harbor Shorepath (p.213)
- Late morning on the Park Loop Road (p.131)
- Lunch at Jordan Pond House (p.160)
- Afternoon Boat Cruise (p.23)
- Sunset at Bass Harbor Lighthouse (p.260)
- Dinner at Thurston's Lobster Pound (p.259)

One Perfect Day for Outdoor Lovers

- Sunrise (see following page)
- Blueberry pancakes at Jordan's Restaurant (p.222)
- Hike the Precipice (p.178) or Penobscot Mountain (p.186)
- Lunch in Northeast Harbor (p.233)
- Afternoon bike ride (p.19) or sea kayaking (p.17)
- Sunset on Cadillac Mountain (p.172)
- Dinner in Bar Harbor (p.221)
- Stargazing at Sand Beach (p.146)

Rainy Day Options

Rainy days are a fact of life in Maine. Fortunately, there are plenty of great indoor activities on Mount Desert Island:

- Abbe Museum (p.217)
- Atlantic Brewing Company (p.207)
- La Rochelle Mansion (p.217)
- Barn Arts Collective (p.259)
- Criterion Theater (p.220)
- George Dorr Natural History Museum (p.217)
- Great Harbor Maritime Museum (p.237)
- ImprovAcadia (p.216)
- Somesville Museum (p.247)
- Mount Desert Oceanarium (p.207)
- Petite Plaisance (p.237)
- Reel Pizza (p.220)
- Seal Cove Auto Museum (p.247)
- Wendell Gilley Museum (p.221)

Sunrise in Acadia

Cadillac Mountain, the tallest peak in Acadia, has long been heralded as "the first place in America to see sunrise." But in spring and summer, that's actually not true. From late March through late September, Mars Hill in northern Maine is the first place in America to see sunrise. That hasn't stopped hundreds of visitors from driving to the top of Cadillac each summer morning, leading to pre-dawn traffic jams and overflowing parking lots. Starting in 2020, the park began requiring permits to visit Cadillac Mountain for sunrise.

So what's an Acadian sun worshipper to do? If you can survive watching sunrise a few seconds after the folks on top of Cadillac, there are plenty of great sunrise spots along the Bar Harbor Shorepath (p.213) and Park Loop Road. My personal favorites are Egg Rock Overlook (p.141) and Otter Cliffs (p.152).

Downeast Maine

Downeast Maine refers to the northeast coastal region that lies between Penobscot Bay and Canada. The term "Downeast" is derived from sailing terminology. Because the region's prevailing winds blow from the west, and because the coast of Maine trends northeast, ships sailing from Boston to Maine would sail *down*wind to travel *east*. Hence the term "Downeast." On a similar note, ships sailing from Maine to Boston sail upwind, which explains why some Mainers still say they're going "up to Boston."

Downeast Maine

Festivals & Events

LEGACY OF THE ARTS FESTIVAL (June)

This week-long festival, held every year in late June, features exhibits, workshops, and an art show on the Village Green.

FOURTH OF JULY

Bar Harbor's biggest celebration includes a pancake breakfast, morning parade, afternoon lobster bake, "lobster races" where live lobsters race each other in salt-water tanks, and evening fireworks at the town pier.

BAR HARBOR TOWN BAND (July, August)

Free concerts Mondays and Thursdays, 8pm Bar Harbor Village Green.

HARBOR HOUSE FLAMINGO FESTIVAL (July)

Southwest Harbor's annual plastic pink flamingo festival features a fun-loving parade followed by food and music.

BAR HARBOR MUSIC FESTIVAL (July)

Since 1967, the Bar Harbor Music Festival has organized weekend concerts featuring classical, jazz, and pop. Times and locations vary. Call or check the schedule online. (207-288-5744, barharbormusicfestival.org)

NATIVE AMERICAN FESTIVAL (July)

This annual festival, co-sponsored by the Abbe Museum, features Native American basketry, beadwork, drumming, and dancing. Held the first Saturday after Fourth of July at College of the Atlantic.

OPEN GARDEN DAY (July)

Every other year, members of the Mount Desert Garden Club showcase their private gardens in late July. (gardenclubofmountdesert.org)

LOBSTER BOAT RACES (July, August)

Lobster boat races are coastal Maine's version of NASCAR. The two closest races are held in Bass Harbor (p.257) in early July and Winter Harbor (p.265) in early August.

ACADIA NIGHT SKY FESTIVAL (September)

Downeast Maine has the darkest skies on the East Coast. This multi-day festival celebrates Acadia's starry skies with fascinating astronomy programs during the day and telescope viewing parties at night. (acadianightskyfestival.com)

Festivals & Events (cont.)

OKTOBERFEST (October)

Nearly two dozen Maine breweries descend on Southwest Harbor for the town's annual Oktoberfest celebration. (acadiaoktoberfest.com)

MDI MARATHON (October)

Named America's "Most Scenic Marathon" by *Runner's World* (mdimarathon.org)

WINTER BEERFEST (January)

A mid-January celebration of Mount Desert Island's rich brewing culture.

ACADIA WINTER FESTIVAL (February)

Hosted by the Schoodic Institute, this mid-winter festival celebrates nature and outdoor activities. (schoodicinstitute.org)

Local Publications

Mount Desert Island's weekly newspaper, *The Islander* (mdislander.com), focuses on local news and has plenty of info geared towards visitors. It's worth picking up a copy for the weekly calendar of events.

I also love the *The Working Waterfront* (workingwaterfront.com), a free monthly paper published by the Island Institute that focuses on fishing, fishermen, and Maine coastal life. Look for free copies of *The Working Waterfront* at local grocery stores.

Mosquitoes, Bugs, & Ticks

Mosquitoes and tiny midges (aka "no-see-ums") are the most common biting bugs on Mount Desert Island. They are most abundant in spring and early summer, but numbers vary each year due to rain (the more rain, the more bugs). If you plan on hiking, biking, or walking in the woods, bring bug repellent with DEET. Red, itchy bug bites are best treated with hydrocortisone cream (1%).

Ticks are a much greater concern because they can transmit a variety of illnesses, most notably Lyme disease, which can cause severe pain and lethargy. Only 3% of tick bites result in Lyme infection, and it takes at least 36 hours from the time an infected tick bites until the disease can be transmitted. The best course of action is prevention. Wear long pants and long sleeves, tuck your pants into your socks, and use bug repellent with DEET. After spending time in the woods, search your entire body for ticks. If you find a tick, pull it out with tweezers as close to the skin as possible without twisting. Avoid crushing the body of the tick or removing the head from the body. Roughly 75% of people who become infected with Lyme develop a red "bull's-eye" rash within one month. Early stage antibiotic treatment is often highly effective.

Charitable Organizations

Acadia was the first national park created entirely from privately donated land, and that spirit of giving continues today. The following organizations offer fantastic ways to give back to this beautiful landscape.

FRIENDS OF ACADIA

Founded in 1986, Friends of Acadia is the nonprofit partner of Acadia National Park. They've raised millions of dollars to maintain Acadia's hiking trails and carriage roads, and they helped create the Island Explorer shuttle. FOA organizes volunteer programs and lobbies on behalf of the park. (friendsofacadia.org)

ALLIED WHALE

Founded in 1972, and affiliated with College of the Atlantic, Allied Whale has been at the forefront of whale and marine mammal research for decades. See page 79 for more info. (coa.edu/allied-whale)

SCHOODIC INSTITUTE

This unique public-private nonprofit advances ecosystem science and education in Acadia National Park. Located on Schoodic Peninsula, the institute brings researchers, educators, and students together to study at one of the world's great natural classrooms. (schoodicinstitute.org)

LAND & GARDEN PRESERVE

This local nonprofit protects over 1,400 acres on Mount Desert Island, including Thuya Garden, Asticou Azalea Gardens, Abby Aldrich Rockefeller Garden, and the Rockefeller family's former estate in Seal Harbor. (gardenpreserve.org)

MAINE COAST HERITAGE TRUST

Founded in 1970, Maine Coast Heritage Trust helped pioneer conservation easements, which limit development on private land in exchange for tax breaks. To date it has helped protect over 130,000 acres in Maine, including more than 275 islands and 3,000 acres on Mount Desert Island. (mcht.org)

ISLAND INSTITUTE

This community development organization focuses on preserving the ecological and cultural heritage of Maine's 15 year-round island communities. Five of those islands—Islesford, Great Cranberry Island, Frenchboro, Swan's Island, and Isle au Haut—lie within sight of Mount Desert Island. (islandinstitute.org)

NATURE CONSERVANCY

The Maine chapter of the Nature Conservancy protects multiple properties near Acadia, including Indian Point Blagden Preserve, Great Duck Island, and Placentia Island. (nature.org)

LOCAL FOOD

Maine Lobster

Maine is home to the freshest, tastiest lobster on earth, so don't even think about visiting without sampling the state's quintessential crustacean. Not only is Maine lobster delicious, it's also healthy. Lobster meat is virtually fat free, has less cholesterol than chicken or beef, and it's packed full of vitamins A, B12, E and Omega-3 fatty acids.

Lobster has been a local delicacy for thousands of years. Native tribes cooked lobster by placing layers of seaweed over hot embers, then piling lobsters, clams, and mussels on top. European colonists copied this technique, which came to be known as a lobster bake. For the most part, however, early settlers thought of lobster as a cheap, inferior fish substitute. Many Mainers claim a state law once existed that prisoners would not be fed lobster more than twice a week. (Scholars who have investigated this claim can find no evidence of its existence.) Then, in the 1800s, diners in Boston and New York developed a taste for fresh lobster. This led to the invention of the lobster smack, a sailboat designed specifically to transport live lobster, which kicked off the commercialization of the lobster industry. Before long, popular dishes like Lobster Newburg and Lobster Thermidor had catapulted the once-lowly crustacean to the height of sophistication.

Today there's no shortage of restaurants serving pricey lobster dinners on Mount Desert Island. But the freshest, best lobster is generally found at laid-back lobster shacks where salt water tanks are built into the ordering counter. Don't be fooled by appearances. These low-key seafood shrines are as good as it gets. My favorite places to eat lobster are Thurston's (p.259), Captain's Galley at Beal's (p.253), and the Trenton Bridge Lobster Pound (p.209).

To learn about the natural history of lobsters, see p.72.

Soft-Shell Clams

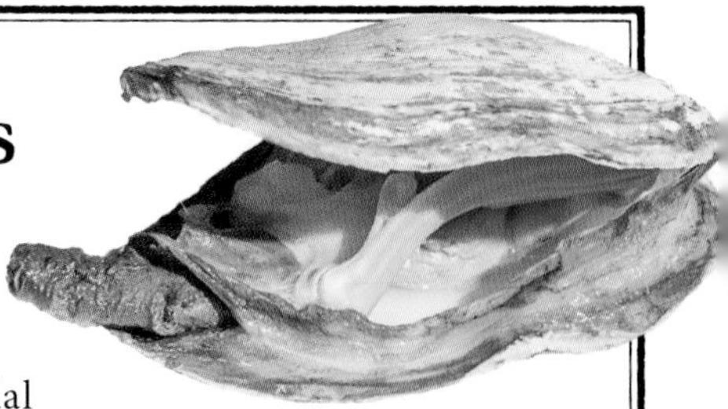

Commonly called "steamers," soft-shell clams (*Mya arenaria*) are the famous "steamed clams" served throughout Maine. They are harvested from tidal mudflats, where they live six to ten inches under the surface, extending long black siphons ("necks") to the surface to filter nutrients from the water at high tide. When steamed, the thin white shells open to reveal soft, tender meat. To eat a steamer, scoop out the innards and peel off the tough, rubbery exterior covering the neck and outer edges. Next, dip the meat in clam broth, which removes any remaining grit. Finally, dip the clam in butter, pop it into your mouth, and enjoy. (Although purists insist on butter, I love steamers dipped in olive oil.) Try the steamers at C-Ray Lobster (p.209), where owner Joshua is one of the few licensed clammers on Mount Desert Island. You can be confident his clams are always fresh.

Hard-Shell Clams

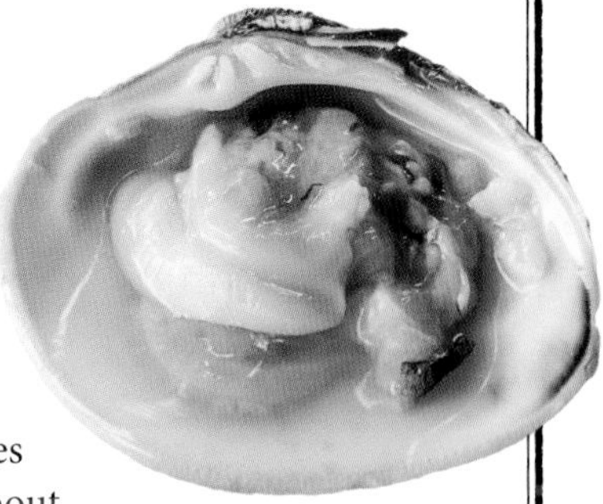

Most East Coast hard-shell clams are the same species, *Mercenaria mercenaria*, but they have different names depending on their size. Littlenecks (named for Little Neck Bay, New York) are less than two inches across. Cherrystones (named for Cherrystone Creek, Virginia) are about two and a half inches across. And quahogs (pronounced *coe*-hogs—a word likely derived from the native word "poquauhock") measure three inches or more across. Clam meat gets tougher with size. Littlenecks are often used in pasta dishes, while cherrystones are enjoyed raw on the half shell. Quahogs are chopped up for clam chowder. Maine clam chowder starts with a milky, brothy base—a stark contrast to the clear clam chowders found in southern New England. Sadly, most clam chowder served on Mount Desert Island is not made from scratch. It's ordered in bulk from large food distributors and arrives in plastic bags. Try the homemade clam chowder at the Fish House Grille (p.223) or Peekytoe (p.221). If you'd like to sample raw cherrystones, head to (where else?) Cherrystones (185 Main Street, Bar Harbor).

Cherrystone

Littlenecks

Oysters

Oysters have complex flavors heavily influenced by their local habitat. Because they are filter feeders that remove plankton and nutrients from seawater—a single oyster can filter up to 50 gallons per day—they concentrate the flavors of their surroundings over time. Oyster farmers refer to this unique taste as *meroir* (a play on the French word *terroir*, which describes how local soil influences the flavor of wine). Maine's pristine inlets and bays are ideal for oyster cultivation, which has flourished in recent decades. Maine oysters need at least three years to reach market size (compared to one year in warmer climates), but they possess a depth of texture and flavor prized by top chefs. Oysters grown near Acadia include Waukeag Neck, Top Notch, Taunton Bay, and Cranberry Oysters. Try the oysters at Peekytoe (p.221), which carries a number of local varieties.

Mussels

The mussels native to Maine, *Mytilus edulis*, are commonly called "blue" mussels due to iridescent blue bands that decorate the otherwise black shells. The most popular way to cook these beautiful bivalves is steaming them with white wine, garlic, and parsley. When the shells open, mussels release a briny liquid, creating a delicious broth that you can scoop up with discarded shells or soak up with crusty bread. Mussels are simple to cook, so go ahead and order them at any decent restaurant.

Pickled Wrinkles

These large carnivorous sea snails are the escargot of Downeast Maine. Traditionally harvested during lean times, these protein-packed snacks are preserved through pickling. Unlike periwinkles, which are found in the intertidal zone (p.65), wrinkles (aka whelks) are found in deeper water below the tide line. Lobstermen often find them in their traps. Pickled wrinkles tend to be hard to find these days, but The Lobstore in Winter Harbor (207-963-8600) sometimes carries them.

Scallops

There are three kinds of scallops on the East Coast. Sea scallops are the most common, with shells that grow up to 12 inches across. Bay scallops and calico scallops grow two to three inches across. Scallops live on the ocean floor, and their beautiful shells (made famous by the Shell Oil logo) have over 100 tiny bright blue "eyes" to help them detect predators. Unlike most bivalves, scallops can swim short distances by clapping their shells, propelling them away from predators such as starfish. Scallops are commonly harvested by dredging—towing heavy metal nets across the ocean floor. The scallop meat prized by cooks is the adductor muscle that holds shells together. This meat is often soaked in the preservative sodium tripolyphosphate to increase bulk and give it a shiny white appearance. Although they look nice in the supermarket, such "wet" scallops are considered inferior to the "dry" scallops that have not been soaked in chemicals. Dry scallops are often hand-harvested by divers, which is more labor-intensive than dredging but far less destructive to marine ecosystems. Try the scallops at the Burning Tree (p.221).

Fiddleheads

The coiled tips of young ostrich ferns (*Matteuccia struthiopteris*) are considered a delicacy in Maine and eastern Canada. When boiled or steamed, they have a texture similar to asparagus with a woodsy aftertaste. European settlers learned to eat fiddleheads from native tribes who foraged for them in spring for food and medicine. Ostrich ferns grow in clusters along the banks of rivers, streams, and marshes. Overharvesting can destroy a patch, so fiddlehead foragers are *very* secretive about their favorite locations. Foragers must be able to distinguish fiddleheads from similar-looking braken ferns, which are toxic. Fiddleheads must be gathered when young—adult ferns are toxic—and fiddleheads must be cooked to remove toxins. If you don't poison yourself trying to eat a fiddlehead, you'll savor a tasty wild vegetable packed with antioxidants, omega-3s, omega-6s, and vitamin D. No matter the season, you can buy pickled fiddleheads at the Atlantic Brewing Company (p.50).

Popovers

These puffy pastries are the unofficial baked treat of Acadia National Park. The basic batter is the essence of simplicity: flour, eggs, milk, salt. When baked in a popover pan, the batter "pops" over the top, inspiring the name. Popovers are essentially an Americanized version of English Yorkshire pudding. For over a century, popovers and tea have been the signature dish at the Jordan Pond House (p.160), where the puffed pastries are served with butter and jam. These days popovers are also available at other restaurants, most notably the Asticou Inn (p.239) in Northeast Harbor.

Whoopie Pies

This iconic Maine dessert is traditionally made by slathering white frosting between two chocolate cake patties. More recently, however, an explosion of new whoopie flavors—pumpkin, gingerbread, blueberry, peanut butter—have flourished, raising the profile of this once-humble treat. What hasn't changed is the ongoing dispute between Maine and Pennsylvania over who invented the whoopie pie. Pennsylvania claims whoopies were first made by Amish housewives, who packed them in their husbands' lunches. When the husbands discovered the tawdry bundle of sin, they shouted out "Whoopie!" Skeptical Mainers don't buy that origin story, and in recent years Mainers have gone to great lengths to prove their whoopie bona fides. In 2009, the town of Dover Foxcroft launched the Maine Whoopie Pie Festival, which now lures several thousand people each year. Then, in 2011, the Maine state legislature declared the whoopie pie the official "State Treat of Maine" (blueberry pie was already the official "State Dessert"). Maine also holds the record for World's Largest Whoopie Pie with a whopping 1,062-pounder. The previous record holder, Pennsylvania, baked a paltry 200-pound whoopie. Whoopie pies are available at stores throughout Mount Desert Island. Try the tasty whoopies at the Pink Pastry Shop (75 Main Street, Bar Harbor).

Wild Blueberries

Wild blueberries are Maine's second most famous delicacy after lobsters. Maine leads the nation in wild blueberry production, and over 40,000 acres of wild blueberries are harvested within 60 miles of Mount Desert Island.

Although smaller than cultivated blueberries, wild blueberries are sweeter and tastier. They also contain twice the antioxidants. Some studies indicate a diet rich in wild blueberries may improve memory, though I don't recall where I read that.

Maine's official state berry is one of a handful of berry species that originated in North America (cranberries and huckleberries are others). Blueberries were an important food for native tribes, who combined dried blueberry powder with cornmeal, honey, and water to make a pudding called *Sautauthig*. They also brewed a strong aromatic tea from the roots of the blueberry bush.

In 1822, Abijah Tabbutt of Sugar Hill, Maine, invented the Blueberry Rake, a hand-held harvesting tool that looks like a metal dustpan with rounded teeth. Tabbutt's invention led to wide-scale cultivation of Maine's blueberry fields. It wasn't until the Civil War, however, that blueberries became famous outside New England. Scurvy-ravaged Union troops desperately needed vitamin C, so Maine sardine canneries were converted to blueberry canneries to send the vitamin-rich berries south. The entire country soon developed a taste for Maine blueberries, and demand continued after the war.

Today Maine harvests over 80 million pounds of wild blueberries each year. Each spring over 30 million bee hives, containing 30,000 to 100,000 bees each, are brought to Maine to pollinate blueberry fields. Harvest starts in late July/early August and runs through the first heavy frost in September or October. These days blueberry picking machines harvest most of the crop, while migrant workers rake areas the machines can't reach. By autumn the green leaves on blueberry bushes turn fiery red.

Wild blueberry bushes grow across Mount Desert Island, turning Acadia's mountains into massive, all-you-can eat buffets in late summer. Around this time roadside blueberry vendors also appear throughout Maine. Buy a bunch and freeze them for later. And here's an old Maine trick: spread the berries on a cookie tray, freeze them, and then put them in a plastic bag. That way the blueberries won't clump together when you take them out of the bag.

Try the blueberry pie at West Street Cafe (p.222) in Bar Harbor and the Blueberry Ale at the Atlantic Brewing Company (p.50).

Atlantic Brewing Company

The "ABC" is the oldest and most famous brewery on Mount Desert Island. Founded in 1990 in Bar Harbor's Lompoc Cafe, its first beer was Bar Harbor Real Ale, a dark, malty beer with a light, crisp finish. Real Ale was an immediate hit, and today it outsells most other beers on the island. In 1998, the brewery moved to a new location several miles west of Bar Harbor. Today it offers a wide variety of beers, including Coal Porter, Blueberry Ale made from local blueberries, and the obligatory IPA. Seasonal beers include Summer Ale, a hybrid English ale/German lager, and Leaf-Peepin Ale, an English-style red ale brewed with German noble hops. Tours of the brewery are offered daily. You can also visit the tasting room at 52 Cottage Street in Bar Harbor, which features additional small-batch beers. (207-288-2337, atlanticbrewingonline.com)

Bartlett Maine Estate Winery

For over 30 years, Bob and Kathe Bartlett have been making top-notch fruit wines from Maine blueberries, blackberries, raspberries, loganberries, apples, and pears. Most of their fruit wines are dry or semi-dry, but they also produce dessert wines and honey meads. The Bartletts create over 20 varieties of wine, and they produce over 7,000 cases each year. Bartlett Maine Estate Winery also distills award-winning pear eau de vie, apple brandy, and Rusticator's Rum—a gold medallist at the San Francisco World Spirits Competition. The winery/distillery is located in Gouldsboro, 23 miles east of Ellsworth near Schoodic Peninsula (p.263). The tasting room is open Tuesday–Saturday, 10am–5pm, Memorial Day through Columbus Day. (207-546-2408, bartlettwinery.com)

Moxie

This carbonated beverage has a bittersweet flavor that divides people into two camps: those who like it and those who hate it. (I like it.) Created in the 1870s by Dr. Augustin Thompson, it was first marketed as "Moxie Nerve Food," a medicine that prevented "paralysis, softening of the brain, nervousness, and insomnia." Dr. Thompson claimed the drink was derived from a secret South American plant (now known to be gentian root), and he chose the name Moxie based on a supposed native word for "dark water." Following extensive advertising, the word "moxie," meaning pluck or energy, entered the popular lexicon. In 2005, Moxie was officially designated the Soft Drink of Maine.

Allen's Coffee Flavored Brandy

For better or worse, this cheap, sweet, coffee-flavored liquor is the unofficial alcohol of Maine. Step into any store that sells booze and notice the unusual amount of shelf space devoted to Allen's, which is the state's top-selling liquor by volume, earning it the nickname "The Champagne of Maine." Allen's 1,750 ml, 1 liter, 750 ml, and 375 ml bottles are consistently among the top ten bestselling liquors in Maine. In no other state does Allen's even crack the top 100—not even Massachusetts where it's made! Annual sales in Maine often tops one million bottles—one for nearly every man, woman, and child in the state. Allen's first became popular with fishermen in the 1960s, but how it rose to its current "prominence" is a bit of a mystery. Mainers like to mix it with milk, a concoction called simply Allen's & Milk or Sombrero. Not long ago, many local bartenders refused to carry Allen's because of its rough and tumble reputation. But as its fame/infamy has grown, Allen's has become a popular ingredient at hipster bars and restaurants—albeit ironically.

GEOLOGY

MOUNT DESERT ISLAND boasts some of the most fascinating geology on the eastern seaboard. Unlike much of the East Coast, which is sandy and flat, Mount Desert Island towers 1,500 feet above a rocky shore. Over two dozen peaks rise above the island, some visible up to 60 miles at sea. How those mountains formed is a fascinating story that involves colliding continents, erupting volcanoes, scouring glaciers, and countless other splendid catastrophes.

Roughly 550 million years ago, Maine was part of the ancient continent Gondwana, which included South America and Africa. North America belonged to another ancient continent, Laurentia, and between Gondwana and Laurentia lay the Iapetus Ocean, which pre-dated the modern Atlantic. (Iapetus was the father of Atlas, "Atlantic").

Over the next 100 million years, narrow slices of land broke off northern Gondwana and drifted across the Iapetus Ocean towards Laurentia. One of those slices, a New Zealand-sized micro-continent called Ganderia, collided with Laurentia roughly 440 million years ago. Today most of Maine and much of New England contain ancient Ganderian rocks.

After Ganderia broke off Gondwana, Ganderian rivers deposited vast amounts of sediment offshore. This sediment—a combination of sand, mud, and silt—piled up in thick layers, and over millions of years the layers compressed into sedimentary rock. As Ganderia continued drifting north, tectonic plates shifted, and heat and pressure transformed the sedimentary rock into schist, a metamorphic rock similar to slate. The schist that formed is called Ellsworth Schist, and today it is the oldest rock on Mount Desert Island. Around 465 million years ago, rivers deposited additional sediments on top of the Ellsworth schist, forming the second-oldest rocks on Mount Desert Island: the Bar Harbor Formation.

Around 420 million years ago (20 million years after Ganderia attached to Laurentia), things really got interesting. Another drifting slice of Gondwana called Avalonia crashed into Laurentia's Ganderian coast. The intensity of the impact pushed up the ancient Acadian Mountains, which stretched from Newfoundland to Georgia. A chain of volcanoes erupted, including one on present-day Mount Desert Island, where a catastrophic eruption left a caldera 10 miles

GANDERIA

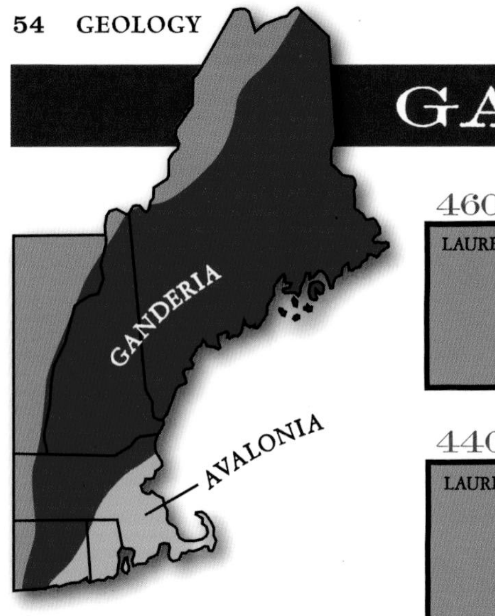

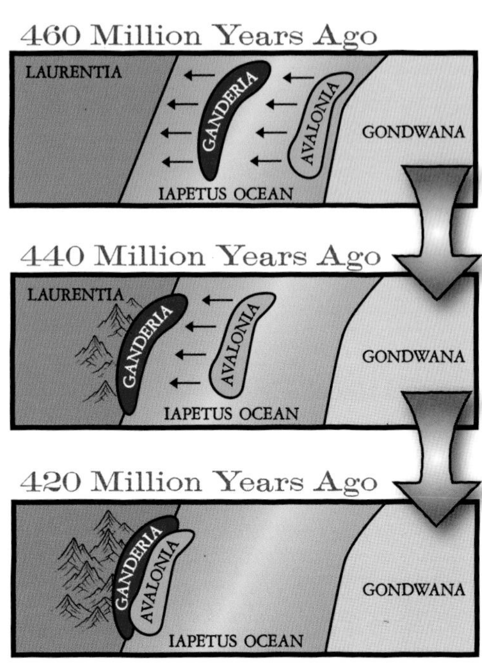

Coastal Maine once belonged to an ancient landmass called Ganderia, which broke off of the northern tip of Gondwana (South America and Africa) 500 million years ago. Roughly 440 million years ago, Ganderia crashed into Laurentia (North America), followed by Avalonia 20 million years later. These collisions pushed up mountains and created massive volcanoes.

wide. After several million years of activity, the Mount Desert Island volcano went dormant. Magma in the heart of the volcano cooled into granite, which would one day form the mountains of Acadia National Park.

Around 300 million years ago, Gondwana collided with Laurentia to form the supercontinent Pangea. The collision pushed up the ancestral Appalachian Mountains, which stretched 2,000 miles across the heart of the supercontinent. At that point, Maine lay near the Equator and enjoyed a warm, tropical climate. Over the next 100 million years, Pangea witnessed the evolution of trees, reptiles, mammals, and flowering plants. When it broke apart roughly 200 million years ago, North America separated from Europe and the Atlantic Ocean formed.

The past 200 million years have seen relatively little tectonic drama in Acadia. As North America drifted from the equator to its present location, erosion removed over two miles of rock above the present landscape. By the start of the Ice Age, Mount Desert Island probably resembled the present-day Great Smoky Mountains, with deep V-shaped valleys carved by mountain streams. It would take one last dramatic act of geology before Mount Desert Island acquired the familiar profile we know today.

THE ICE AGE

AROUND TWO MILLION years ago, earth entered the Ice Age. Thick layers of snow accumulated in the Arctic, compacting into massive ice sheets that eventually started moving under the pressure of their own weight. As massive glaciers pushed south, they consumed everything in their path. Boulders, soil, trees—everything but the bedrock was picked up and carried along.

But even the bedrock did not escape unscathed. The glaciers, essentially dirty ice full of loose debris, acted like giant sheets of sandpaper, grinding down the bedrock and smoothing it out. The glaciers advanced over much of North America, then retreated abruptly. Then they advanced and retreated again. And again. And again. All told, glaciers advanced and retreated nearly a dozen times in North America. The most recent glacial advance, called the Wisconsin glaciation, ended around 12,000 years ago.

Scientists are unsure what triggered the Ice Age, or why glacial advance has followed somewhat regular cycles. One culprit is a small wobble in the earth's orbit that affects how much solar radiation reaches the surface. When the wobble goes one way, solar radiation increases, temperatures rise, snowfall decreases, and glaciers melt. When the wobble goes the other way, solar radiation decreases, temperatures drop, snowfall increases, and glaciers advance. This cycle—the earth wobbling, glaciers advancing, the earth wobbling, glaciers retreating—generally lasts about 120,000 years. Cool periods of glacial advance last about 100,000 years, while warm, interglacial periods last about 10,000 to 20,000 years. (We are currently about 15,000 years into the current interglacial period.)

Before the Ice Age, a chain of jagged mountains rose above Mount Desert Island. Streams tumbled down the mountains, cutting deep V-shaped valleys between the peaks. When the glaciers arrived, they flowed into the valleys and gouged them out, sculpting graceful U-shaped valleys. Eventually, advancing glaciers covered the mountains entirely, rounding down the jagged peaks, smoothing them out, and creating the graceful profiles we know today.

The most recent period of glacial advance started about 100,000 years ago. Around 25,000 years ago, a massive glacier reached the coast of Maine. At its maximum extent, roughly 20,000 years ago, Mount Desert Island was buried under 5,000 feet of ice. The glacier covered every mountain in New England, stretched 150 miles past the present shoreline, and reached as far south as Long Island. So much of the world's water was frozen in glaciers that global ocean levels dropped 300 feet. The weight of the glacier covering Mount Desert Island was so tremendous—one cubic mile of ice weighs 4.5 *billion* tons—it compressed the land 600 feet below present-day levels.

Around 18,000 years ago, the earth's temperatures warmed and the glacier started to melt. Within 5,000 years, it had retreated as far as central Maine. Three thousand years later, it disappeared from the state entirely. The melting glacier released massive amounts of water, forming huge rivers that cut deep channels into the land. Many of those Ice Age channels continue to guide the paths of major rivers flowing through present-day Maine.

As glaciers melted, ocean levels rose 300 feet, flooding the compressed land and sending saltwater up to 60 miles inland. Free of the weight of the glaciers, the compressed land slowly rebounded and rose back toward its original levels. The rising land drained the interior of the state and formed the modern shoreline. Remnants of the former shoreline can still be found on the mountains of Mount Desert Island, including cobblestone beaches stranded hundreds of feet above present-day sea levels.

Before the Ice Age, the coast of Maine was covered in sandy beaches—the result of waves grinding down a once rocky shore. When the glacier descended, it pushed sand and other sediments out to sea. The weight of the glacier also permanently tilted land near the coast, which was covered in rolling hills before the Ice Age. When ocean levels rose, those tilted hills, scraped bare by the ice, formed hundreds of rocky inlets and bays along Maine's coast.

Erosion continues to chip away at Mount Desert Island today. Geologists estimate that roughly two inches erode from the island every 1,000 years. A million years from now, the forces of geology will have rendered Mount Desert Island unrecognizable to modern eyes. So consider yourself lucky. You're alive for that brief moment (geologically speaking) when you can enjoy one of earth's loveliest creations.

Georges Bank

Roughly 18,000 years ago, when a vast glacier extended nearly 150 miles past the present Maine shoreline, it pushed a vast accumulation of rocks and loose debris. When the glacier retreated, it left the rocks and debris behind to form what geologists call a terminal moraine. At the time, sea levels were roughly 200 feet below present levels, and the terminal moraine formed a gravelly ridge connected to the mainland. As massive Ice Age glaciers melted, ocean levels rose and flooded the terminal moraine, creating a shallow underwater ridge known today as Georges Bank. (Another part of the terminal moraine, Cape Cod, remains above sea level.) Georges Bank is one of the defining features of the Gulf of Maine, effectively separating the gulf from the Atlantic Ocean. From time to time, fishing trawls drag up mammoth bones from Georges Bank—a reminder of the giant Ice Age creatures that once roamed the Gulf of Maine.

ICE AGE GLACIERS

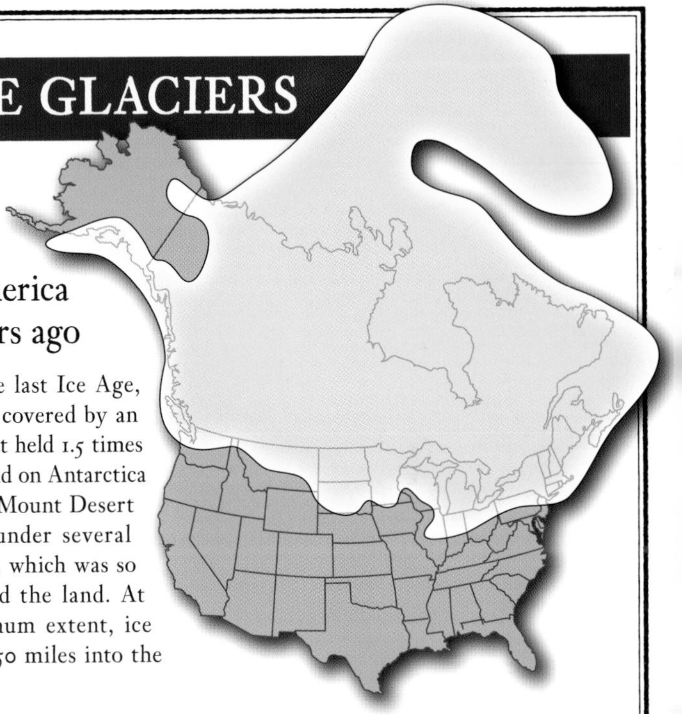

North America 18,000 years ago

At the peak of the last Ice Age, North America was covered by an enormous glacier that held 1.5 times more ice than is found on Antarctica today. At the time, Mount Desert Island was buried under several thousand feet of ice, which was so heavy it compressed the land. At the glacier's maximum extent, ice stretched roughly 350 miles into the Gulf of Maine.

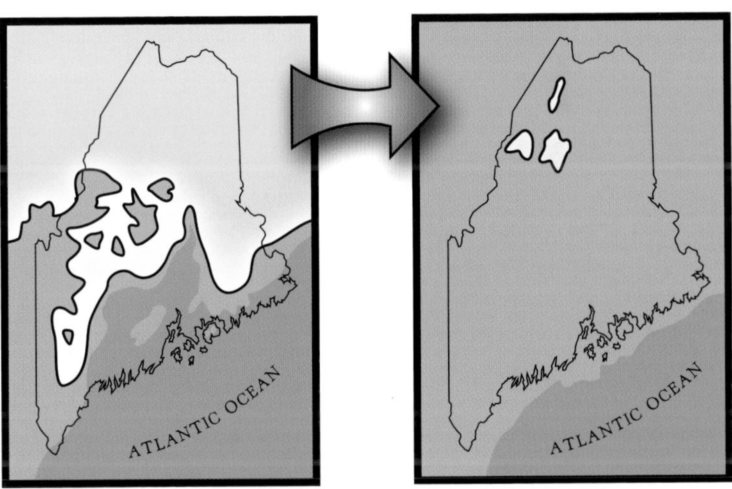

13,000 years ago

As temperatures continued to rise, the glacier continued to melt and retreat. The huge volumes of melting ice caused sea levels to rise, flooding the compressed land in Maine.

11,000 years ago

Free of the weight of the glaciers, the land in Maine began to rise. But with so much ocean water still trapped in retreating glaciers, sea levels remained below present-day levels.

ECOLOGY

ACADIA IS ONE of America's most ecologically fascinating places. With elevations ranging from sea level to 1,500 feet, a location at the boundary of two of North America's major botanical zones, and a landscape filled with forests, lakes, and wetlands, Acadia is home to an astonishing number of plants and animals. Over 50 mammal species, 338 bird species, and 1,000 flowering plant species have been identified in the park, in addition to hundreds of marine creatures offshore. Perhaps most amazing, Acadia's biodiversity is packed into less than 48,000 acres. Outside of a tropical rainforest, there are few places in the world with so many species packed into such a small space.

Mount Desert Island lies at the boundary of North America's northern boreal forest, found in northern Maine and much of Canada, and the eastern deciduous forest, found in southern Maine and much of the eastern U.S. The boreal forest is dominated by evergreens such as red spruce and balsam fir—hardy trees that grow in thin, poor soil. Thriving in cool, damp climates, they create a dense canopy that blocks sunlight and drops needles to the ground, creating acidic soil. As a result, spruce-fir forests tend to go unchallenged by other trees that require abundant sunlight and rich soil to grow. The nutrient-poor floor of spruce-fir forests is often covered with mosses and lichens.

In 1947, fire burned much of the eastern half of Mount Desert Island, clearing out 17,000 acres of spruce-fir forest. This allowed deciduous trees like birch, poplar, oak, and other hardwoods to grow. In contrast to evergreens, deciduous trees drop their leaves each fall, enriching the soil and allowing other plants to thrive. Today, over 30 tree species grow in Acadia National Park, including pitch pines at the northeastern limit of their range and jack pines at the southern limit of their range. Scattered through Acadia's forests are dozens of shrubs and hundreds of wildflowers.

Hike the island's tallest mountains and forests give way to bare rocky peaks. Small populations of alpine plants grow on the summits, scraping out a living in tiny pockets of soil. Because there is very little vegetation on Acadia's barren peaks, there is very little soil development—a self-reinforcing process that prevents larger plants from growing. Lying exposed at high elevations, Acadia's peaks experience cooler than average year-round temperatures. This creates excellent habitat for plants normally found much farther north, including Alpine clubmoss and mountain sandwort.

In summer, Acadia's mountains are often bathed in thick coastal fog, which provides moisture for plants near the summit. Any rain that falls tends to rush off the peaks immediately because there is so little vegetation to absorb the water or slow it down. Cascading down rocks, rainwater forms dozens of temporary waterfalls, then gathers into creeks and streams that flow to the island's lakes, ponds, and marshes.

Roughly 20 percent of Acadia is classified as wetland such as saltwater marshes, freshwater marshes, bogs, and swamps. Because wetlands attract plants and animals from both land and water, they are extremely important to the park's ecology. Wetlands boost Acadia's biodiversity and provide important stopover points for birds migrating on the Atlantic flyway.

Mount Desert Island is one of New England's premier birding locations. James Audubon, founder of the Audubon Society, did much of his research here, and birders from around the world flock to the island. Lying on the boundary of North America's temperate and sub-arctic zone, Mount Desert Island attracts over 330 bird species. Many are migrants that arrive in spring, including 21 nesting wood warbler species, which has earned Acadia the nickname "Warbler Capital of North America." In autumn the migrants fly south, and by winter the island's bird population is reduced to a fraction of its summertime high. Some interesting northern migrants arrive in winter, including snowy owls, great gray owls, and king eiders.

Seabirds bob in the waters along the shore, including common eiders and black guillemots. Further offshore, small islands characterized by cool climates and rocky terrain shelter sub-arctic species normally found farther north. The lack of predators on these islands makes them ideal for breeding seabirds. Great Duck Island, six miles south of Mount Desert Island, supports 20 percent of Maine's nesting seabirds. Petit Manan Island, nine miles east of Schoodic Peninsula, is home to a breeding puffin colony.

A wide range of mammals call Mount Desert Island home. Some, such as snowshoe hares and white-tailed deer, are strict vegetarians, nibbling on grasses and shrubs. Others, such as red foxes and eastern coyotes, are predators that feed on smaller animals. Acadia also contains 11 of Maine's 19 amphibian species, including six-inch-long bullfrogs and thumbnail-sized spring peepers, a tree frog that chirps up to 4,500 times per night in spring. Because Mount Desert Island is located so far north, there are very few reptiles, which are cold-blooded and prefer warmer climates. Only two species of turtles and five species of snakes are found in the park. None of the snakes are poisonous.

Autumn Foliage

New England is famous for autumn foliage, which is particularly dramatic in Acadia. But what causes the leaves to change color? The answer is chlorophyll—or rather, lack of chlorophyll. In spring, new leaves contain a variety of pigments—red, yellow, orange, purple—but green chlorophyll dominates. As autumn days grow shorter, chlorophyll production drops and green pigments fade. For a few glorious weeks, the remaining pigments flaunt their true colors before the leaves fall to the ground.

Interestingly, we may have Florida to thank for New England foliage. Twenty thousand years ago, advancing glaciers pushed North American ecosystems hundreds of miles south. Deciduous trees ended up at the tip of Florida, clinging to suitable habitat. When temperatures warmed, the glaciers retreated, and deciduous trees slowly migrated back to New England.

Acadia's foliage normally peaks in mid-October. The exact timing varies from year to year depending on weather conditions in summer and early autumn. For up-to-date foliage conditions and forecasts, visit mainefoliage.com.

"Before the land rose out of the ocean, and became dry land, chaos reigned; and between high and low water mark, where she is partially disrobed and rising, a sort of chaos reigns still, which only anomalous creatures can inhabit."

—Henry David Thoreau

INTERTIDAL ZONE

When people think of marine ecology, they often picture whales and sharks swimming in the open ocean. But between water and land lies another amazing ecosystem: the intertidal zone. This fascinating region, encompassing the shore between high and low tide, is a world unto itself. Its creatures are among the most rugged on earth, surviving daily threats that include dehydration, extreme temperature fluctuations, and pounding waves. During winter storms, crashing waves produce pressures up to 500 pounds per square inch!

Thanks to Maine's rocky coast and unusually large tides, which average 8–12 feet in Acadia, its intertidal zone is particularly dramatic. Unfortunately, much of Maine's coast is inaccessible to the public because so much is privately owned. In Acadia National Park, however, over 40 miles of rocky shoreline are open to exploration, revealing the wonders of this fascinating ecosystem.

Intertidal zones vary dramatically from top to bottom. Near the top, organisms live most of their lives above water. Only at high tide are they fully submerged, and only for a few hours. Organisms at the bottom of the intertidal zone are only exposed to air at low tide, and most will perish if exposed for too long. In between these extremes lies a wide range of plants and animals adapted to specific amounts of time above and below water.

No animal showcases the intertidal zone's evolutionary variety quite like the periwinkle, a marine snail that grazes on algae. Three types of periwinkles live in Acadia, and each is adapted to different parts of the intertidal zone. Smooth periwinkles live at the bottom of the intertidal zone, and they barely tolerate air. Common periwinkles, found in the mid-intertidal zone, tolerate some air, but not much. And rough periwinkles, which live at the top of the intertidal zone, spend little time underwater. Both smooth and common periwinkles lay eggs in the water, but rough periwinkles give birth to live young on the rocks. In fact, some scientists believe rough periwinkles are slowly evolving into land snails. At some point in the future, rough periwinkles may disappear from the intertidal zone entirely.

Tide pools are some of the best places to explore the intertidal zone. These temporary water pockets, exposed on the rocks at low tide, shelter lifeforms as small as plankton and as large as starfish and sea anemones. A tide pool's location has a dramatic effect on the plants and animals living there. Tide pools at the top of the intertidal zone are exposed to more sunlight, which heats and evaporates water throughout the day, causing drastic fluctuations in temperature, water level, and salinity. Tide pools at the bottom of the intertidal zone, by contrast, receive much less sunlight, so their daily fluctuations are far less extreme.

INTERTIDAL ZONE

SPLASH ZONE: Although splashed by waves and spray at high tide, this zone is never fully submerged. It is sometimes called the Black Zone due to a dark algae that grows on the rocks. Small marine snails called rough periwinkles feed on the dark algae.

BARNACLE ZONE: This easily identified zone is home to countless tiny white barnacles, which spend their lives glued to a single location. When submerged at high tide, barnacles extend feathery legs to feed on floating food particles. When exposed to air at low tide, barnacles retract their legs and close a "trap door" at the tip of their conical shells.

ROCKWEED ZONE: Large strands of rubbery rockweeds cover this mid-intertidal zone. As the tide rises, tiny air bladders in rockweeds lift them toward the surface where they can better photosynthesize. At low tide, rockweeds draped over the rocks provide moist protection for mussels, crabs, and dog whelks.

IRISH MOSS ZONE: This loosely defined zone often overlaps with the zones above and below it. Its namesake plant, Irish moss, has beautiful iridescent tips and grows in small, dense clumps. Sea anemones, whose tentacles shoot microscopic spears that paralyze victims, live in the Irish moss zone.

KELP ZONE: Thick curtains of kelp define the lowermost zone, home to sea stars, sea urchins, and sea cucumbers. Kelp anchors itself to the rocks and sends up belt-like ribbons that grow up to 20 feet long.

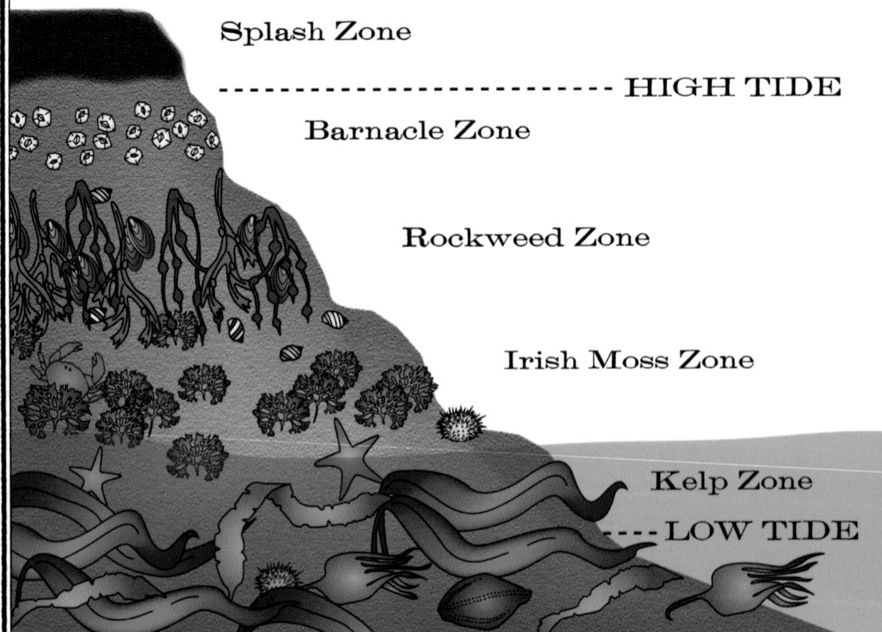

Sea Stars

Sea stars (aka starfish) are found in lower intertidal zones. They grow up to ten inches across and come in a rainbow of colors. Their arms are covered with hundreds of tiny tube feet, which they use to wander around and pry open mussels. After opening a mussel, a sea star disgorges its stomach into the open shell, digesting the victim from the inside. Sea stars can regenerate lost arms, and the tip of each arm has a tiny, primitive "eye."

Dog Whelks

These predatory sea snails, distinguished by pointed spires on their shells, rove around mid-intertidal zones and feast on stationary victims. Dog whelks use a tongue-like organ called a radula to drill into the shells of barnacles and mussels. It takes roughly one hour to drill into a barnacle and 10–20 hours to drill into a mussel. The dog whelk then injects digestive enzymes directly into the victim's shell, creating a nutritious soup. Mussel sometimes fight back by attaching threads to a dog whelk, immobilizing the snail until it starves to death.

Sea Cucumbers

Growing up to ten inches long, these strange, leathery creatures thrive in the lower intertidal zones where they filter nutrients from ingested sediments. Sea cucumbers can loosen and firm their bodies at will. If a sea cucumber wants to squeeze through a small gap, it can essentially liquefy its body to do so. When seriously threatened, sea cucumbers disgorge their internal organs to confuse predators. New organs regenerate later. A sea cucumber "breathes" by drawing water in and out of its anus.

Sea Urchins

These prickly creatures, found in lower intertidal zones, have spiny, limestone shells that protect their soft organs from predators. Sea urchins use tiny tube feet to "walk" along rocks while grazing on algae. Seagulls pluck urchins from the intertidal zone, then drop them on rocks to crack open their hard shells.

GULF OF MAINE

One of the most fascinating aspects of Acadia's ecology is the Gulf of Maine, a shallow region (on average 500 feet deep) covering 69,000 square miles from Cape Cod to Nova Scotia. About 150 miles off the coast lies Georges Bank, the gulf's most important physical feature. Only 13 feet deep in places, Georges Bank is a 10,000 square-mile shallow ridge that acts as a barrier between the Gulf of Maine and the open Atlantic. With the help of Browns Bank to the northeast, Georges Bank creates a semi-enclosed sea. Over 60 rivers flow into the Gulf of Maine, depositing an average of 250 billion gallons of freshwater each year. Georges Bank and Browns Bank help retain this freshwater, creating, in effect, a massive estuary. The mixing of freshwater and saltwater greatly enhances the biological productivity of the Gulf of Maine.

In addition to freshwater deposited by rivers, cold arctic water cycles into the Gulf of Maine via the Labrador Current, which flows down the east coast of Nova Scotia. This cold, dense, nutrient-rich water enters the Gulf of Maine via the Northeast Channel, a deep underwater valley between Georges Bank and Browns Bank. The Northeast Channel formed at the end of the last Ice Age, when so much of the world's water was frozen in glaciers that sea levels lay hundreds of feet below present levels. As global temperatures rose and glaciers melted, a massive river flowed across the exposed Gulf of Maine and carved a deep valley. When sea levels rose, the deep valley became the underwater Northeast Channel.

After nutrient-rich arctic water from the Labrador Current enters the Gulf of Maine, it settles in undersea basins up to 1,500 feet deep. In winter, when surface water cools to near freezing, it sinks and stirs up the arctic water below. By spring, the Gulf of Maine is swirling with nutrients. As days grow longer, abundant sunlight triggers massive phytoplankton blooms, which give the Gulf of Maine its characteristic murky green hue. (A single teaspoon of Maine seawater holds over one million phytoplankton.) The phytoplankton are devoured by zooplankton, which form the foundation of a thriving food chain. Herring and mackerel feed upon zooplankton, and tuna and sharks feed on herring and mackerel. Migrating whales, which arrive in summer to feast on the bounty, eat up to 5,000 herring per day. Meanwhile, the craggy floor of the Gulf of Maine creates ideal habitat for lobsters. Just above the seafloor lurk bottom-dwelling fish such as cod, haddock, and flounder. All told, the Gulf of Maine is home to over 3,000 species, including 652 fish, 32 mammals, and over 700 species of microscopic plants.

In summer, when the Gulf of Maine's surface temperature warms to the mid-60s° F, mixing between surface and bottom slows. Cold, nutrient-rich water settles to the bottom of the gulf, and phytoplankton density drops. Closer to shore, however, large tides ensure continuous mixing of nutrients. Although tides rise and fall an average of three to six feet across much of the planet, Maine tides rise and fall up to 28 feet. Farther north in Canada's Bay of Fundy, a long channel con-

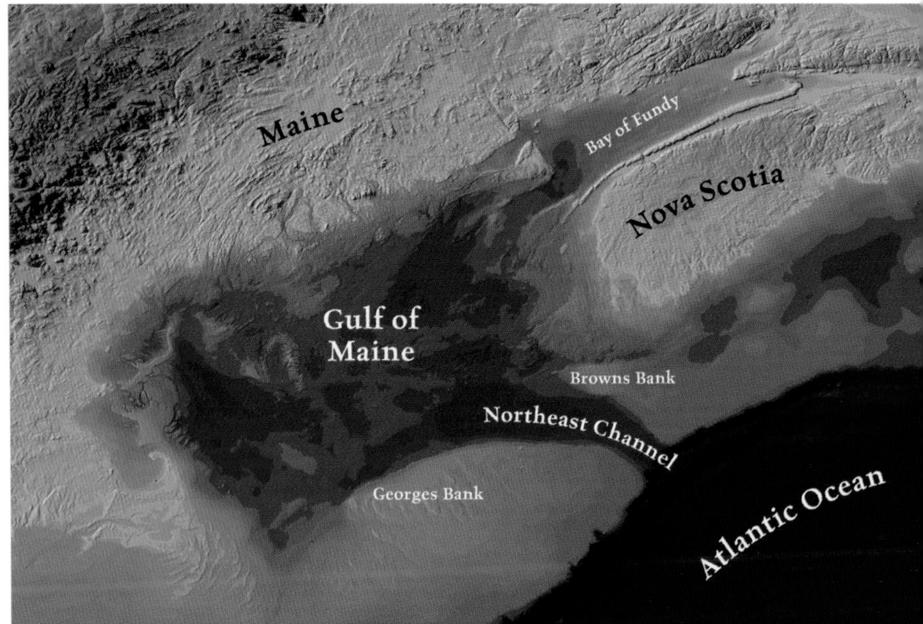

nected to the northern tip of the Gulf of Maine, tides rise and fall an astonishing *50 feet*—the largest tidal fluctuations in the world. The Bay of Fundy's massive tides create, in effect, a giant nutrient pump. Twice a day, over 100 billion tons of water is sucked into the Bay of Fundy and injected back into the Gulf of Maine.

These dramatic tides are due to the region's shallow underwater topography. As tides in the Atlantic Ocean rise and fall, water sloshes back and forth across the Gulf of Maine like water in a bathtub. This sloshing water amplifies the gulf's tidal range, a phenomenon called tidal resonance. The unique shape of the Bay of Fundy has even greater tidal resonance, which further amplifies its tides.

The Gulf of Maine's high tides create abundant mixing close to shore, and sinking surface water stirs up deep nutrients offshore in winter. But another phenomenon mixes the water further still: a powerful counterclockwise current that cycles around the Gulf of Maine every three months. The current not only ensures mixing of nutrients, it disperses the eggs and larvae of marine animals, scattering biodiversity throughout the Gulf.

Taken together, these unique aspects of the Gulf of Maine—its shallow depth, estuary-like quality, nutrient-rich waters, and powerful circulation patterns—create one of the most productive ecosystems in the world. According to some scientists, the Gulf of Maine is richer in nutrients than almost any other body of saltwater on earth.

HUMAN IMPACT

For thousands of years, native tribes altered Maine's environment through hunting, harvesting, and intentional fires to clear brush. But their activities—limited by small populations and lack of technology—had relatively little impact on the land. When Europeans settled coastal Maine in the late 1700s, their impact was swift and dramatic.

The most obvious change was to the forest. Settlers chopped down oaks, cedars, and chestnuts for shipbuilding and construction. But the most important tree was the white pine. Growing up to 250 feet high, white pines tower above all other trees in New England. Once referred to as "skyscrapers" (before steel buildings commandeered the name), white pines are perfect for ships masts. But aggressive harvesting quickly wiped out white pines along the coast. As loggers pushed farther inland in search of white pines, settlers chopped down forests along the coast to farm and graze cattle. By the mid-1800s, much of Maine's coast was nearly treeless.

Hunting and trapping also took a toll on wildlife. As trade between natives and Europeans increased in the 1600s, natives harvested animals in far greater numbers than their pre-contact lifestyles required. Soon many animals, particularly beaver, dissappeared from much of the region. Coastal residents also hunted seabirds for their meat, feathers, and eggs. Because seabirds reproduce in relatively small numbers, their populations were devastated. One species, the penguin-like great auk, was hunted to extinction. Unable to fly away from humans, great auks were rounded up by hunters and clubbed to death on shore. Eventually public pressure, including the founding of the National Audubon Society, encouraged protection of the remaining seabird population. The landmark Migratory Bird Treaty Act of 1918 banned seabird hunting, and conservationists established multiple bird sanctuaries along Maine's coast. Over time, many seabird populations slowly recovered.

On Mount Desert Island, the environment has also been altered in more subtle ways. Today nearly one-quarter of plants in Acadia are non-native "exotics." Free from diseases and pests that keep their populations in check in their native habitats, some exotics have thrived in Acadia. Purple loosestrife, a beautiful European plant with magenta flowers that bloom in July and August, flourishes in wetlands throughout the park. When purple loosestrife takes root, it muscles out native plants. Within Acadia's boundaries, park employees keep purple loosestrife populations under strict control. Outside the park, however, the plant is thriving. About a dozen other non-native species are currently considered a disturbance to the park's native ecosystem.

But the ecosystem most in peril is the Gulf of Maine. For centuries the Gulf of Maine was one of the world's richest offshore fisheries. Over the past half-century, however, once-abundant fish such as cod, haddock, swordfish, and bluefin tuna have seen their populations collapse due to overfishing.

In the 1950s, fears of a global food shortage were widespread, and the U.N. encouraged dramatic increases in fishing to avert the looming catastrophe. Around the same time, modern technology allowed fish catches to skyrocket. In the 1960s, dozens of industrial fishing vessels from the Soviet Union, Western Europe, and Japan arrived in the Gulf of Maine. The foreign vessels, which measured up to 400 feet long, stayed for months at a time and hauled astounding catches. In 1968 alone, foreign vessels harvested 1.2 billion tons of seafood, compared to 556 million tons harvested by U.S. vessels. At the time, the U.S. only had jurisdiction over waters within 12 miles of its coast, which meant foreign vessels were legally entitled to fish there.

Alarmed by the situation, Congress passed the Fisheries Conservation and Management Act in 1976, which extended control of U.S. waters from 12 to 200 miles offshore. With the stroke of a pen, lawmakers prohibited foreign vessels from plundering the Gulf of Maine. The legistlation did not, however, prohibit American vessels from plundering the Gulf of Maine—which is exactly what happened next. To boost fishing harvests, federal subsidies expanded the U.S. fishing fleet, and the devastation continued. When fisherman adopted electronic fish-finding technology in the 1980s, harvesting ability vastly exceeded available stocks, and by the end of the decade fish populations had collapsed.

In the 1990s, environmental groups lobbied for, and achieved, strict fishing regulations to save the remaining fish. But the one-size-fits-all regulations were poorly suited to the complex, dynamic ecology of the Gulf of Maine. Some regulations had the tragic, unintended consequence of incentivizing unsustainable fishing practices. Limits on days at sea encouraged fishermen to stay close to shore, where they overfished critical spawning grounds. The new regulations also tended to favor large fishing operations over small independent fishermen.

Across Maine, fishermen abandoned species that had sustained their communities for generations and switched to lobster, which still boasted healthy populations. But dependence on a single species is fraught with hazard. Any disturbance to Maine's lobster population could jeopardize the state's entire fishing industry and wreak havoc on small coastal communities.

Meanwhile, federal regulations have failed to rebuild fish populations in the Gulf of Maine. But after decades of mutual mistrust, fisherman, lawmakers, and environmentalists could be at a turning point. They are starting to share the blame for past mistakes and work together to devise a new framework. Today some prominent thinkers have concluded the top-down nature of federal regulations is ineffective. A new solution, based on community-centered management and local stewardship, could be more successful. This radical idea, it turns out, is not so radical after all. Local stewardship has worked exceptionally well over the past several decades to protect Maine's signature crustacean: lobster.

LOBSTERS

Lobster is the quintessential symbol of Maine. Although billboards are proudly banned throughout the state, it's impossible to drive through a coastal town without encountering dozens of wooden signs painted with lobsters. And rightly so. There are roughly 30 species of clawed lobsters in the world, but no seafloor on the planet is as densely populated with lobsters as the Gulf of Maine. And the species found here, *Homarus americanus*, is one of the ocean's most unusual and fascinating creatures.

American lobsters live on ocean floors from North Carolina to Newfoundland, but they thrive in the Gulf of Maine due to cold, shallow water and a rocky, craggy seafloor. Lobsters seek shelter among rocks. Large lobsters commandeer the best hiding spots and defend them vigorously. Smaller lobsters are sometimes forced to burrow into the sand like rodents. In some parts of the Gulf of Maine, the density of lobsters is roughly one per square meter.

Lobsters are almost neutrally buoyant, and they tiptoe across the sea floor with ease. Each spring, millions of lobsters migrate towards the warmer water close to shore. In autumn, when cold winds chill water near the shore, lobsters migrate offshore to spend winter in relatively warmer water. During this migration, lobsters travel up to four miles per day. When threatened they flap their powerful tail, propelling them backward at speeds topping 16 feet per second!

Young lobsters start out with two claws of equal size. As they mature, lobsters develop a preference for one claw or the other, much like people become right- or left-handed. The preferred claw becomes the powerful "crusher" claw, used to crush the shells of prey. The smaller "shredder" claw shreds flesh. When lobsters bring food close to their face, a vast array of tiny appendages near the mouth are employed as forks, clamps, brushes, and shredders. Teeth-like grinders finish the job in the lobster's stomach. Lobsters feed on just about anything, including mussels, crabs, and starfish. Lobsters, in turn, are preyed upon by skates, sharks, and groundfish that swallow them whole.

Because lobsters grow throughout their lives, they periodically shed their shells to accommodate larger bodies. This process, called molting, is similar to how a snake sheds its skin. In a lobster's first five years, it molts roughly 25 times, gaining 15 percent body length and 50 percent volume each time. As adults grow larger, molting decreases. A three- to four-pound lobster generally molts every three to five years.

Prior to molting, a new shell forms under the lobster's old shell. The lobster drains calcium out of the old shell and stores it in a reservoir to be recycled into the new shell. When ready to molt, the lobster secretes enzymes to soften its old shell. It then swells its body with saltwater and splits the old shell open. The lobster backs out of its old shell, but its large claw muscles sometimes get stuck in the

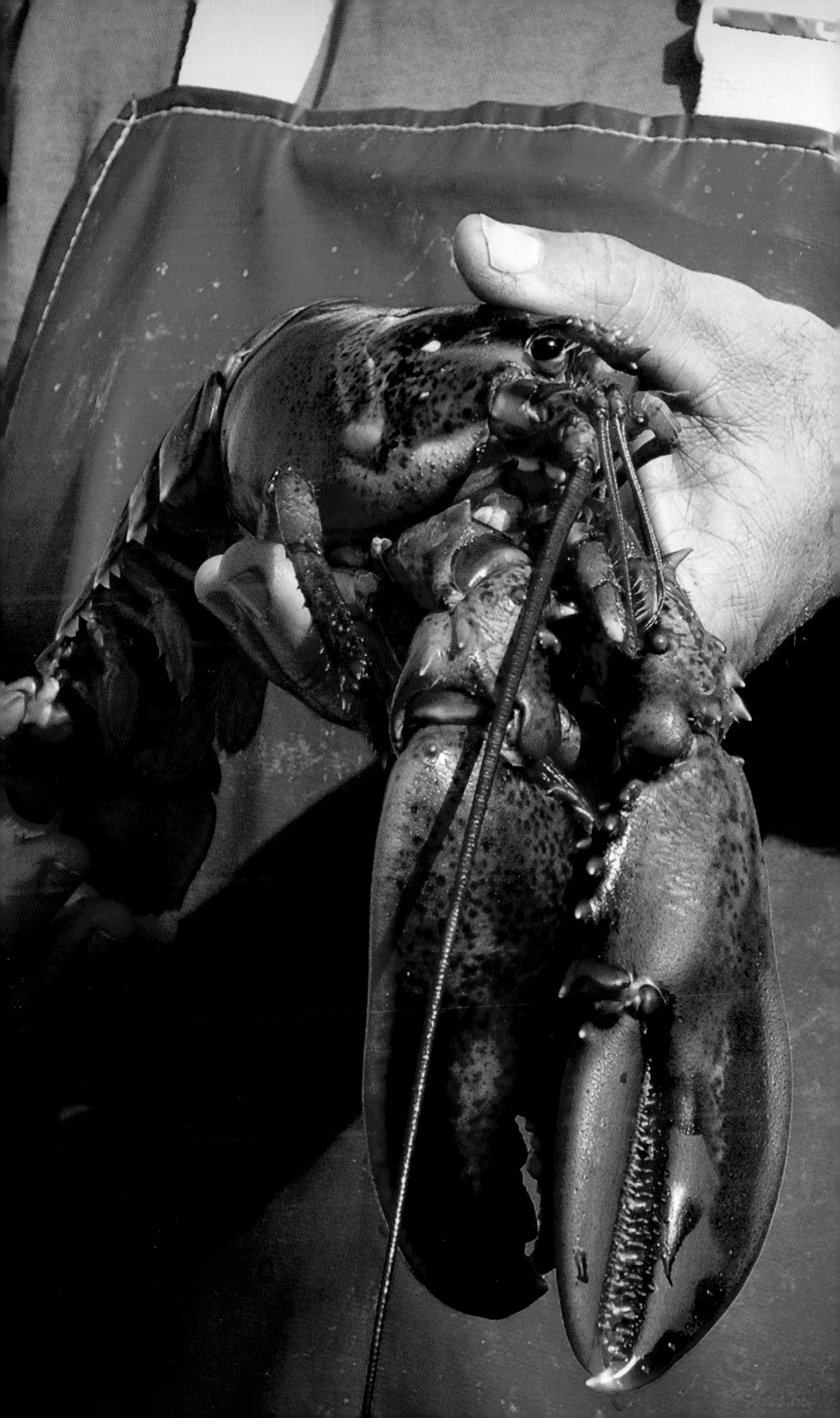

narrow claw joints. Occasionally, claw muscles won't fit through the claw joints and tear off. But claws, like all other lobster appendages, can regenerate over time. The complete molting process takes anywhere from five minutes to half an hour. After a molt, the lobster's soft, squishy muscles are almost completely exposed. The lobster is rendered defenseless and enters one of the most dangerous phases in its life. The lobster quickly eats its old shell to absorb additional calcium and minerals, then seeks shelter while waiting several days for its new shell to harden.

A lobster's shell offers terrific defense, but it also poses unique challenges. Hard shells reduce access to a female's anatomy, so lobsters only have sex after the female has molted. During courtship, an alpha male wanders the ocean floor and evicts females from their shelters, then returns to his shelter. Interested females, who only mate with dominant alpha males, wander by the male's shelter and pee inside. The alpha male then happily swirls the urine around himself. (If this isn't strange enough, lobsters pee through an opening in their face.) Eventually the female moves in with the male, sheds her shell, and the lobsters copulate. For the next week or so, as the female waits for her new shell to harden, she stays in the male's shelter under his protection. When she leaves, a new female immediately takes her place.

Females can carry sperm for several month before using it. They can also store sperm for a second batch of eggs. Eggs develop inside the female, then attach to the underside of her tail. Depending on the size of the female, her tail can carry anywhere between 5,000 and 100,000 eggs.

When eggs hatch, tiny lobster larvae disperse into the ocean and float where the current takes them. Only a handful of larvae survive this dangerous period; most are eaten by predators. After molting four times in three weeks, tiny half-inch lobsters settle to the ocean floor. Baby lobsters that settle on sandy bottoms are often eaten by predators. Baby lobsters that settle on cobble bottoms—of which there are many in the Gulf of Maine—have a much better chance of growing to adulthood.

Some scientists believe lobsters are one of a handful of species that don't die of old age. If lobsters can survive predation, disease, and entrapment, they can grow to monstrous proportions. The largest known lobster, caught in Nova Scotia in 1977, weighed 44 pounds and was estimated to be over 100 years old. In the early 1800s, before lobsters were commercially harvested, reports exist of four-foot lobsters weighing 50 pounds or more.

A lobster's shell has multiple dark pigments. When lobster is cooked, its dark pigments break down and a bright red pigment is all that remains. In rare cases, lobsters are born with a genetic mutation that gives them just one pigment. Every few years, a blue or yellow lobster is harvested to much local fanfare. In extremely rare cases, a lobster's coloration splits down the middle—half yellow, half blue.

ANATOMY OF A LOBSTER

Shredder Claw
This sharp, slender claw shreds the flesh of victims. It is composed of fast muscle fibers, which contract rapidly but tire easily.

Crusher Claw
This large, powerful claw crushes the shells of prey such as clams and mussels. It is composed of slow muscle fibers, which produce strong contractions of long duration.

Antennules
A lobster's antennules contain hundreds of chemical receptors that give lobsters an extraordinary sense of smell. Lobsters "sniff" by flicking the antennules up and down.

Carapace
This large backplate stretches from the eye socket to the top of the tail. Lobstermen measure the carapace to determine legal size.

Legs & Feet
Lobsters have ten legs, including the claws, which are covered with thousands of tiny hairs that sense touch and function as taste buds.

Antennae
These whip-like antennae are highly mobile, moving swiftly from side to side to detect motion. The two antennae can also sense bidirectional movement to determine water current direction.

Tail
A lobster's powerful tail propels it backwards at speeds up to 16 feet per second. Female lobsters carry eggs on the underside of their tails, and they have wider tails to accommodate more eggs. Large females carry up to 100,000 eggs.

MAINE LOBSTERMEN

Proud, tough, independent minded—lobstermen are the cultural and economic heart of Maine's coastal communities. But it wasn't always this way.

Until the 1800s, lobster was considered a "garbage fish" barely worthy of harvesting. Lobster was collected close to shore by old men and young boys who lacked the strength to fish at sea. Then New Yorkers discovered the taste of fresh lobster, and demand increased. The 1840s saw the invention of the "lobster smack," a sailboat that could transport live lobsters over long distances, and by the 1870s canned lobster had become big business. In the 1840s, there were only a few dozen lobstermen in Maine. By 1880, there were over 1,800.

When settlers first arrived in Maine, they could gather large lobsters among the rocks at low tide. When harvesting reduced lobster populations along the shore, settlers built wooden traps and launched them from rowboats. As the industry grew, lobstermen abandoned rowboats for sailboats—most notably Friendship sloops built in Friendship, Maine. Then, in the 1930s and 1940s, lobstermen abandoned sailboats for diesel-powered motorboats.

The next major change came in the 1970s, when durable metal traps replaced wooden traps. Today lobster traps, which measure roughly four feet long, are divided into two chambers. The first chamber, the "kitchen," has twin, funnel-shaped openings where lobsters enter the trap. From the kitchen a third funnel-shaped opening leads to a "parlor," where lobstermen place a bag of smelly bait. Once a lobster wanders into the parlor, it's effectively trapped.

Each trap is connected by rope to a floating buoy, which is painted with a color pattern unique to each lobsterman. After snagging a buoy, the lobsterman hauls the trap onboard with the aid of an electric motor. He then removes any lobsters, puts a fresh bag of bait in the trap, and throws the trap overboard. In Maine, lobstermen are allowed a maximum of 800 traps.

According to the Gulf of Maine Research Institute, the average lobsterman is 50 years old and has been lobstering for 30 years. His boat is 32 feet long, 17 years old, and has a 260-horsepower engine. If he works with

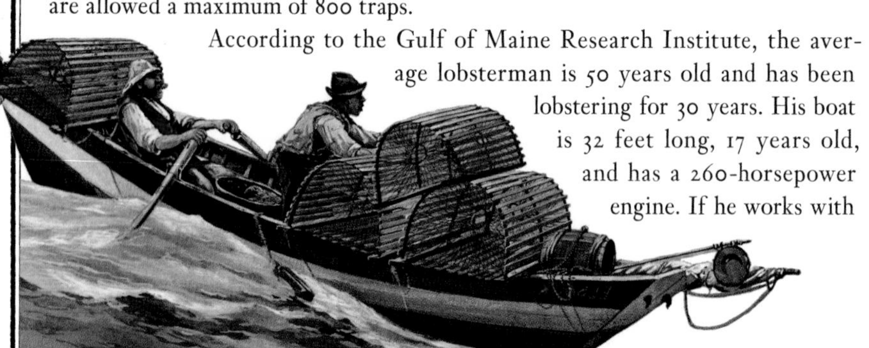

a sternman (assistant), he lands roughly 24,000 pounds of lobster. Lobstermen earn anywhere from $25,000 to $250,000 per year, depending on the price of lobster, the price of gas, and their work ethic.

Today nearly every fisherman in Maine is a lobsterman. After fish populations collapsed in the early 1990s, lobstering took up the slack. Today there are roughly 7,000 lobstermen in Maine—up from 2,500 lobstermen in the 1970s. Annual harvests have skyrocketed from 20 million pounds in the 1980s to over 100 million pounds today. Amazingly, lobster populations in Maine appear to be stable. This is due, in large part, to the lobstermen themselves, who adhere to strict conservation measures that allow lobsters to flourish.

Lobster conservation laws first appeared in the late 1800s, but back then they were largely ignored. When lobster catches collapsed in the 1920s, averaging 5–7 million pounds, lobstermen reluctantly embraced conservation. Today all lobsters are measured, and lobstermen only keep lobsters with a carapace between 3.25 and 5 inches. All other lobsters are returned to the sea. This allows small lobsters to reach sexual maturity and big lobsters (which produce exponentially more eggs) to reproduce. When lobstermen catch an egg-bearing female they cut a permanent V-notch on the tip of her tail. Once a female lobster acquires a V-notch, she can never be harvested.

Perhaps most fascinating, these conservation measures are almost entirely self-regulated. Lobstermen belong to unofficial "gangs" that work specific harbors or territories. If anyone breaks the rules, they face the wrath of the gang. Likewise, if a lobsterman encroaches on another gang's territory, subtle warning signals are sent. At first, knots are tied on the offending lobsterman's buoy. If violations continue, trap ropes are cut. In severe cases, lobster boats are vandalized. This social pressure, it turns out, is far more effective than government intervention, especially when there are only 32 wardens to patrol 2,500 miles of Maine coast. It also helps that lobstermen have good working relationships with government officials and a strong personal sense the system works for them.

The unusual success of Maine's lobster industry has drawn the attention of prominent researchers. Elinor Ostrom became the first woman to win the Nobel Prize in Economics in 2009 for her work on the management of common property by common ownership, which examined Maine lobstermen. Someday, the unorthodox solutions pioneered by Maine lobstermen may help conserve other natural resources around the world.

WHALES

The Gulf of Maine's cold, nutrient-rich water and shallow depth make it one of the most biologically productive marine habitats in the world. In summer, when nutrients are at their peak, hundreds of migrating whales arrive to feast on the natural bounty. From 85-foot finback whales to 5-foot harbor porpoises, the Gulf of Maine is filled with extraordinary cetaceans.

Whales are warm-blooded mammals that breathe air, have hair, and nurse their young. Although mammals evolved roughly 200 million years ago, whales did not appear until roughly 50 million years ago. Around that time, some land mammals began spending more and more time in the ocean. After several million years, they evolved into purely marine animals—the ancestors of modern whales. Even today, whale fetuses develop a pair of rear legs that are genetic remnants of their land-dwelling ancestors. Although these tiny legs fail to fully develop, tiny "leg bones" are visible in the skeletons of many whales.

Whales are divided into two major categories: toothed whales and baleen whales. Toothed whales (such as sperm whales) have teeth, while baleen whales (such as humpbacks) have mouths filled with hundreds of fibrous, closely-spaced baleen plates. The plates, which are made of keratin—the same substance found in human fingernails—allow whales to filter out plankton and fish from seawater. Although there are over 70 species of toothed whale and only 12 species of baleen whales, baleen whales are the most commonly spotted large whales in the Gulf of Maine.

Because whales are warm-blooded, they must maintain a constant body temperature of 98.6° F, which is a major challenge in the frigid Gulf of Maine. To help retain warmth, whales have a thick layer of blubber (fat) under their rubbery skin. In large baleen whales blubber layers can measure up to two feet thick. Although blubber helps whales survive in cold water, it nearly resulted in their extinction in modern times.

Three hundred years ago, people relied on oil rendered from whale blubber to fuel lamps and lubricate machines. In the 1700s, New Englanders aggressively hunted whales offshore. When local populations declined, they sailed around the planet in search of new whales to harvest. By the early 1800s, global whale populations were in steep decline. The development of petroleum in the late 1800s saved whales from complete annihilation.

Within a few decades, however, motorized boats and exploding harpoons allowed whalers to hunt species that had previously been too fast to catch. At the same time, new chemical processes allowed whale oil to be rendered into a variety of products, including margarine and soap. Blue whales and finback whales suffered massive population declines before a commercial whaling moratorium was established in 1986. Today some whale populations are recovering, but many remain threatened by fishing nets and accidental boat strikes.

Allied Whale

Over the past five decades, researchers at Allied Whale have studied migrating whales and other marine mammals off Mount Desert Island. Founded in 1972 as a nonprofit research arm of Bar Harbor's College of the Atlantic, Allied Whale pioneered identifying humpback whales by their unique tail markings. Allied Whale maintains a database of tens of thousands of whale photos to help track population and migration patterns. In 2010, researchers used Allied Whale photos to identify a humpback whale that traveled over 6,000 miles between Brazil and Madagascar—the largest mammal migration ever documented. Allied Whale also operates the most remote field research station on the Eastern Seaboard: Mount Desert Rock (p.111), a tiny island 20 miles south of Mount Desert Island. To learn more about Allied Whale, visit the George B. Dorr Natural History Museum (p.217).

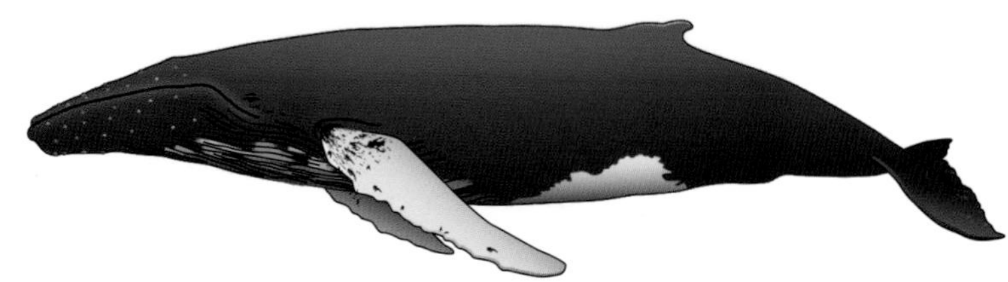

Humpback Whale
Megaptera novaeangliae

Famous for their acrobatic displays and crooning songs, humpback whales grow up to 60 feet long and weigh up to 45 tons. Over 10,000 humpbacks spend their summers in the western North Atlantic, eating up to 3,000 pounds of fish and krill each day and often doubling their weight by fall. After accumulating thick layers of blubber, humpbacks migrate to the Caribbean to breed and raise calves. During this time calves consume up to 100 gallons of mother's milk each day, but adults do not feed at all. A pronounced back arch gives humpbacks their common name. Long flippers—the longest of any whale—inspired their scientific name: *Megaptera novaeangliae*, "Big Wing of New England." (Humpbacks were first studied in New England.) Humpbacks, which swim in all the world's oceans, have the longest migration of any animal: 5,000 miles.

Northern Right Whale
Eubalanea glacialis

The northern right whale is one of the rarest animals in the world. Fewer than 350 remain in the North Atlantic. Among the bulkiest of whales, they are slow-moving giants that grow up to 60 feet long and weigh up to 100 tons. This made right whales the main target of whalers in the 1800s. Right whales (which earned their name because they were the "right" whales to hunt) nearly went extinct by the 1930s, when hunting was banned. Sadly, their populations have barely recovered since then. In winter, mothers and calves migrate to the warm waters off northern Florida and Georgia. The heads of right whales are often covered in large skin growths called callosities, which contain several species of whale lice.

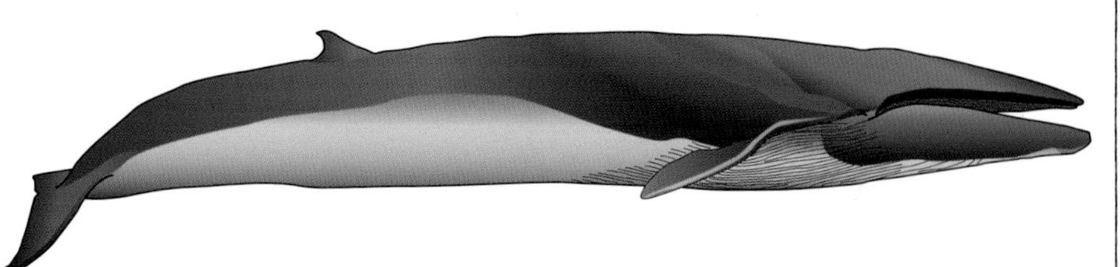

Finback Whale

Balaenoptera physalus

Finbacks are the second-largest whales in the world after blue whales. They grow up to 85 feet long and weigh up to 70 tons. Named for their prominent dorsal fin, which is located two-thirds of the way down their back, finbacks are the most commonly spotted whales off Mount Desert Island. After coming to the surface for air, a finback breathes 5 to 15 times in a row, diving a short distance between breaths. Each breath raises their back and dorsal fin higher and higher out of the water. The final breath leads to a "terminal dive," when the finback arches its back five to six feet above water, then dives underwater up to 15 minutes. During this time, finbacks reach depths up to 750 feet. Finbacks return to the same North Atlantic feeding areas year after year, but where they mate and give birth remains a mystery. Today there are roughly 16,000 finback whales in the North Atlantic.

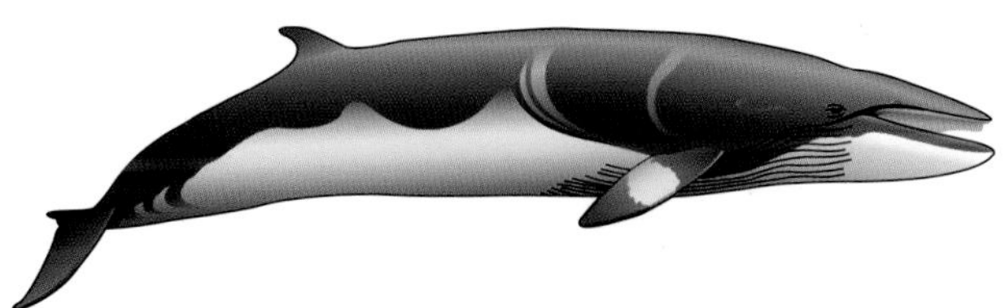

Minke Whale

Balaenoptera acutorostrata

Minke whales are relatively small, growing "just" 30 feet long and weighing 11 tons. Because of their size, they were not aggressively hunted by whalers. Today there are an estimated one million minke whales, making them the world's most common baleen whale. Minke whales live in every ocean in the world, but they prefer cold environments like the North Atlantic. In summer, larger minke whales migrate farther north than smaller minke whales, and adult females migrate farther north than adult males. In the Gulf of Maine, the majority of minke whales are small juveniles. Because they venture closer to shore than larger whales, minke whales can sometimes be seen in harbors and bays.

Harbor Seals & Gray Seals

Harbor seals (*Phoca vitulina*) swim in the waters off Mount Desert Island and bask on offshore ledges. Growing up to six feet long and weighing up to 290 pounds, they come in a wide range of colors including black, gray, tan, and white. Harbor seals have large, round eyes that give them superior vision in dark, murky water. Because they lack ducts to drain eye fluids, tears flow continuously down their eyes. Harbor seals swim up to 12 mph, dive up to 300 feet, and can stay submerged for half an hour. While diving their heart rate decreases from 120 to six beats per minute to conserve oxygen.

Gray seals, which are much larger than harbor seals, grow up to eight feet long and weigh up to 800 pounds. They are identified by distinctive horse-like faces and prominent curved noses. The gray seal's scientific name, *Halichoerus gryphus*, means "hook-nosed sea pig."

In the late 1800s, fishermen put a $1 per head bounty on seals to reduce competition for fish. By the time the bounty was repealed in 1905, seals were nearly exterminated along much of Maine's coast. In 1972, the Marine Mammal Protection Act banned hunting of all marine mammals, and seal populations have slowly rebounded since then.

BIRDS

Acadia National Park is a birdwatching paradise. Over 330 bird species have been identified in the park—roughly one-third of all bird species in the United States. Acadia's impressive diversity is due to the park's diverse habitat. Onshore there are lakes, ponds, and marshes surrounded by extensive conifer and hardwood forests. Offshore there are dozens of pristine islands surrounded by the biologically rich Gulf of Maine, which attracts both northern and southern seabirds. Over two dozen seabird species have been identified near Acadia, including rarely seen pelagic (open ocean) species that only venture onshore to nest.

If you're a serious birder looking for a great guide, contact Rich MacDonald (207-266-9461, thenaturalhistorycenter.com) or Michael Good (207-288-8128, downeastnaturetours.com). Seasonal events include the Acadia Birding Festival (acadiabirdingfestival.com) in late spring, Peregrine Watch at the Precipice in spring and early summer, and Hawk Watch on Cadillac Mountain in autumn. Cadillac Mountain offers some of the best views on the East Coast, making it a great place for Hawk Watch volunteers to study annual raptor migrations.

Peregrine Falcon
Falco peregrinus

Peregrine falcons are legendary hunters that can spot birds from thousands of feet above, then dive-bomb them at speeds topping 200 mph—the fastest speed of any animal. The collision creates an explosion of feathers, and victims that don't die upon impact have their necks broken by the peregrine's powerful beak. During World War II, Allied troops trained peregrine falcons to kill Nazi carrier pigeons. By the early 1970s, however, peregrine populations collapsed due to the toxic effects of the pesticide DDT. When ingested by birds, DDT fatally weakened eggshells, and mothers accidentally crushed their own brittle eggs. After DDT was banned, peregrine populations began to recover, and in 1999 peregrine falcons were removed from the federal endangered species list. Today peregrine falcons nest on several cliffs in Acadia, most notably the Precipice (p.144). Adult peregrines weigh up to 3.3 pounds and have a 3.9-foot wingspan.

Atlantic Puffin

Fratercula arctica

These adorable seabirds, famous for their colorful beaks, spend most of their lives on the open ocean. They return to land only to raise chicks in spring and summer. Amazing swimmers, puffins use their wings to "fly" underwater and hunt fish. Puffins can carry up to 60 fish in their beak at one time. When flying through the air they flap their wings up to 400 times per minute. Early Maine settlers hunted puffins, and by 1900 just one colony remained. In the 1970s, conservationists reintroduced puffin chicks from Newfoundland to Maine islands, and today there's a breeding colony on Petit Manan Island near Schoodic Peninsula. (Bar Harbor Whale Watch offers puffin tours, p.218.) Atlantic puffins grow up to one foot long. Their scientific name, *Fratercula arctica*, means "little friar of the north," a reference to their robe-like coloration.

Common Loon

Gavia immer

Famous for their haunting call, which echoes across lakes in summer, loons are one of Acadia's most recognizable birds. Their summer range includes most of Canada and the northern United States. Loons spend winters in coastal areas as far south as Mexico. Summer plumage is striking: jet black feathers covered with bright white points. Winter plumage is drab brown. Unlike most flying birds, loons have relatively solid bones that help them dive deep underwater. They can hold their breath up to 90 seconds and reach depths up to 150 feet. Bright red eyes give them superior vision underwater. Loons pursue fish with dagger-like bills, which they use to stab and grasp prey. Loons also use their bills against other loons, engaging in underwater fights to defend territory. Although loons are powerful swimmers, they are famously clumsy on land. The word "loon" is supposedly derived from the Scandinavian word *lom* ("clumsy person"). Chicks often take to the water within hours of hatching.

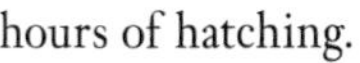

Osprey

Pandion haliaetus

Osprey fly high above water in search of fish, which make up the vast majority of their diet. When an osprey spots a fish—sometimes from as far as 130 feet in the air—it swoops down and snatches the fish out of the water with powerful talons. Up to 80% of osprey strikes are successful. They can even catch two fish at once using each talon. Backwards-facing scales on the talons act as barbs to grasp slippery fish. Osprey wingspans measure up to six feet across, and their nests can exceed twelve feet in height. Their call is a sharp, high-pitched *cheep cheep*. Osprey are found along the entire East Coast in summer, but those north of South Carolina spend winter in the tropics. Osprey from Mount Desert Island have been recorded as far south as Haiti and Honduras. Their only natural predators are great horned owls, golden eagles, and bald eagles.

Bald Eagle

Haliaeetus leucocephalus

One of the largest birds in North America, bald eagles weigh up to 14 pounds and boast 7.5-foot wingspans. Their tree nests—the largest of any animal—measure up to eight feet across, 13 feet high, and weigh up to 2,000 pounds. The bald eagle's call is a high-pitched *kleek kik ik ik*. Fish constitute the majority of their diet, but bald eagles also prey on birds and small mammals. When attacking they dive at speeds up to 100 mph. In 1782, bald eagles became the national bird of the U.S. (Ben Franklin didn't like the choice because of the bird's "bad moral character.") By the 1960s, however, there were fewer than 900 bald eagles in the lower 48 states. Populations plummeted due to hunting, habitat loss, and the toxic effects of the pesticide DDT. Today, following effective conservation programs, there are over 300,000 bald eagles in the lower 48 states.

Blackburnian Warbler

Setophaga fusca

With its vibrant orange and black plumage, the Blackburnian warbler is one of the most striking birds in Acadia. Their summer breeding range extends from southeastern Canada down the Appalachian Mountains as far south as North Carolina. In winter they migrate to Central America and northern South America, where they live in tropical montane forests between 2,000 and 8,000 feet. Their winter range extends down the Andes Mountains as far south as Peru. Blackburnian warblers measure up to five inches long with 8.5-inch wingspans. Their song is a series of high simple notes, often ascending in pitch, sometimes described as *zip zip zip zip zip zip zip zip*. They spend much of their time in high treetops, and their diet consists almost entirely of insects. Blackburnian warblers have a particular fondness for caterpillars. Their annual migration corresponds with the vast number of insects that thrive in North America in summer.

Herring Gull

Larus argentatus

The most commonly spotted bird in Acadia is, without question, the herring gull. From the park's rocky shoreline to its highest peaks, these medium-sized birds are ubiquitous. Adult birds, which grow up to two feet long, have white bodies, gray wings and black wing tips. Juveniles are mottled brown. Herring gulls eat just about anything, including fish, shellfish, garbage, and baby seabirds. To crack open the shells of clams and mussels, herring gulls drop them onto hard surfaces. Like all gulls, herring gulls have unhinged jaws, allowing them to swallow large prey. The red spot on a gull's yellow bill is a target for chicks, who peck at it to indicate hunger. When pecked, adults regurgitate food into the chick's mouth. Although common today, herring gull populations collapsed in the 1800s due to egg poaching, habitat loss, and feather harvesting for ladies' hats. Conservation laws helped gull populations rebound, and today there are over 200,000 herring gulls in Maine.

Great Shearwater
Puffinus gravis

These seabirds spend most of their lives on the open ocean, and they circumnavigate the Atlantic each year. From September to May great shearwaters breed on a handful of small islands (Gough, Nightingale, Tristan da Cunha) in the middle of the South Atlantic, then migrate up the coast of South America. By June they are common in North American waters. In late summer they migrate to Europe, then head down the African coast en route to winter breeding grounds. This migration pattern—breeding in the Southern Hemisphere, flying to the northern hemisphere—is the reverse of most long-distance migrants. Great shearwaters measure up to 1.7 feet long and have four-foot wingspans. Like all shearwaters they have stiff wings that enable them to "shear" across wave fronts, reducing physical exertion with a minimum of active flight.

Common Eider
Somateria mollissima

The common eider is the largest duck in the Northern Hemisphere, growing up to 28 inches long and weighing up to five pounds. Adult eiders feed primarily on shellfish, swallowing mussels and crabs whole. Their stomachs are specially designed to crush shellfish, digesting both the shell and its contents. During spring breeding season, adult males sport dramatic black and white plumage with white cheeks and yellow/greenish coloration on the back of the neck. Females eiders are completely brown year-round. Males leave immediately after breeding, and females are solely responsible for incubation of the egg. Females work cooperatively raising "crèches" of 60 or more chicks. Although common today, Maine eider populations plummeted in the late 1800s. Eiders were aggressively hunted for their soft down, which was used in pillows and quilts. By the early 1900s, just one breeding population remained in Maine. Following a hunting ban, eider populations slowly recovered. Today they gather in large "rafts" of several thousand birds on the open water.

Arctic Tern

Sterna paradisaea

This remarkable bird has the longest annual migration of any animal. Arctic terns spend June, July and August in the arctic and subarctic regions of North America, Europe, and Asia. When temperatures drop, they migrate to Antarctica—a minimum distance of 12,000 miles. Some arctic terns travel up to 56,000 miles *each year.* Those that live 30 years or more can travel over 1.5 million miles during their lifetimes. This "Endless Summer" migration—enjoying both northern summer and southern summer—means arctic terns see more daylight than any other creature on the planet. Those that summer in Maine follow a migration route along the west coast of Europe and North Africa, crossing the North Atlantic to reach North America. Arctic terns breed and raise chicks in their northern range. Fierce defenders of their nests, they attack any animals, including humans, that wander too close. From beak to tail, arctic terns measure up to 14 inches and have 2.5-foot wingspans.

Black Guillemot

Cepphus grylle

The black guillemot is one of Acadia's most easily identifiable seabirds. In summer, look for a medium-sized black body with bright red feet, striking white patches on the top and underside of the wings, and a rapid flapping motion in flight. Winter plumage is whitish/gray. Black guillemots grow up to 15 inches long with 23-inch wingspans. They are found on both sides of the North Atlantic, but Maine marks the southern limit of their North American range. Black guillemots are members of the alcid family, which includes puffins. Unlike puffins, black guillemots prefer foraging for fish and crustaceans in relatively shallow waters near shore. Black guillemots are non-migratory birds that spend winters near the rocky cliffs and islands where they breed.

White-Tailed Deer

Odocoileus virginianus

White-tailed deer are the most abundant large mammal in North America. Their range extends from Canada to Peru, but the largest whitetails live in the U.S. and Canada. The flash of their tail, which sports a bright white underside, serves as a warning to other deer when danger is present.

Bucks (males) are distinguished by antlers, which grow up to two feet across. Bucks use antlers as sparring weapons during the fall rut, and the most dominant bucks breed with the most does (females). During this time bucks are so focused on finding does they rarely eat or rest. Bucks shed their antlers each winter, then regrow them the following spring.

In spring does give birth to one to three fawns, which are virtually defenseless when born. During their first month, fawns lie hidden in vegetation while their mothers forage. To avoid detection by predators, fawns have white spots on their backs that provide camouflage with the sun-dappled forest floor. After one month, fawns follow their mothers on foraging trips, and by summer their spots have disappeared. Bucks leave their mother after one year. Does leave after two years. When fully grown, does weigh up to 200 pounds and bucks weigh up to 350 pounds.

Deer are ruminants with four-chambered stomachs. This allows them to digest rough vegetation such as shoots and leaves. They can also eat mushrooms and plants that are toxic to other animals. Although classified as herbivores, white-tailed deer opportunistically feed on small animals.

Highly adaptable, white-tailed deer live in forests, swamps, deserts, plains, mountains—even in densely populated cities. Prior to European colonization, North America's white-tailed deer population may have numbered as high as 40 million. By the mid-1800s, however, hunting reduced that number to roughly one million. Hunters, alarmed at the decline, pushed for wildlife management practices that allowed populations to bounce back. But the near extermination of natural predators such as mountain lions and wolves means that white-tailed deer are now entirely dependent on humans to keep their population in check. Without adequate hunting, deer populations would explode to unsustainable levels.

Moose
Alces alces

Weighing up to 1,800 pounds, moose are the largest animals in Acadia National Park. Some stand 7.5 feet tall at the shoulder, and the tips of their antlers tower 10 feet above ground. Despite their large size, moose are surprisingly nimble. They can run up to 35 mph—nearly as fast as white-tailed deer—and swim up to six mph. Their long, gangly legs are well-adapted to walking through deep snow.

Moose are solitary animals that do not form herds. Bulls (males) are distinguished by massive antlers, which can stretch six feet across and weigh nearly 80 pounds. Antlers start growing in spring and are shed each winter. They grow progressively larger each year until a bull reaches about five years in age. Antlers are used to mark territory, dig plants from the bottom of ponds, and fight with other males. During the autumn rut, when bulls are stoked by testosterone, spectacular fights erupt among bulls competing for cows (females). About eight months after mating, cows give birth to one or two offspring. Newborns weigh up to 35 pounds. Adult moose live up to 20 years in the wild.

Moose require 50 to 60 pounds of vegetation each day. They feed by wrapping thick, rubbery lips around a twig, then stripping away the leaves, bark, and buds in a single motion. The name "moose" comes from the Algonquian word *moosu*, which has been translated as "twig eater" or "he who strips off." Moose meat was a staple of native diets, and moose hides were used to make leather moccasins.

In the depths of the Ice Age, Asian moose crossed the Bering land bridge and spread across North America for the first time. Today 80 percent of North America's moose population lives in Canada. Although once common throughout New England, moose populations plummeted by the late 1800s due to hunting and habitat loss. Populations have since rebounded, and today Maine has an estimated 75,000 moose—the most south of Canada. Although rarely seen on Mount Desert Island, moose are occasionally spotted on Schoodic Peninsula or swimming among the islands of Blue Hill Bay.

Black Bear

Ursus americanus

Black bears are rarely seen in Acadia National Park, but they are the most common bear species in North America. There are nearly one million black bears in the U.S. and Canada. Of North America's three bear species—black, grizzly, and polar—black bears are the smallest. They grow up to six feet long and weigh up to 600 pounds. Despite their roly-poly appearance, black bears can reach top speeds of 30 mph over short distances. They are also excellent tree climbers.

Black bears are highly intelligent, and their sense of smell is roughly 100 times more powerful than a dog's. Opportunistic omnivores, black bears eat just about anything: grass in spring, berries in summer, and pine seeds in autumn. Roughly 80 percent of their diet is vegetation, but bears also eat ants, termites, and insect larvae. Black bears have a particular fondness for human trash, which is why bear-proof trash cans are found throughout the park.

In autumn, black bears consume up to 20,000 calories per day in preparation for winter "hibernation." But black bears are not true hibernators. After snuggling into their dens in October or November, black bears enter a "light" hibernation referred to as seasonal lethargy. During this time, black bear heartbeats drop from roughly 70 beats per minute to as low as eight beats per minute. Compared to true hibernators, black bear body temperatures drop relatively little. During winter dormancy, which lasts three to five months, black bears lose roughly 25–30 percent of their total body weight.

Between the ages of three and five, females produce their first offspring. They breed about every two years after that. Mating season peaks in May and June, but embryos don't develop until autumn, when mothers have put on adequate weight to survive winter. Mothers give birth in the den after a two- to three-month gestation. Most litters consist of one to three cubs, which weigh less than a pound at birth. Youngsters stay with their mother throughout their first year while learning how to fend for themselves. Black bears live about 20 years in the wild.

Coyote
Canis latrans

Coyotes roam Acadia by day, and their haunting howls echo through the park at night. One long, high-pitched howl calls a pack of coyotes together. When the pack has gathered, a cacophony of yips and yelps are often added to the mix. Coyotes have brownish-gray fur and long, bushy tails. Unlike dogs and wolves, coyotes run with their tails hanging down.

Coyotes currently range from Canada to Panama, but historically they were confined to the open spaces of the western U.S. and Mexico. Following the extermination of wolves in the 1800s, coyotes spread rapidly throughout North America. Coyotes first appeared in New England in the 1930s and '40s. Eastern coyotes mixed with the remaining wolf population, and today they are considered a genetically distinct subspecies. Intelligent, adaptable animals with a knack for scavenging, coyote populations have held steady and even increased in places despite years of being hunted, poisoned, and trapped.

Although coyotes often forage alone, they sometimes travel in packs of six or so closely related family members. Their diet, which is 90 percent animals, consists mostly of rodents and small mammals. But coyotes eat just about anything, including birds, snakes, insects, carrion, and trash. Working in packs, coyotes hunt larger animals such as deer. While pursuing prey, they reach top speeds of over 40 mph and jump up to 13 feet horizontally.

Coyotes are strictly monogamous. They mate in winter, and mothers give birth to five to seven pups in spring. Newborn coyote are hairless and sightless, and pups don't leave the den until eight to ten weeks of age. Young coyotes are extremely vulnerable. Up to two-thirds do not survive to adulthood, but those that survive can live 10 years or longer in the wild. Adult coyotes measure up to four feet long and weigh up to 50 pounds.

Coyotes often play a central role in the legends and myths of native tribes. Among a small cast of human and animal characters, Coyote is portrayed as a scheming trickster that scrapes by on cunning and charm. The word "coyote" is derived from the Aztec word *cóyotl*. Coyote's Latin name, *Canis latrans*, means "barking dog," a reference to its famous vocalizations.

Beaver
Castor canadensis

Weighing 40 pounds or more, beavers are the largest rodents in North America. They use large incisors to topple trees and drag them to streams to build dams. The resulting wetlands create prime habitat for beavers and boost the area's biodiversity. Beavers construct dams with logs, sticks, and rocks cemented with mud. They build a living space, called a lodge, by heaping together a separate pile of debris, then gnawing out a roomy chamber from below. Beavers are excellent swimmers that can remain submerged up to 15 minutes. Large, webbed hind feet aid in swimming. They use their long, flat tails as rudders while towing trees and branches in water. Native tribes considered roasted beaver tail a delicacy, and European settlers paid high prices for beaver pelts. By the 1800s, however, beaver populations were in serious decline. They recovered following the collapse of the beaver trade and protective laws enacted in the 1900s. Beavers were reintroduced to Acadia in 1920. Since then, North American beaver populations have recovered to roughly 10–15 million animals—a fraction of the 100–200 million beavers present before Columbus.

Raccoon
Procyon lotor

Famous for the black "mask" that covers their face, raccoons are intelligent, crafty creatures. Their eyes are incredibly well adapted to darkness, allowing them to carry out mischievous deeds at night, such as removing trash lids and prying open coolers to steal food. Raccoons eat just about anything, including frogs, birds, fruits, nuts, worms, slugs, and garbage. They are especially ravenous in autumn, increasing their body fat up to 50 percent to prepare for the lean winter months. Although raccoons prefer wooded areas near streams, they have adapted remarkably well to urban environments, traveling along sewage pipes and living in attics and chimneys. Despite their cute and cuddly appearance, raccoons have a nasty disposition and a tendency to carry rabies. They should never be approached. The name raccoon is supposedly derived from the Algonquian *arakunem*, which means "one that scratches with its hands."

Red Fox
Vulpes fulva

Sleek and swift, crafty and cunning, the red fox is a highly adaptable animal. Its range includes much of North America, Europe, Asia, North Africa, Iceland and Japan. Although members of the dog family, foxes display many feline characteristics such as stalking, pouncing, and toying with wounded prey. Their elliptical cat-like pupils shrink to a narrow slit, giving them exceptional vision in bright light. A reflective membrane at the back of the eye causes light to pass over the retina twice, which also gives them excellent night vision. Their superior vision, combined with exceptional hearing and a sense of smell 100 times greater than that of humans, makes foxes highly skilled hunters. They eat virtually anything they can catch, including grasshoppers, crickets, small birds, squirrels, rabbits, and lizards. Mothers bring partially dead animals back to the den so pups can sharpen their survival skills. While still less than a month old, pups fight among themselves to establish dominance. Parents feed the most dominant pups first.

Snowshoe Hare
Lepus americanus

Snowshoe hares are masters of disguise. In summer they sport a grayish brown coat that helps them blend in with grasses and shrubs. As winter approaches, their coat turns white, providing excellent camouflage in snow. They are preyed upon by foxes, coyotes, owls, and hawks. When a hare senses a predator, it freezes to avoid detection. If necessary, it can flee at speeds up to 30 mph, making sharp zigzags and hopping 12 feet in a single bound. Snowshoe hares often spend their days sleeping in hidden locations, becoming active only at night or in the low light of dawn or dusk. They mate and give birth year-round. Females produce up to eight young per litter, up to four times per year. Young hares run within hours of birth. Snowshoe hare populations are cyclical, becoming plentiful every 10 years or so, then plummeting dramatically. During population booms, some areas contain up to 10,000 snowshoe hares per square mile.

HISTORY

NOT LONG AFTER ice age glaciers retreated from New England, humans settled the land. Around 11,000 years ago, paleo-Indian hunters arrived in Maine and scraped out a living on the tundra left in the glacier's wake. At the time, mammoths, mastodons, and six-foot beavers roamed the land. Hunters chased game throughout the interior and hunted seals and walrus on the coast.

As temperatures warmed, trees such as spruce and fir took root, followed by birch, alder, and other hardwoods. Around 5,000 years ago, the modern ecology of Maine began to take shape. By that point many large ice age mammals had gone extinct (possibly due to overhunting), and many arctic and sub-arctic species migrated north. Taking their place in Maine's forests were deer, moose, and a variety of small mammals.

By the time of European contact, French explorers called the tribes living in Downeast Maine "Etchemins." The name may have been derived from the native word *skicin*, which translates as "the real people." Following the upheaval of European contact, Etchemins merged with neighboring tribes to become the Wabanaki—an Algonquian-speaking group that includes the Penobscot, Passamaquoddy, Mi'kmaq, and Maliseet. *Wabanaki*, loosely translated, means "People of the Dawnland," a reference to Maine's eastern location. The Wabanaki were highly mobile, with seasonal patterns adapted to plant and animal lifecycles. They paddled birch-bark canoes and established villages on the banks of rivers, lakes, and along the coast.

Of the four Wabanaki tribes, the Penobscot and the Passamaquoddy are the two most closely associated with Mount Desert Island. They call the island *Pesamkuk*, and for centuries they lived in seasonal villages in present-day Northeast Harbor and Bar Harbor.

The Wabanaki enjoyed abundant seafood. They used nets, bone hooks, and harpoons to catch cod, swordfish, flounder, and salmon. At night they hunted sturgeon from canoes, using birch bark torches to attract the large fish. The Wabanaki gathered clams, mussels, and shellfish near the shore. (They call Bar Harbor *moneskatik*, "The Clam-Gathering Place.") Surplus seafood was smoked and stored for winter use.

Native Crafts

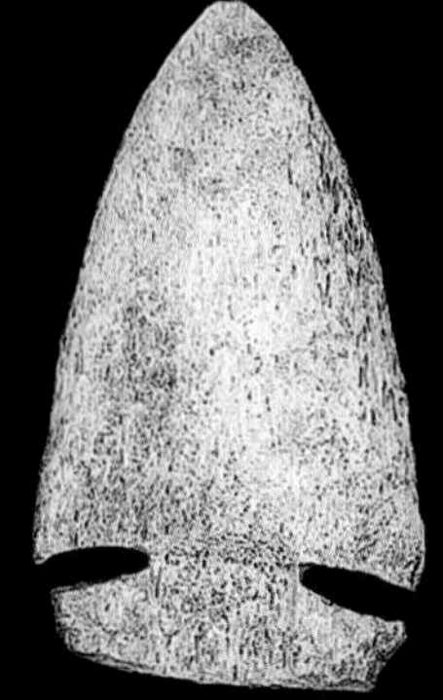

Spear Points

The first people to arrive in Maine 11,000 years ago hunted with spears and spear-throwers. Most spear points were made from stone that, when struck with another stone, flaked off to form sharp edges. Some points were carved from animal bones, such as the whale bone point pictured here. Native tribes hunted large Ice Age animals like mastodons with large spear points. When those animals went extinct, tribes hunted smaller animals with smaller spear points.

Arrowheads

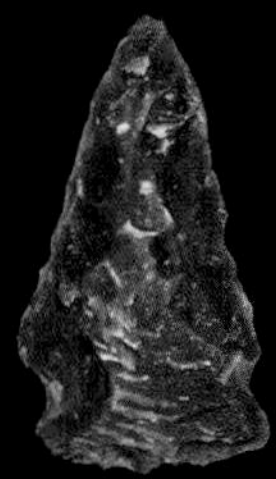

Sometime between 2,000 and 1,000 years ago, bows and arrows replaced spears and spear throwers as primary hunting weapons. Arrows travel up to 300 feet—much farther than the 90-foot range of spear throwers. Hunters made bows from beechwood or rock maple, then strung them with animal sinew. Hunters fashioned arrows from ash, fletched them with crow or hawk feathers, then tipped them with flaked stone points.

Birch Bark Canoes

These elegant boats were so important to local tribes that early European settlers often referred to Wabanaki as "Canoe Indians." Maine is crisscrossed with lakes, rivers, and streams, making water transport superior to overland travel. The earliest people made dugout canoes, but these cumbersome vessels were eventually replaced by birch-bark canoes, which are lighter and easier to portage. Large canoes, which reach 20 feet in length and hold 12 people, weigh just 85 pounds. Birch-bark is waterproof, rot-resistant, and flexible. Canoe makers harvest birch bark in winter when it is thickest, then sew it over a beechwood frame using split spruce root. Leaks are fixed with a mixture of spruce gum and animal fat.

Penobscot tribal members N.M. Francis and his wife

Pottery

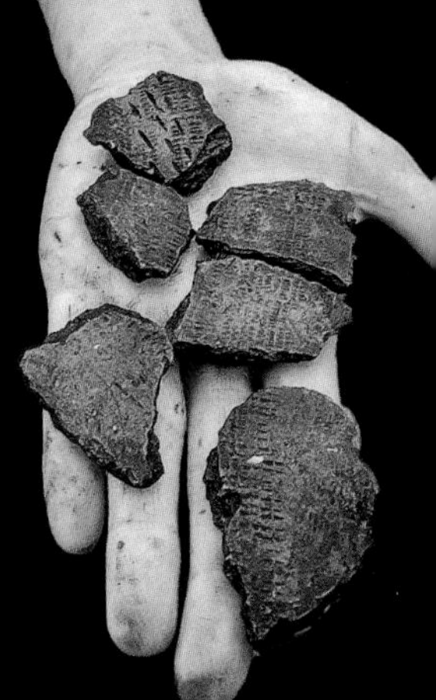

Clay pottery first appeared around 3,000 years ago. Prior to pottery, native tribes used bark, wood, and animal skin containers for cooking and storage. To boil liquids, they heated rocks in a fire, then dropped the hot rocks in a liquid-filled container. Pottery, by contrast, could be placed directly over a fire to boil liquids and cook soups and stews. Pottery is fragile, however, and it tends to fragment over time. Today pottery shards provide archaeological evidence of this ancient craft.

Baskets

Wabanaki weave beautiful baskets from sweetgrass and thin strips of ash trees, which they call "basket trees." Basketmaking is one of the most important aspects of Wabanaki culture. One myth tells how Gluskabe, the creator, split an ash tree with an arrow, and from that tree emerged the ancestors of the Wabanaki. Baskets and birch bark containers are sometimes decorated with dyed porcupine quills.

Wigwams

Wabanaki lived in portable wigwams, which measured 8–12 feet across and were easily assembled in a few hours. Wooden poles form a basic conical framework, and birch bark panels are lashed to the poles. Moose or deer hide are hung as a door. Inside there is a central fire pit surrounded by sleeping areas carpeted with fragrant balsam tips and soft animal hides. An overhead platform provides extra storage space for utensils, dried food, and extra furs. A hole in the roof allows smoke to escape. During bad weather, the hole is covered with a birch bark flap. When it's time to move on, wigwams are disassembled and birch bark panels are rolled up for easy transport.

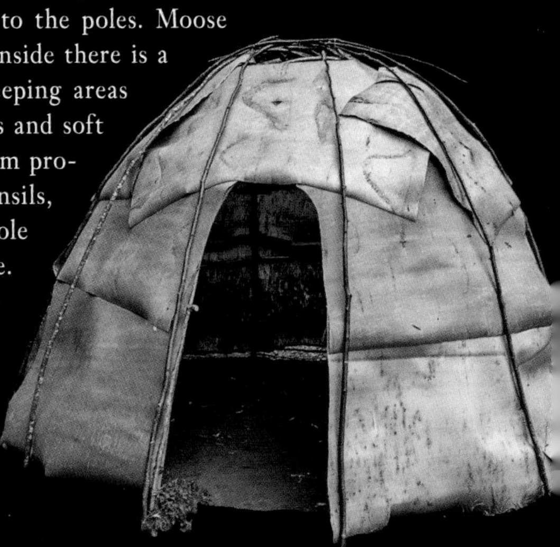

On land, Wabanaki supplemented their diet with nuts, berries, and maple sap. They hunted moose and deer with arrows and spears, and they trapped smaller animals such as beaver and otter. In winter, Wabanaki used snowshoes to chase game across deep snow. Unlike tribes to the west, Wabanaki in Downeast Maine did not practice agriculture. Wild food was abundant, and they were happy to trade surplus meat and animal hides for beans, corn, and squash grown by neighboring tribes.

When European explorers arrived in the early 1600s, there were an estimated 32,000 Wabanaki living in Maine and Canada (about 41 people per 100 square miles). As one explorer noted, "I should consider these Indians incomparably more fortunate than ourselves ... their lives are not vexed by a thousand annoyances ... They mutually aid one another in their needs with much charity and without selfseeking. There is a continual joy in their wigwams." Another observer claimed the Wabanaki "start off to their different places with as much pleasure as if they were going on a stroll ... for their days are all nothing but pastime."

Physical differences were also noted. One early European explorer observed the Wabanaki "have no beards, the men no more than the women ... They have often told me that at first we seemed to them very ugly with hair both upon our mouths and heads; but gradually they have become accustomed to it, and now we are beginning to look less deformed."

Europeans did not settle coastal Maine until the mid-1700s, but European contact had an immediate impact on native life. By the early 1600s, Mi'kmaqs learned to sail European "shallop" boats, venturing as far south as Cape Cod. They were happy to trade beaver pelts for European guns and metal weapons, which gave them a strategic advantage over rival tribes. As trade with whites increased, native tribes began to abandon traditional lifestyles.

At the same time, European diseases such as smallpox, cholera, and influenza ravaged native communities. Europeans had been exposed to those pathogens for centuries, but North American tribes were completely vulnerable. In 1618, a plague killed nearly three-quarters of coastal Maine's native population. Within a few decades, up to 90 percent of Wabanakis perished. Their communities decimated, many Wabanaki abandoned traditional religious beliefs in favor of Christianity introduced by missionaries.

By the late 1700s, Maine's Wabanaki population had fallen to just 1,200 people. The white population, meanwhile, exploded to nearly 300,000. Wabanaki survivors lost access to much of their traditional territory, including parts of Mount Desert Island. But despite the upheaval, many Wabanaki continued to fish, hunt, and gather food along the coast. As late as the early 20th century, seasonal Wabanaki camps were common on Mount Desert Island.

EUROPEAN ARRIVAL

Some historians believe Vikings were the first Europeans to visit Maine. Others speculate that European fisherman secretly fished Maine's waters long before Columbus set sail. (Some believe Columbus overheard fishermen discussing North America, thus inspiring his historic voyage.) But the first recorded voyage to Maine comes from Giovanni De Verrazano, an Italian navigator who led a French expedition to the New World in 1524.

By the time Verrazano set sail, Spain and Portugal had explored the New World from Florida to the tip of South America, and John Cabot had led an English expedition to Newfoundland. But most of North America remained a mystery. Searching for a northern passage to Asia, Verrazano landed at present-day North Carolina and named it "Archadia" after a mythical landscape described by the Greek poet Virgil. He then sailed north to explore the unknown coast.

When Verrazano reached Maine, he encountered Wabanaki tribes, whom he described as "of such crudity and evil manners, so barbarous, that despite all the signs we could make, we could never converse with them." As Verrazano's boat approached the shore, Wabanaki men yelled and shot arrows at them. They were eager, however, to trade with the Europeans for metal tools—with the aide of a basket on a line shuttled safely between ship and shore. When Verrazano's ship departed, the Wabanaki sent them off by "exhibiting their bare behinds." Verrazano returned the favor by naming the Maine coast *Terra Onde di Mala Gente*, "Land of Bad People."

The Wabanaki's less than hospitable *bon voyage*, and their desire to trade for metal tools, indicates they had encountered Europeans before. But Verrazano became the first to officially map the region. Included on his map was a spot near Mount Desert Island labeled "Oranbega."

Despite Verrazano's successful exploration, no permanent settlement was attempted in New England for almost a century. Europe, preoccupied with wars at home and the plunder of Central and South America to the south, paid little attention to chilly, remote New England. Although Maine's rich coastal waters were filled with fishermen by the late 1500s, they did little more than set up seasonal camps on offshore islands.

Before long, however, rumors of a fantastic city of gold located somewhere in Maine began to spread through Europe. The rumor is believed to have originated from a group of English sailors who were stranded in Mexico in 1567 and spent the next three years traveling on foot to New Brunswick, Canada. From there they hopped a fishing boat back to England and immediately hit the pubs, telling drunken stories of a fabulous city of gold located somewhere in Maine. They called the city "Norumbega"—a name strikingly similar to "Oranbega" on Verrazano's map.

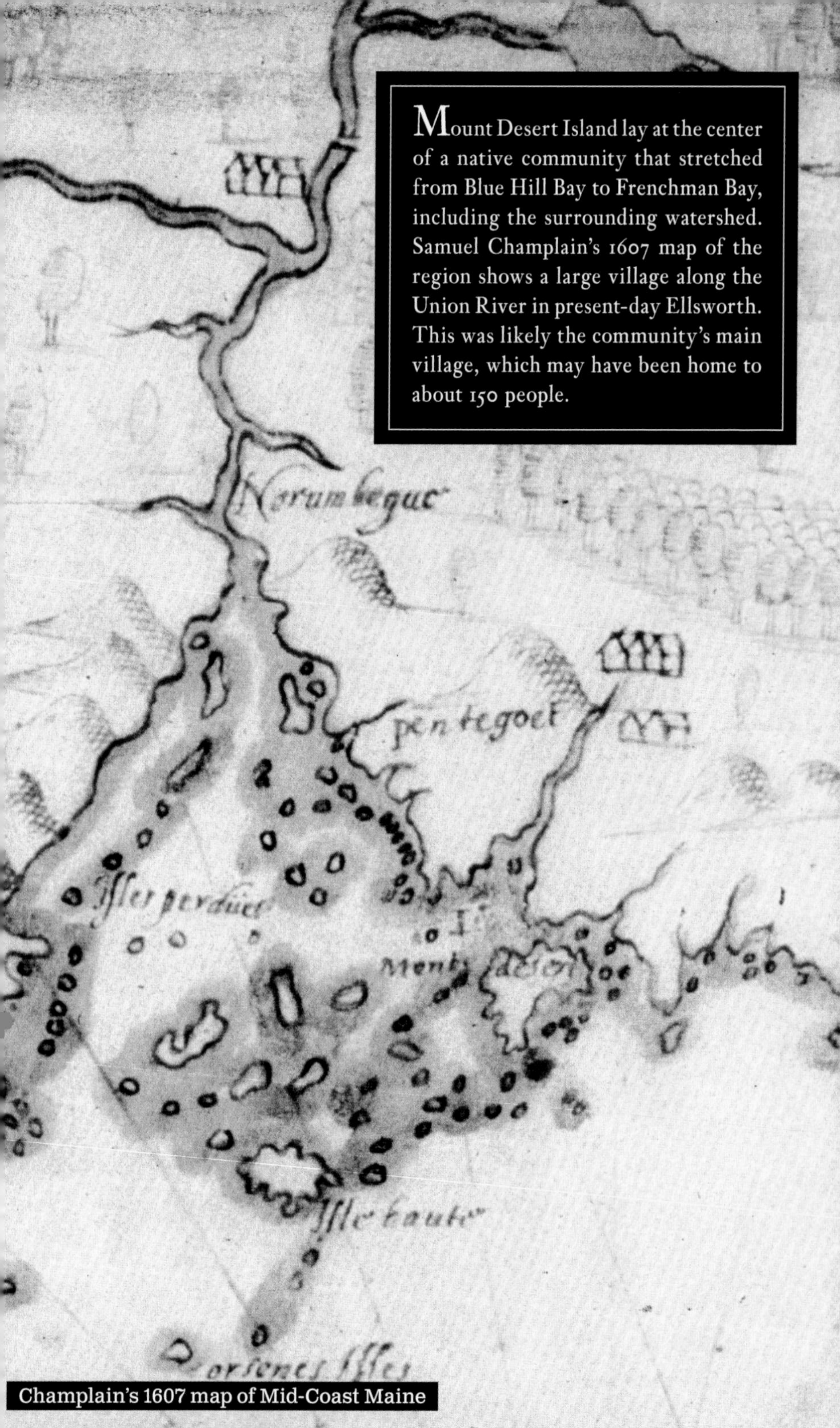

Mount Desert Island lay at the center of a native community that stretched from Blue Hill Bay to Frenchman Bay, including the surrounding watershed. Samuel Champlain's 1607 map of the region shows a large village along the Union River in present-day Ellsworth. This was likely the community's main village, which may have been home to about 150 people.

Champlain's 1607 map of Mid-Coast Maine

In the mid-1500s, the idea of a golden city in Maine would not have seemed far-fetched. Spain hauled away enormous quantities of gold from the Aztecs and Incas, and it seemed logical that more riches lay awaiting discovery in the New World. In 1579 and 1580, England sent two expeditions to mid-coast Maine to search for Norumbega. Although the expeditions failed to find the golden city, the British named the entire region "Norumbega." (In 1606, the name Norumbega was changed to "Virginia," and 14 years later Virginia was changed to "New England.")

England wasn't the only country with an eye on the region. And dreams of easy riches were not so quickly forgotten. In 1603, 17 years before the Pilgrims landed at Plymouth Rock, France sent an expedition to North America led by Samuel Champlain. After landing at the mouth of the St. Croix River in Canada, Champlain sailed south to explore the coast of Maine. When he spotted the bald peaks of Mount Desert Island, he noted in his log:

"The island is very high and notched in places, so that there is the appearance to one at sea, as of seven or eight mountains extending along near each other. The summit of most of them is destitute of trees, as there are only rocks on them. The slopes are covered with pines, firs, and birches. I named it *L'isle des Monts-déserts* [Island of Barren Mountains]."

Although earlier explorers had noticed the island before, Champlain was the first to give it a name. He was also the first to note that Mount Desert is, in fact, an island—previous maps showed it connected to the mainland.

Continuing on, Champlain sailed up the Penobscot River, which empties into the Atlantic southwest of Mount Desert Island. If Norumbega existed, he hoped to find it there. Champlain made his way as far as present-day Bangor, where he found, to his dismay, a small village with no gold. Frustrated, he concluded the city of Norumbega was a myth. He did point out, however, that the region as a whole was "marvelous to behold."

By the time of Champlain's voyage, Verrazano's name for North Carolina, Archadia, had migrated north on French maps. As Verrazano's map was drawn and redrawn by map makers, Archadia became "L'Acadie" and began to refer to the region between Philadelphia and Montreal—a region that would soon become a major point of contention between the English and French.

SAMUEL CHAMPLAIN

FRENCH JESUITS

Although there was no gold in Maine, the region was overflowing with natural resources. "The aboundance of Sea-Fish," wrote one early fisherman, "are almost beyond beleeving." Cod grew up to six feet long and could be gathered by simply dropping a bucket into the water. Sturgeon were so numerous near the shore they were considered a navigational hazard. The natural bounty was all the more dramatic compared with Europe's own depleted resources. And the items that Europe needed most—timber, cod, beaver, and sassafras (mistakenly thought to cure syphilis)—were among the most abundant in New England. For over a century, Europe had virtually ignored the region. But once New England's natural resources were recognized, it began to look a lot more promising.

By the time of Champlain's voyage, both England and France claimed *they* were the rightful owner of North America. But with no English settlements in the New World, and only a handful of French settlements in Canada, there were no actual conflicts over the land. Then, in 1607, England established a permanent settlement at Jamestown, Virginia. In response, France's Louis XIII granted North America to French noblewoman Antoinette de Pons, Marquise de Guercheville, who proposed a Jesuit mission on the Maine coast.

In May of 1613, two Jesuits and 48 settlers set sail from France, hoping to establish a mission along the Penobscot River. As they neared the coast, they were surrounded by a thick fog. Unable to see more than a few feet ahead, the Jesuits grew terrified. If their ship ran aground it could easily sink, and they would be stranded with no supplies. Poor winds prevented the boat from retreating to deeper water. The helpless French settlers simply huddled together and prayed. For two days, their ship drifted aimlessly through the fog. When it finally lifted, they found themselves staring at Mount Desert Island.

Overjoyed, the settlers rowed to shore and raised a cross. Not long after they landed, they were approached by a group of Wabanaki who introduced themselves and encouraged the Frenchmen to stay—presumably to benefit from the lucrative fur trade. But the Jesuits insisted on continuing to the Penobscot River. The Wabanaki then informed them that their leader, Sagamore Asticou, was mortally ill and wished to be baptized before he died. Eager to save a soul, the Jesuits climbed into Wabanaki canoes and paddled to the southern end of the island.

When the Jesuits met Asticou, they found him suffering from nothing more than a common cold. Some historians speculate that Asticou actually faked sickness to draw the Jesuits near and convince them to stay. If that was the case, it worked. The Jesuits baptized Asticou and established a small settlement, Saint Sauveur, just north of present-day Southwest Harbor.

Unfortunately for the French, English settlers in Jamestown, Virginia, caught wind of their plans, and a 14-gun warship was dispatched to deal with the problem. When the warship's captain, Samuel Argall, reached Penobscot Bay, he encountered a group of Wabanaki fishing among the offshore islands. The Wabanaki, assuming the white men were friends of the French, tipped them off to the Jesuits' settlement. By the time they realized their mistake, it was too late. Argall's ship sailed toward Mount Desert Island ready to attack.

The French, caught entirely by surprise, fired off a single shot before their settlement was laid to waste. Argall allowed 14 Frenchmen to flee to Nova Scotia in an open boat, but the rest were taken to Jamestown as prisoners. Upon arriving in Jamestown, the governor threatened to hang the prisoners, but they were ultimately sent back to France.

The battle on Mount Desert Island was one of the first skirmishes between the English and the French in North America. It would hardly be the last. For the next 150 years, as the two countries battled over the region, Mount Desert Island became a virtual no man's land.

The Original Cadillac

In 1688, the king of France granted 100,00 acres along the coast of Maine to a young French lawyer named Antoine Laumet. Undaunted by the violent land disputes in the region, the ambitious Laumet sailed to Mount Desert Island to oversee his new domain. Upon arriving, he changed his name to the noble sounding, yet completely fabricated, "Antoine de La Mothe, Sieur de Cadillac" and created a noble-looking coat of arms. But Mount Desert Island offered little in the way of social mobility, and Cadillac headed west after only one summer. He later founded Detroit, Michigan, and today a modernized version of his fake coat of arms still graces the hood ornaments of Cadillac automobiles.

In 1786, Cadillac's granddaughter, Maria Teresa de Gregoire, contacted American authorities and claimed *she* was the rightful owner of Mount Desert Island. Although her claim was legally dubious, the newly independent American government granted her the eastern half of the island as a show of goodwill toward the French. De Gregoire and her husband then moved to the island and started a real-estate company, selling land at $5 per 100 acres. Today, there are only two places in the United States where real estate titles can be traced back to the king of France: Louisiana and Mount Desert Island.

SETTLEMENT BEGINS

Ongoing battles between England and France kept many would-be settlers out of Maine until the late 1700s. During this time, Mount Desert Island was used primarily as a navigational tool. (On clear days its mountains can be seen up to 60 miles at sea.) As one Englishman put it, the region north of the Penobscot River was "a Countrey rather to affright then delight one, and how to describe a more plaine spectacle of desolation, or more barren, I know not." But shortly before the 1763 Treaty of Paris, which granted England control of New England, Mount Desert Island received its first permanent settlers.

In 1761, 22-year-old Abraham Somes sailed north from Gloucester, Massachusetts, and settled the town of "Betwixt the Hills" (later named Somesville) on Mount Desert Island. At the time, Mount Desert Island was owned by Francis Bernard, the royal governor of the Province of Massachusetts. Following the Revolutionary War, Bernard fled to England and the Americans confiscated his land. Bernard's son, who sided with the Americans, ultimately petitioned the new government for his father's land, which he was granted. But shortly after the transaction, the young Bernard sold the land and hightailed it back to England to join his father.

By the late 1700s, fertile land near the coast was in short supply in southern New England, and ambitious settlers headed north to undeveloped harbors in Maine. Before long, Mount Desert Island was growing at a healthy clip. Initial development took place in Somesville, but settlement soon spread throughout the island. In 1796, the town of Eden (later named Bar Harbor) was incorporated. Fishing, shipbuilding, and lumbering were the primary occupations of island residents, who soon numbered several thousand. For the most part, islanders led peaceful, industrious lives. As one observer noted, "The women do the most of what there is in the way of farming, while the men, from early boyhood, are upon or in the water, chiefly as fishermen, but always as sailors, and unquestionably the best sailors in the world."

Mount Desert Island's economy revolved around the sea, and each day hundreds of sailboats plied the waters offshore. Local sailors shipped goods around the world. Many knew the coastlines of Europe and South America as well as the coast of Maine. But sailing and fishing were rugged occupations. Men spent up to eight months of the year at sea, leaving wives and children to fend for themselves at home.

Although Mount Desert Island continued growing throughout the mid-1800s, access remained challenging. Traveling to the remote island was a multi-day affair that required a train ride to Portland, a steamboat cruise to Castine, and a schooner trip to Mount Desert Island. As a result, few outsiders knew about this lovely landscape. But following the arrival of a handful of landscape painters from New York, all that was about to change.

Lobstermen, 1800s

Fitz Hugh Lane, *Entrance of Somes Sound from Southwest Harbor*, 1852

BOOM to BUST
Coastal Maine in the 1800s

As the Industrial Revolution swept across North America in the 1800s, demand for natural resources boomed. And everything America needed—fish for food, lumber for ships, granite for construction—Maine had in abundance. In an era when virtually everything was transported by ship, Maine also boasted a coast filled with sheltered, deep-water harbors and thousands of offshore islands. After plodding along for centuries as an economic backwater, Maine finally hit the jackpot.

The fishing industry in Maine, which had always been big business, revolved around cod, which were easily caught, cured, and transported. As American and European populations grew, demand for dried cod skyrocketed. Fishing villages flourished, and new settlers cut down trees at a furious rate for fuel, building material, and farmland. After coastal forests were plundered, lumber barons turned their eyes to the state's vast interior. By 1880, lumberjacks had chopped down nearly half of Maine's forests.

Granite also became big business, and many entrepreneurs (including my own great-grandfather) set up quarries on offshore islands. Because the islands were located along popular shipping routes, transportation was easy. On Mount Desert Island, Hall Quarry churned out enough granite to fill 10 to 15 schooners *each day*. Hall Quarry granite was used, among other things, to construct the Library of Congress.

Even the ice was valuable. In winter, men carved huge blocks of ice from rivers and ponds, covered the blocks in sawdust, then shipped them around the world. From Bourbon Street to Bombay, Maine ice was a delicacy.

For a few decades, it seemed like everything in Maine turned to gold. But the same economic forces that showered Maine with easy riches took them away just as quickly.

It started with railroads, which opened up the vast virgin forests west of the Appalachian Mountains. Railroads also reduced America's reliance on coastal shipping routes. Maine's offshore islands, previously the best places to live and work, soon became the worst places to live and work. Coastal commerce collapsed, and hundreds of islands were abandoned.

At the same time, many independent fisherman found they couldn't afford new, modern technologies used by larger fishing operations. Maine's fishing fleet, once the nation's largest, shrank by over 70%. When reinforced concrete became widely available, the granite industry collapsed. And mechanical refrigeration destroyed demand for Maine ice. As the decades wore on, coastal Maine watched its once vibrant economy collapse. It wasn't long before people turned to the only lucrative industry that remained: tourism.

LIGHTHOUSES

Before trains, planes, and automobiles, the world relied on boats to transport nearly all commercial goods. And in the days before radar and GPS, boats depended upon lighthouses for navigational guidance. Due to the craggy, treacherous nature of Maine's shoreline, 68 lighthouses were constructed along the coast. By the late 1800s, it was possible to sail from one end of the state to the other and always be within sight of a beacon. The earliest beacons were lit with whale oil and attended by a keeper who lived at the lighthouse full-time. Lighthouse keepers and their families lived on remote islands for months or even years at a time. Infrequent supply ships provided their only link to the mainland. By the late 1970s, however, all lighthouses were automated and lighthouse keepers were no longer necessary.

Bass Harbor Light (p.260) is the only lighthouse on Mount Desert Island. Nearby lighthouses include Bear Island (p.240), Egg Rock (p.141), Baker Island (p.291), Winter Harbor (p.265), Burnt Coat Harbor (p.297), Isle au Haut (p.275), and Petit Manan (right), at 96 feet the second tallest lighthouse in Maine.

Mount Desert Rock Lighthouse

Mount Desert Rock is one of Maine's most famous lighthouses due to its remote location (20 miles south of Mount Desert Island) and the island's exceptionally small size (1.5 acres, with a maximum height 15 feet above sea level). Originally built in 1830, the lighthouse was later fortified with granite walls four feet thick to withstand pounding waves. During particularly fierce storms, keepers took shelter in the tower. In the 1880s, three keepers lived here with their families and a schoolteacher visited in summer to teach the children. One keeper's family lived on the island for eight straight years without visiting the mainland. The last keepers left in 1977. Today the lighthouse is used as a whale research station by Allied Whale.

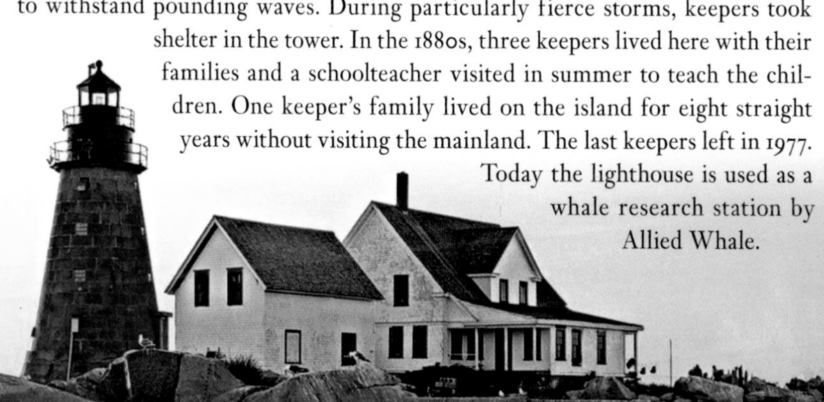

HUDSON RIVER SCHOOL PAINTERS

In the mid-1800s, American cities faced immense growing pains. Overpopulation and the effects of the Industrial Revolution transformed previously pleasant cities such as Boston, New York, and Philadelphia into filthy, wretched urban nightmares. Indoor plumbing did not exist, and people left trash and human waste in the street to rot.

The art world experienced an overwhelming demand for landscape paintings during this time. City dwellers, disgusted with the stink and grime of city life, were desperate for wholesome scenes of unspoiled nature—hung conveniently on their townhouse walls. At the same time, railroads created an entirely new industry: tourism, which further fueled demand for paintings of scenic destinations.

One of the first artists to visit Mount Desert Island was Thomas Doughty, who worked his way up the Maine coast in the early 1830s, booking passages on small sailing vessels. Doughty exhibited his paintings in New York, where they received moderate acclaim. They also caught the eye of his student, Thomas Cole, who was maturing into one of America's leading landscape artists.

In 1844, Cole traveled to Mount Desert Island with fellow artist Henry Cheever Pratt. The pair stayed at a farm near Schooner Head and painted dramatic scenes of Sand Beach, Otter Cliffs, and Frenchman Bay. Cole was in awe of the rugged, coastal scenery. His diary from the trip includes passages describing "threatening crags, and dark caverns in which the sea thunders" and "a range of mountains of beautiful aerial hues."

When Cole exhibited his work in New York the following summer, it opened to mixed, but predominantly negative, reviews. One critic chided Cole for painting red rocks, noting "the rocks are of a kind that no geologist would find a name for; the whole coast of Maine is lined with rocks nearly black in color." (In fact, the rocks on Mount Desert Island do have a reddish hue.) Another critic opined that "the ocean appears like a vast cabbage garden."

Despite the poor reviews, Cole's paintings were a hit with the public. Several years later, Cole's aspiring young student, Frederic Church, set off to create his own paintings of Mount Desert Island. Only 24 years old, Church was considered something of a prodigy. He spent his days exploring the island's rugged terrain, producing a series of dramatic paintings that achieved enormous success when he exhibited them the following year.

In the days before television or photography, landscape painting offered a rare glimpse of exotic destinations, and top landscape painters were bona fide celebrities. Church's stunning depictions of Mount Desert Island created a public frenzy. Thousands of people lined up outside galleries in New York to view his work, and ambitious painters rushed to follow in his footsteps. Suddenly, Mount Desert Island found itself thrust into the national spotlight.

the Hudson River School

FREDERIC CHURCH

The painters of the Hudson River School, who helped popularize Mount Desert Island as a travel destination in the 1800s, were among America's first conservationists. Two hundred years earlier, when Puritans arrived in New England, most people viewed wilderness as a sinister, dangerous place. The Puritans believed it was their moral duty to tame the wilderness so religious communities could flourish. But even after the landscape was tamed, their harsh view persisted, and generations of Americans grew up viewing the frontier as an obstacle to be conquered. As more and more pristine wilderness disappeared, however, a philosophical backlash took root.

Leading the charge were landscape painters such as Frederic Church and Thomas Cole, members of the Hudson River School of Art (which was not an actual school but an artistic movement). Cole rallied against the "apathy with which the beauties of external nature are regarded by the great mass, even of our refined community." Another artist declared, "Yankee enterprise has little sympathy with the picturesque, and it behooves our artists to rescue from its grasp the little that is left before it is for ever too late."

Hudson River School artists painted dramatic scenes of American wilderness that ignited public passions. They also used subtle visual techniques to convey their belief that wilderness was an extension of God—not an obstacle to His progress. One of their favorite tricks was hiding human features in the contours of rocks. This not only turned picture viewing into a kind of game, but it also established a direct link between man and nature, and by extension God.

By portraying American wilderness as a spiritual destination, Hudson River School artists hoped to dispel the notion that nature was an obstacle to be conquered. They also wanted to prove that American landscapes were just as beautiful as European landscapes, creating a much needed sense of national pride for the young democracy. On both counts, they succeeded. Hudson School exhibitions drew huge crowds and lured thousands of tourists to beautiful destinations such as Mount Desert Island.

The Artist Sketching at Mount Desert, Maine, 1864–1865, Sanford Robinson Gifford

"The ladies wear wide-brimmed hats and picturesque costumes ... cut short above the feet and ankles, which, in turn, are incased in stout walking shoes. The gentlemen appear in warm, rough clothing, which will stand the wear and tear of a tramp over the rocks."

—*Harper's Magazine*, 1872

THE RUSTICATORS

Church's paintings generated a flurry of interest in Mount Desert Island, and before long artists and tourists were making the multi-day journey to see the landscape firsthand. In the summer of 1855, Church returned to Mount Desert Island with 26 friends, a group that included artists, writers, businessmen, and their families. The group stayed at a Somesville tavern and spent their days hiking, fishing, sailing, picnicking, and otherwise thoroughly enjoying themselves.

Although artists like Church were present, the excursion was first and foremost a social expedition. What little drawing was done generally consisted of humorous sketches mocking members of the party. At the end of their month-long stay, the group threw a large party. They invited dozens of locals and imported a piano—the island's first—for the event. Church held forth at the piano, indulging in his "perfectly inexhaustible" capacity for entertainment late into the night.

What seemed like nothing more than a satisfying summer actually set the tone for the first wave of visitors to Mount Desert Island. Later named "Rusticators," these early tourists—for the most part artists, professors, and other intellectuals with leisure time on their hands—came to experience the simple pleasures of rugged, outdoor coastal life.

Rusticators required no fancy accommodations. They often rented attic space from locals and paid for an extra spot at the family's dinner table. Locals, eager for extra cash, were more than happy to accommodate the easy-to-please visitors, creating a wonderfully symbiotic relationship. An 1872 travel article in *Harper's Magazine* summed up the rusticator's lifestyle: "Now, most of the visitors to Mount Desert, even the prosaic folk, go prepared to enjoy the picturesque, the beautiful, the sublime."

Another article that year stated that "During the day parties of several persons, ladies and gentlemen, start off on a walking expedition of five, ten, and fifteen miles to one or another of the many objects of interest on the sea-shore or up the mountains. There is a vigorous, sensible, healthy feeling in all they do, and not a bit of that overdressed, pretentious, nonsensical, unhealthy sentimentality which may be found at other places."

But changes to the rusticator lifestyle were already under way. Several years earlier, a New York journalist named Robert Carter chartered a fishing sloop in Boston and took a pleasure cruise to Mount Desert Island. At the time, there were no summer homes on the island and just two small inns. Carter reported that "of late years [Mount Desert Island] has become attractive to artists and summer loungers, but it needs the hand of cultivated taste." Although he could hardly have imagined it at the time, the arrival of a "cultivated hand" was near, and it would forever change the character of the island.

THE COTTAGERS

As stories, artwork, and magazine articles about Mount Desert Island continued to spread, interest in the island soared. But tourism was limited by the physical challenge of actually getting there. Few would-be tourists had the time, money, or patience required for the multi-day journey. Then, in 1868, direct steamboat service was offered between Boston and Mount Desert Island. The new steamboat route dramatically reduced the time it took to get to the island. It also dramatically increased the reliability of the voyage because travelers were no longer at the mercy of the wind. Within a few years, Mount Desert Island had become a major tourist destination.

Between 1868 and 1882, at least one hotel was built or thoroughly expanded on Mount Desert Island each year. The largest, Rodick House in Bar Harbor, had over 400 rooms and was the largest hotel in Maine. Locals welcomed the flood of cash, but some were left feeling a bit perplexed. When one visitor told a local innkeeper that "It's the scenery we wish to see," the innkeeper replied, "Yes, I know, it's what them artist men come here for. But what it amounts to, after all their squattin' and fussin', I don't know."

In 1882, luxuries such as electricity and telephones arrived on Mount Desert Island. This was followed, two years later, by train service from Boston to Hancock Point, which was a short ferry ride away from Bar Harbor. The new train service cut travel time to Mount Desert Island down to a single day. The result was predictable: the number of summer visitors quadrupled.

The tourist explosion quickly changed the face of Bar Harbor. As more and more wealthy visitors arrived, upscale development proceeded at a breakneck pace. Luxury hotels sprouted up on Bar Harbor farmland, and quaint general stores were replaced with boutiques showcasing the latest Parisian fashions.

An 1886 article in *Harper's* neatly summed up the situation: "For many years [Bar Harbor] had been frequented by people who have more fondness for nature than they have money, and who were willing to put up with wretched accommodations, and enjoyed a wild sort of 'roughing it.' But some society people in New York, who have the reputation of setting the mode, chanced to go there; they declared in favor of it; and instantly, by an occult law which governs fashionable life, Bar Harbor became the fashion."

The writer went on to describe a typical day at Rodick House: "The first confused impression was of a bewildering number of slim, pretty girls, nonchalant young fellows in lawn-tennis suits, and indefinite opportunities in the halls and parlors and wide piazzas for promenades and flirtations ... The big office is a sort of assembly room, where new arrivals are scanned and discovered, and it is unblushingly called the 'fish-pond' by the young ladies who daily angle there."

Hoping to distance themselves from hotel life, which was becoming increasingly less exclusive, the wealthiest visitors built giant mansions along the shore. So as not to appear pretentious, they referred to their mansions as "cottages." The name fooled no one, however, and before long the social epicenter had shifted from hotel lounges to private dinner parties. Some of the wealthiest families in America added Bar Harbor "cottages" to their portfolio of homes, and their arrival cemented Bar Harbor's reputation as one of America's most exclusive summer resorts.

By 1896, when there were nearly 200 mansions in Bar Harbor, the tone of the town had completely changed. As longtime summer resident Edward Godkin put it, "The Cottager has become to the boarder what the red [squirrel] is to the gray, a ruthless invader and exterminator ... caste has been established ... the community is now divided into two classes, one of which looks down on the other."

SCHOOL ST.
MT DESERT
COTTAGE
MAIN ST.

Bar Harbor, late 1800s

Lost "Cottages" of BAR HARBOR

WINGWOOD

Wingwood was Bar Harbor's most extraordinary summer cottage. It belonged to Edward T. Stotesbury, who grew up poor in Philadelphia, started working at age 12, and eventually became a senior partner at J.P. Morgan & Company. In 1925, flush with cash, Stotesbury purchased a large mansion in Bar Harbor. His wife Eva took one look at the new property, hired an architect, and spent over one million dollars remodeling the house. When the remodel was complete, Wingwood boasted 80 rooms, 26 hand-carved marble fireplaces, 52 telephone lines, and a 30-room servants' wing. Some of Wingwood's bathrooms (28 total) featured gold fixtures, which Eva claimed were "economical" because "they saved polishing." Edward considered his wife's excesses overwhelming. He once remarked to his gardener that he would have been content with a small cottage and a supper of beans.

Instead, his meals were served on one of two 1,200-piece dining sets. Eva's spending habits were legendary. She hired gardeners to move plants around Wingwood's grounds on a weekly basis, and she employed a full-time fashion designer and "costume secretary." At one point, Eva organized a $500,000 alligator safari to gather leather for a set of matching luggage. Despite her lavish pretensions, Eva was fondly remembered as an exemplary hostess who "made every guest feel as if he or she were the only one invited." After her death in 1946, Wingwood fell into disrepair. The once-grand mansion was demolished in 1953.

CHATWOLD

Chatwold was the summer home of famed millionaire Joseph Pulitzer, Bar Harbor's strangest cottager. After making a fortune in the newspaper business—where he introduced such revolutionary concepts as the daily sports page and color comic strip—Pulitzer added Chatwold to his collection of mansions in New York, Georgia, and the French Riviera. His idiosyncrasies were legendary. Pulitzer was pathologically sensitive to noise, and the sound of a nut cracking is said to have made him wince. When Pulitzer stayed in hotels, he required the rooms above, below, and on either side of him to be vacant. To combat the irritating sounds of everyday life, Pulitzer spent $100,000 constructing the "Tower of Silence"—a massive granite structure on the right side of Chatwold designed to be 100 percent soundproof. The mansion also boasted the first heated swimming pool in Bar Harbor and a master bedroom that rotated on ball bearings.

Despite Pulitzer's legendary aversion to noise, he required a servant to read him to sleep each night—and continue reading, in monotone, for at least two hours after he fell asleep. Legend has it he would awaken at the slightest change in pitch. Pulitzer also spent at least 12 hours a day in bed, dictating letters to his secretaries in a self-devised code that contained over 20,000 names and terms (Pulitzer was "Andes," Theodore Roosevelt was "Glutinous"). Chatwold was ultimately demolished in 1945, several decades after Pulitzer's death.

JOSEPH PULITZER

ACADIA NATIONAL PARK

By the turn of the century, New Yorkers could hop a train in the morning and arrive in Bar Harbor by evening. As more and more tourists flooded the island, some citizens grew alarmed at the speed of development. Speculators were snatching up real estate, and the lumber industry, equipped with modern machinery, was eyeing the island's vast untouched forests.

Among the citizens most alarmed was former Harvard president and longtime summer visitor Charles Eliot. With the help of his friend, wealthy island resident George Dorr, Eliot organized a group of private citizens dedicated to preserving Mount Desert Island for future generations. As savvy as they were civic-minded, the Hancock County Trustees of Public Reservations (as they later came to be called) obtained a tax-exempt charter and quickly set to work purchasing land. Dorr enthusiastically took charge and acquired Eagle Lake, Cadillac Mountain, Otter Cliffs, and Sieur de Monts Spring—all told over 6,000 acres.

Things went well until 1913, when the Maine Legislature, under pressure from a variety of sources, attempted to revoke the trustee's tax-exempt charter. Worried their charter might ultimately be dissolved, Dorr suggested the trustees donate their land to the federal government. This was easier said than done. More government land meant more government spending, and Dorr traveled to Washington to convince lawmakers it was worth the extra money.

Using his considerable wealth and influence, Dorr pulled strings and cashed in on personal favors to arrange a meeting with President Woodrow Wilson. He also convinced the editors at *National Geographic* to publish an article about Mount Desert Island that generated tremendous public support. Two years later, Woodrow Wildson created a national monument by presidential proclamation.

Dorr's next move was to elevate the national monument to a national park, which required an act of Congress. Despite the government's preoccupation with World War I, Dorr wrangled congressional support, and on February 26, 1919, Wilson signed the bill creating Lafayette National Park. (The name Lafayette was chosen to reflect America's pro-French sentiment in the wake of World War I.) Lafayette became the first national park east of the Mississippi and the first national park donated entirely from privately owned land.

Dorr became the park's first superintendent—at a salary of one dollar per year—and continued working to expand its holdings. In the late 1920s, a family of Anglophiles donated Schoodic Peninsula with the stipulation that the name of the park be changed to something less French. And so, in 1929, Lafayette National Park became Acadia National Park. (Ironically, Acadia was based on an early French name for the region.) A decade later, the park acquired the southern half of Isle au Haut, a small island 15 miles south of Mount Desert Island.

the Father of Acadia
GEORGE DORR

Without George Dorr, Acadia National Park would not exist as we know it today. His tireless lobbying in Washington, D.C., was responsible for the creation of the national park in 1919, and he devoted the rest of his life to preserving and expanding Acadia's holdings.

Dorr first visited Mount Desert Island in 1868 when his wealthy family purchased a summer home in Bar Harbor. As a young man, Dorr attended Oxford University and traveled extensively throughout Europe, exploring the Scottish highlands and hiking the Swiss Alps. When Dorr inherited his family's vast textile fortune at the turn of the century, he could have lived anywhere in the world he wanted. His choice: Mount Desert Island, where he spent his days immersed in outdoor pursuits. When he wasn't hiking or biking across the island, he was hard at work building new trails and paths. Locals marveled at his boundless energy, which included a frigid swim in the Atlantic each morning until Christmas. As his good friend Charles Eliot once put it, "George Dorr is an impulsive, enthusiastic, eager person who works at high tension, neglects his meals, sits up too late at night, and rushes about from one pressing thing to another. But he is very diligent, as well as highly inventive."

In 1944, at the age of 94, Dorr died an impoverished man. He spent his entire fortune, once valued at over $10 million, purchasing additional land for Acadia National Park. Toward the end of his life, shabby clothes replaced once expensive suits, and he could not afford to buy new books. The only reason Dorr's estate had $2,000 for a funeral was because its trustees had secretly set the money aside, preventing Dorr from giving it all away.

Reflecting on the creation of Acadia National Park, Dorr once noted, "It never will be given up to private ownership again. The men in control will change. The government itself will change. But its possession, by the people, will remain."

Millionaire's Row, after the 1947 fire

THE GREAT FIRE OF 1947

By the time Acadia National Park was established, Bar Harbor was a town in decline. The Cottage Era began to fade following the introduction of the personal income tax in 1913, and its fate was sealed by the Great Depression. By the late 1940s, many of Bar Harbor's once grand mansions had fallen into disrepair.

The next tumultuous chapter in the island's history began on a dry October day in 1947, when a record drought engulfed the state. That summer and fall, Maine received just 50 percent of its normal rainfall. By mid-October, Mount Desert Island experienced its driest conditions ever recorded. On October 17, at the height of the drought, a small fire broke out in the town dump north of Bar Harbor. Firefighters managed to control the blaze, but they were unable to put it out. When the fire started to grow, firefighters from across the state were dispatched to prevent a possible catastrophe.

For six days, firefighters battled the stubborn blaze. Then, just when the fire was about to be declared out of control, gale-force winds descended on the island, whipping up flames with 60 mph gusts. It was a nightmare scenario. At 4 p.m., the fire covered 2,000 acres. Eight hours later, over 16,000 acres had burned. "It looked like two gigantic doors had opened and towering columns of roaring flames shot down," recalled one firefighter. Many trees in the fire's path simply exploded as extreme heat pressurized their moist interior.

Fueled by howling winds, the fire raced along the northeastern shore of Mount Desert Island and approached Bar Harbor. A lucky shift in wind pushed the fire south, sparing downtown Bar Harbor, but the fire's destruction blocked all roads leading out of town. Fishermen from nearby harbors motored to the Bar Harbor town pier to evacuate trapped citizens. Over 400 people escaped by boat before bulldozers cleared a path through the rubble north of town. Shortly thereafter, a caravan of 700 cars fled to safety along Route 3, sparks from the lingering fire shooting past their vehicles.

South of Bar Harbor the fire continued to rage, roaring around the eastern edge of the island with no signs of slowing down. As it approached Sand Beach, another fortunate shift in wind pushed the fire to the tip of Great Head Peninsula. With winds pounding the inferno, flames leapt nearly a mile over the ocean. Nearby sailors were forced to turn away to avoid igniting their sails. But confined to the peninsula, the fire's progress was finally contained.

On October 27, firefighters officially declared the fire under control. Despite two weeks of rain and snow, scattered fires continued smoldering below ground. Then, on November 14, the fire was finally extinguished. It had burned over 17,000 acres, including 10,000 in Acadia National Park, and caused five deaths. The fire also destroyed nearly $20 million worth of property, including five hotels, 127 homes, and 67 mansions along "Millionaires Row."

PRESENT DAY

As scars from the fire slowly healed, the island took on a new character that defined it for decades. The Cottage Era was over, which meant Bar Harbor could finally shed its reputation as a faded bastion of wealth. With Acadia National Park acting as the main draw, Mount Desert Island attracted a new type of visitor: vacationing middle-class families.

To accommodate the new arrivals, dozens of budget hotels and campgrounds sprang up around the park. Bar Harbor reinvented itself as a sleepy tourist town filled with fried seafood shacks and nautical trinket shops. But as visitation slowly increased, the town grew increasingly less sleepy. By the end of the century, it had become one of New England's most popular summer destinations.

Today Mount Desert Island's economy is largely defined by tourism. Acadia National Park now draws over 4 million visitors each year, and over 100 cruise ships drop anchor off Bar Harbor. Summer is the busiest season, but more people are discovering the charms of autumn. Not long ago, Labor Day was considered the end of the tourist season. Today many hotels and restaurants stay open through October to accommodate leaf-peepers. When the leaves disappear, so do the tourists, and by November Mount Desert Island is back in local hands.

Year-round residents have a surprisingly wide variety of career options. In addition to fishing and boat building—occupations that have thrived here for centuries—Mount Desert Island is now a hotbed of scientific research. Hundreds of scientists work at Jackson Lab (JAX), a biomedical research facility specializing in genomics. Since its founding in 1929, over 26 Nobel Prizes have been linked to JAX, which has made enormous strides in the treatment of cancer, Alzheimer's, and other devastating diseases. With over 1,700 employees, JAX is the largest employer in Downeast Maine. Weekly tours of its Bar Harbor facility are offered from June to September (jax.org).

The Mount Desert Island Biological Laboratory (mdibl.org) is another non-profit genomic research center. By studying organisms that regenerate damaged tissues, organs, and limbs—such as zebrafish and salamanders—they hope to someday bring these capabilities to humans.

Bar Harbor's College of the Atlantic (COA) is another significant patch in the island's cultural quilt. Founded in 1969, it offers just one major: human ecology, which explores how humans interact with the environment. COA has been named the "Greenest College in America" by both the Sierra Club and Princeton Review. Not surprisingly, its 350 students have a passion for the outdoors, which they indulge on Mount Desert Island. Students volunteer for Acadia National Park and assist researchers at Allied Whale (p.79). COA also maintains wildlife research stations on two remote islands: Mount Desert Rock (p.111) and Great Duck Island.

College of the Atlantic

For many locals, the problem these days isn't finding a job, it's finding a house. As wealthy individuals have snatched up summer homes, real-estate prices have skyrocketed. The total value of all private property on Mount Desert Island is now several *billion* dollars. As a result, high property taxes have pushed many locals and businesses off-island. Lobstermen might launch their boats from island harbors, but many commute from the mainland.

The dramatic influx of wealth means Mount Desert Island is now firmly in the grip of a second Cottage Era. The Bar Harbor Airport is crowded with private jets on weekends, and megayachts routinely drop anchor offshore. But the new Cottage Era seems distinctly different from the first. For starters, there's considerable social pressure from old money families to downplay wealth (after climbing out of their Gulfstreams, of course). And the shameless social climbing that defined Bar Harbor in the late 1800s remains blissfully absent. Ostentatious displays are frowned upon, hiking is the distinguished activity of choice, and L.L. Bean fleece is considered haute couture.

These days the island's biggest challenge is a dramatic spike in visitation. In 2021, over 4 million people visited Acadia National Park—a 60% increase over the past decade. Summer traffic jams, once a holiday weekend rarity, are now common mid-week, even on the western "Quiet Side" of the island. After decades of flying under the radar, Mount Desert Island must once again contend with something Mainers have always distrusted: fame.

ACADIA NATIONAL PARK

As NATIONAL PARKS go, Acadia is posh. Real posh. The wealthy families that flooded Mount Desert Island in the late 1800s brought plenty of blue-blooded attitude, but they also brought plenty of cash. And when they created Acadia National Park, no expense was spared. Hiking trails were constructed with hand-cut stones. The Park Loop Road was designed by Frederick Law Olmsted Jr., one of America's leading landscape architects. And John D. Rockefeller Jr. personally commissioned a network of gravel roads through the forest for horse-drawn carriages!

Despite these extravagances, Acadia remains bold and sublime. The park's rugged scenery is scattered in chunks along the coast of Downeast Maine. Acadia's largest and most famous section covers 30,000 acres on Mount Desert Island, protecting roughly 40% of the island. The park also includes over 3,000 acres on Schoodic Peninsula (p.263), 2,700 acres on Isle au Haut (p.275), and roughly a dozen small offshore islands.

If you're only visiting for a weekend, focus on Mount Desert Island, where you'll enjoy two dozen dramatic mountains and the park's most spectacular sights. The Park Loop Road (p.131) is Acadia's most famous attraction, but there are also 125 miles of hiking trails (p.15) and 47 miles of Carriage Roads (p.197) in the park. Wherever you go, ride the free Island Explorer Shuttle (p.30), which removes the hassle of driving and parking.

If you're here for a week—or you've already explored Mount Desert Island—Schoodic Peninsula and Isle au Haut boast similar scenery with a fraction of the crowds. Although Schoodic Peninsula is growing in popularity, remote Isle au Haut remains delightfully uncrowded.

All Acadia visitors—including hikers on trails and bicyclists on carriage roads—must purchase an entrance pass. Seven-day passes, annual passes, and interagency passes (which grant access to all U.S. national parks and monuments for one year) are available at the following locations: Hulls Cove Visitor Center, Thompson Island Visitor Center, the Bar Harbor Village Green, Sand Beach Entrance Station (on the Park Loop Road), Blackwoods Campground, Seawall Campground, and Schoodic Woods Campground.

PARK LOOP ROAD

THE PARK LOOP ROAD is Acadia's top attraction. Twisting 27 miles through the eastern half of Mount Desert Island, it showcases towering mountains, rocky shorelines, dense forests, and pristine lakes. Saving the best for last, it twists and turns to the top of Cadillac Mountain—the highest point on the Eastern Seaboard—where you'll enjoy panoramic views.

The Park Loop Road is Acadia's main artery, pumping millions of visitors through the park each year. But no matter how crowded it gets—and during peak season it can get *very* crowded—the Park Loop Road is always worth it. If you only have one day to spend in the park, spend it on the Park Loop Road.

There are three popular ways to explore the Park Loop Road: drive your own car, pay for a guided bus tour, or take the free Island Explorer shuttle. Taking your own car offers the most flexibility, but traffic and parking can be a hassle. Guided bus tours (p.218) offer narrated commentary and remove the hassle of driving and parking, but they whisk you through the park on a set schedule with little time to explore interesting sights on your own. The Island Explorer Shuttle (p.30) offers flexibility (it stops at popular destinations about every 30 minutes) and relaxation (no driving, no parking), but it doesn't follow the Park Loop Road in a continuous loop (it's broken up into two separate routes) and it doesn't go to the top of Cadillac Mountain.

Whatever you choose, plan on at least three hours to explore the Park Loop Road. If you want to drive your own car, the best place to start is Hulls Cove Visitor Center (p.132), north of Bar Harbor off Route 3.

The Park Loop Road was the brainchild of John D. Rockefeller Jr., who championed a new motor road over the opposition of some who felt it would ruin the park. The way Rockefeller saw it, automobiles were inevitable. The park could either plan wisely for their arrival or ignore the issue until it was too late. Not surprisingly, the deep-pocketed Rockefeller, who donated much of the land that became Acadia, won the battle. To ensure the new road blended in with the scenery, he commissioned renowned landscape architect Frederick Law Olmsted Jr. (whose father designed New York's Central Park) to oversee the project. Construction began in 1922 and finished in 1953. Today, the Park Loop Road is considered one of the most beautiful drives in America.

Hulls Cove Visitor Center

Acadia National Park's main visitor center is located at the start of the Park Loop Road in Hulls Cove, just north of Bar Harbor. A 52-step stone staircase heads from the large parking area to the visitor center. A wheelchair-accessible parking area is located toward the south end of the main parking area. The visitor center, which opened in 1968 as part of the Mission 66 program to modernize parks for the National Park Service's 50th birthday, was renovated in 2019. Inside you'll find a help desk, information on free ranger programs, maps, restrooms, and a store with books and maps. From late June to mid-October, the visitor center parking area is a hub for multiple Island Explorer routes. Hulls Cove Visitor Center is open mid-April through October. In July and August, up to 10,000 people visit each day. It's busiest between 10am and 2pm, so try to arrive earlier or later if possible.

Rules of the Park Loop Road

- The speed limit never exceeds 35 mph, and it is strictly enforced
- When parking, all four tires must be on pavement and in a designated parking spot. Failure to comply risks a ticket.

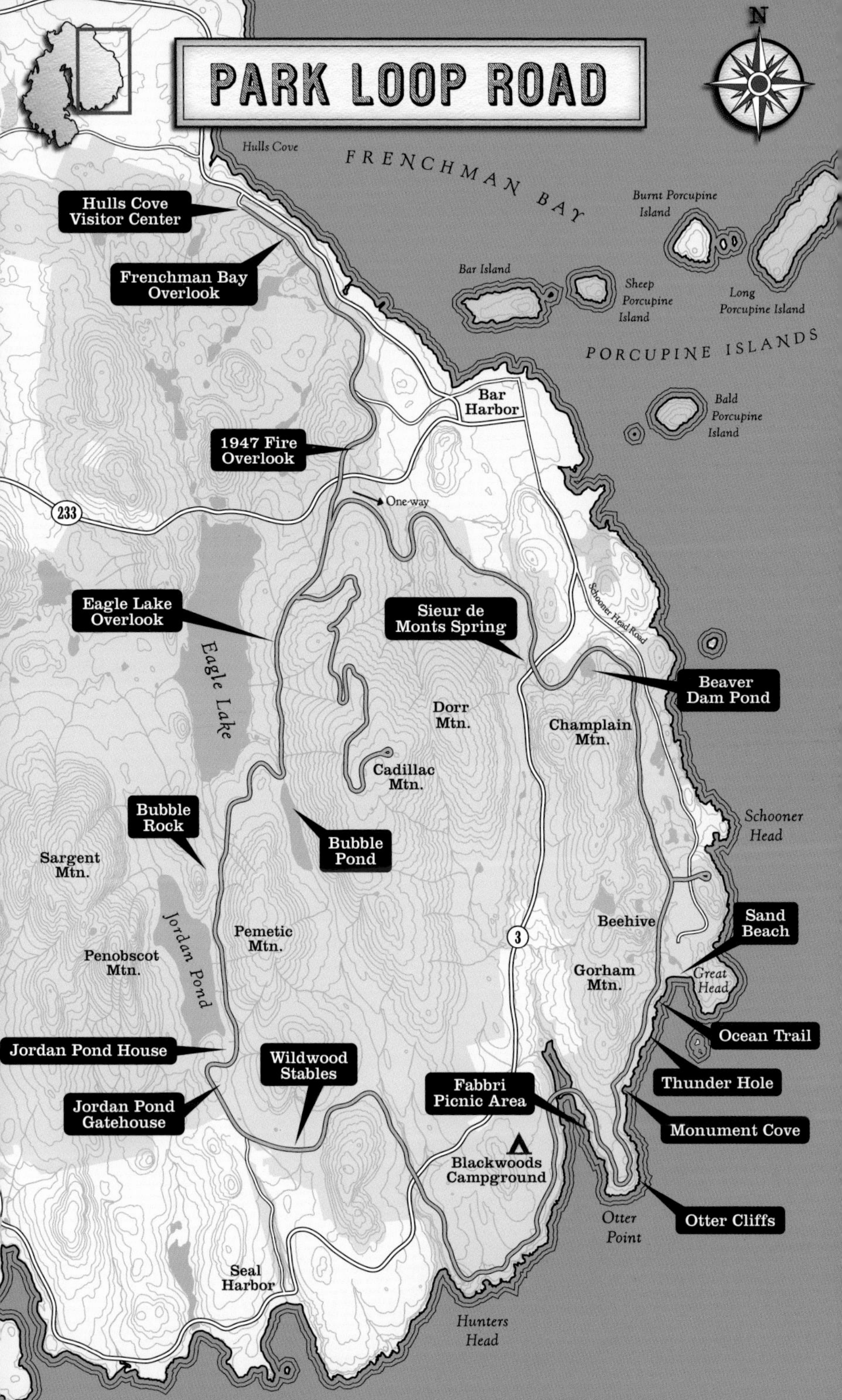
PARK LOOP ROAD
N
Hulls Cove
FRENCHMAN BAY
Hulls Cove Visitor Center
Frenchman Bay Overlook
Burnt Porcupine Island
Bar Island
Sheep Porcupine Island
Long Porcupine Island
PORCUPINE ISLANDS
Bar Harbor
Bald Porcupine Island
1947 Fire Overlook
233
One-way
Eagle Lake Overlook
Sieur de Monts Spring
Schooner Head Road
Eagle Lake
Beaver Dam Pond
Dorr Mtn.
Champlain Mtn.
Cadillac Mtn.
Bubble Rock
Bubble Pond
Schooner Head
Sargent Mtn.
Jordan Pond
Pemetic Mtn.
Beehive
Sand Beach
3
Penobscot Mtn.
Gorham Mtn.
Great Head
Ocean Trail
Jordan Pond House
Wildwood Stables
Thunder Hole
Fabbri Picnic Area
Jordan Pond Gatehouse
Monument Cove
Blackwoods Campground
Otter Point
Otter Cliffs
Seal Harbor
Hunters Head

Frenchman Bay Overlook

The Park Loop Road's first viewpoint overlooks Frenchman Bay, which lies between Mount Desert Island and Schoodic Peninsula to the east. From the overlook you can see several of the Porcupine Islands (p.169), which lie just off Bar Harbor. The closest island to the overlook is Bar Island, which connects to Bar Harbor twice a day at low tide by a shallow sandbar (p.214). Frenchman Bay Overlook is nice, but you'll be treated to much better views of the Porcupine Islands farther down the Park Loop Road.

Frenchman Bay

Grammar nerds take note! The name of the beautiful bay just east of Mount Desert Island is Frenchman Bay, *not* Frenchman's Bay (with a possessive "s"). Acadia National Park, being a good grammatical citizen, always spells it right. But as you wander outside the park on Mount Desert Island, you'll undoubtedly encounter maps, signs, and menus referring to "Frenchman's Bay."

1947 Fire Overlook

In 1947, Maine suffered its worst drought in decades. After a summer and autumn with very little rain, Mount Desert Island experienced the driest conditions ever recorded. Then, in mid-October, a massive fire broke out that burned over 17,000 acres—nearly half the eastern side of Mount Desert Island (p.125).

Before the fire, the island was covered with evergreen spruce-fir forests. For decades these dark, shady forests deterred the growth of sun-loving deciduous trees. But the fire dramatically altered the landscape. Blueberry bushes, wildflowers, and small ground plants grew in the massive fire's charred wake. Later, a wide range of sun-loving, broad-leafed deciduous trees such as birch and poplar flourished in the sunny, open spaces. The new deciduous trees diversified the landscape, created new habitat for deer and songbirds, and resulted in brilliant autumn foliage. The deciduous trees also created a nursery for shade-loving spruce and fir. At some point in the future, dark spruce-fir forests will likely reclaim their lost territory.

From the 1947 Fire Overlook you can still trace the path of the fire. In summer, light green patches of deciduous leaves stand out against dark green evergreens. This contrast becomes particularly dramatic in autumn, when brilliant foliage seems to reenact the historic blaze.

Sieur de Monts Spring

This peaceful, wooded setting is home to a natural spring used by native tribes and early settlers. In many ways, it is the spiritual home of the park. It was one of the first places George Dorr (p.123) acquired to create Acadia National Park. Dorr purchased the property in a last-minute deal, snatching it away from real-estate speculators who, aware of Dorr's interest in acquiring land for a park, hoped to buy it first and drive up the price. Dorr later described Sieur de Monts Spring as "one of the foundations on which the future park was built."

Today the spring is covered by an arched dome built by Dorr, who also had "Sweet Waters of Acadia" inscribed on a nearby rock. The inscription was inspired by Dorr's travels in Turkey, where he saw springs labeled "Sweet Waters of Europe" and "Sweet Waters of Asia." Sieur de Monts Spring was one of Dorr's favorite places, and Dorr Mountain, which rises above the spring to the southwest, was named in his honor. Due to its wet, wooded location, the area around Sieur de Monts Spring is excellent for bird-watching.

The Acadia Nature Center, located adjacent to the parking area, explores "the science behind the scenery." Inside you'll find exhibits about native species and efforts to preserve Acadia's natural resources. Park rangers answer questions inside, and ranger talks are sometimes offered outside.

Just up the hill from the nature center is the small Abbe Museum, which displays artifacts from native tribes, including stone tools, weapons, pottery, and animal bone flutes. The artifacts were collected by summer resident Robert Abbe, who founded the museum in 1928. Although now overshadowed by its larger, modern sister museum in downtown Bar Harbor (p.211), the Abbe Museum at Sieur de Monts is definitely worth a visit. The artifacts are fascinating, and a small gift shop sells baskets and jewelry by native artists.

The Wild Gardens of Acadia, located adjacent to the parking area, have over 400 species of native flowers, trees, shrubs, and plants. A series of rambling paths twists through the gardens, which are divided into 13 sections representing different native plant communities. Open dawn to dusk.

Beaver Dam Pond

This small pond provides habitat for beavers, which are most active at dawn and dusk. Keep your eyes out for ripples in the water. Beaver dams are visible toward the southern end of Beaver Dam Pond. Although trappers exterminated beavers from Mount Desert Island by 1900, George Dorr successfully reintroduced beavers to the park in the 1920s. Across the Park Loop Road from Beaver Dam Pond are several large buildings that belong to the Jackson Lab (p.126).

Sieur de Monts Spring

Beaver Pond

Egg Rock Overlook

Marked by a large pull-off on the left side of the road, this overlook provides sweeping views of Frenchman Bay, Egg Rock Lighthouse, and Schoodic Peninsula beyond. Egg Rock was named by early coastal settlers who gathered seabird eggs on its rocky ledges. Egg gathering was later banned when several seabird species, including eider ducks and herring gulls, nearly went extinct.

In 1875, Egg Rock Lighthouse opened to help boats navigate the rocky entrance to Frenchman Bay. Because Egg Rock is so small, the lighthouse beacon was built on top of the keeper's residence to conserve space. (Most lighthouses place their beacon in a separate tower). For over a century, Egg Rock was manned by lighthouse keepers who lived on the island year-round and rowed four miles to shore for supplies. The beacon was originally lit by whale oil, which was stored in barrels in the adjacent shack. Whale oil was ultimately replaced by kerosene, which was later replaced by electricity from gas-powered generators. Today Egg Rock Lighthouse is fully automated. An underwater cable delivers electricity from Bar Harbor, and solar panels provide backup energy.

As guardian of Frenchman Bay, Egg Rock has seen some remarkable comings and goings over the years. During World War II, a 250-foot German submarine snuck past Egg Rock and deposited two spies at Hancock Point, just north of Mount Desert Island. The spies, carrying $60,000 cash and a bag of diamonds, made their way to New York City before they were captured.

Highseas

This spectacular brick mansion, perched above the ocean just south of Egg Rock Overlook, was built in 1912 by Princeton professor Rudolf Brunnow. The 32-room mansion was intended as a wedding gift for Brunnow's fiancée, who was living in Europe. Sadly, she booked her passage to America on the *Titanic* and perished on the ship's maiden voyage.

In 1924, wealthy New York City divorcée Eva Van Cortland Hawkes purchased Highseas for $25,000. Mrs. Hawkes kept a large staff at Highseas that included a butler, two footmen, a downstairs maid, upstairs maid, kitchen maid, personal maid, cook, laundress, cleaning woman, chauffeur, and gardener. During World War II, Mrs. Hawkes threw lavish parties at Highseas for the American and British navies that called to port in Bar Harbor. Champagne flowed freely and lobster Newburg was cooked in 30-gallon drums.

When the great fire of 1947 swept through this part of the island, Highseas was spared destruction by a faithful gardener who doused the mansion with water. Following Mrs. Hawkes' death, the estate was donated to the Jackson Lab. Today it's used as a dormitory for high school and college students participating in the Jackson Lab's Summer Student Program. The program counts three Nobel Prize winners among its alumni.

Champlain Mountain

Past Egg Rock Overlook, the Park Loop Road descends alongside the eastern flank of Champlain Mountain, which rises nearly 1,000 vertical feet above the road. Champlain's cliffs—the steepest on the island—are home to the Precipice Trail (p.178), which starts from a small parking area on the right side of the Park Loop Road. In spring and early summer, the Precipice Trail is often closed to protect nesting peregrine falcons. During this time the park sets up viewing scopes in the parking area from 9am to noon.

Peregrine falcons (p.84) are one of Acadia's most remarkable birds. In the first half of the 20th century, their populations plummeted due to hunting and the toxic effects of the pesticide DDT. The last known nesting pair on Mount Desert Island was seen in 1956, and by 1969 peregrines disappeared from the island entirely. Following passage of the Endangered Species Act, conservationists set out to restore peregrine populations. In 1984, a captive breeding program reintroduced peregrine chicks to Acadia National Park. The chicks, which hatched in captivity, were transferred to nesting sites in Acadia when they were three to four weeks old. Over the next several weeks, trained specialists monitored the chicks and made "food drops" through long tubes, which were designed to prevent chicks from associating food with humans. Eventually, when their wings were strong enough to fly, the chicks fledged and hunted on their own.

Between 1984 and 1986, specialists raised over 20 chicks in Acadia. In 1987, some of the captive-bred chicks returned to Acadia as adults, but none produced any young. Then, in 1991, a pair of peregrines successfully nested in Acadia for the first time in 35 years. Over the past three decades, nesting peregrines have produced over 160 chicks in the park, many of which fledged from the Precipice. Recovery efforts like those in Acadia have been so successful that peregrine falcons were removed from the federal endangered species list in 1999.

Schooner Head

Just before the park entrance station, a short spur road heads left to an overlook with dramatic views of Schooner Head and Egg Rock Lighthouse. Schooner Head is named for white markings on the rocks that resemble the sails of a ship when viewed from sea. During the American Revolutionary War, a British warship supposedly fired upon Schooner Head during a snow squall, mistaking the white markings for an American ship. A short path descends from the Schooner Head parking area to some rocky cliffs below.

The giant, modern house perched on top of Schooner Head belongs to Dan Burt, a wealthy attorney-turned-poet. Burt once told a local newspaper that he had traveled all over the world, but "I've never seen a piece of land or area more beautiful than Mount Desert."

Peregrine falcon chicks

Sand Beach

Lying at the far end of Newport Cove, Sand Beach is one of the highlights of Acadia National Park. On clear summer days, hundreds of visitors flock to the beach to soak in the sunshine and scenery. If the water wasn't so teeth-chatteringly cold, Sand Beach would be perfect. But this is Maine, and even in summer ocean temperatures rarely crack 60 degrees. Whether you find a swim here refreshing or masochistic, you can rest assured the beach will be packed on sunny days in July and August. Finding a parking spot in one of the two adjacent parking areas feels like winning the lottery (yet another reason to ride the Island Explorer shuttle).

A staircase descends to the beach from the lower parking area. The fragile sand dunes behind the beach are protected by a long wooden fence. On the far, eastern side of the beach, a moderate, 1.8-mile trail rises above the beach and loops around the rocky promontory called Great Head. Another popular hike, the Beehive (p.176), starts across the road from Sand Beach.

Why, on the otherwise rocky coast of Mount Desert Island, did a sandy beach form here? The answer is Newport Cove, which shelters Sand Beach from powerful waves and currents, allowing small particles to accumulate over time. The beach is composed of sand and crushed seashells. A close examination of the grains reveals colors such as blue, green, purple, and cream that came from the shells of mussels, urchins, and barnacles.

Although Sand Beach is generally protected from powerful waves and currents in summer, winter storms often pull sand away. At times enough sand disappears to reveal the hull of the schooner *Tey*, which crashed on Old Soaker (the rock ledge at the head of Newport Cove) and washed up on Sand Beach in 1911. Back then, the beach was privately owned by financier J.P. Morgan. In 1949, Morgan's granddaughter donated Sand Beach to Acadia National Park.

The Ocean Trail

This easy, two-mile path parallels the Park Loop Road and offers fantastic views of the rocky shoreline between Sand Beach and Otter Cliffs. A stroll on the Ocean Trail is the best way to enjoy this magnificent stretch of the Park Loop Road, known as Ocean Drive. Walking the trail allows you to get out of your car, breathe the pine-scented air, and enjoy the scenery at nature's pace. On days when the tide is low and the ocean is calm, you can wander the rocky shore and explore tide pools. You might even catch a glimpse of a local lobsterman hauling traps offshore.

The Ocean Trail starts from the far end of the upper parking area at Sand Beach. If you're riding the Island Explorer, you can follow the Ocean Trail to Thunder Hole, which is the next shuttle stop.

Thunder Hole

Thunder Hole is a narrow rock crevice that booms like thunder when waves hit it just right. But you must visit at just the right time (about two hours before high tide) during just the right seas (three- to six-foot waves). With luck and timing, you might hear the famous boom. What causes the sound? A small cave at the end of the crevice. When waves rush into the cave, they compress the air inside. If enough pressure builds, air explodes outward in a burst of spray, producing a deep, thundering boom.

But don't get your hopes up. Although Thunder Hole is one of Acadia's most famous sights, many visitors walk away disappointed. Expecting dramatic booms, they only encounter weak gurgles and sloshes. But "Sloshing Hole" or "Hole That Thunders Only Occasionally" is no name for a star attraction.

When seas are stormy, Thunder Hole is one of the most spectacular—and terrifying—sights on the island. Unlike much of Mount Desert Island, which is sheltered by offshore islands, this stretch of coast is exposed to the open ocean. In high seas, waves crash into Thunder Hole with fury. If you happen to visit during a storm, use extreme caution and *do not wander onto the rocks*. I took these photos on August 23, 2009, when the remnants of Hurricane Bill kicked up 15- to 20-foot seas in the Gulf of Maine. Against the warnings of park rangers, dozens of people wandered onto the rocks. At one point, with little warning, a large wave swept a father and his 7-year-old daughter into the 55-degree water. Although the Coast Guard rescued the father, the little girl drowned.

Monument Cove

Monument Cove

Most people drive past Monument Cove without realizing it's there. But this tiny cove, sheltered by tall pine trees on either side, is a testament to the power of erosion. The "monument" is an obelisk-like spire at the cove's north end. Over thousands of years, erosion widened natural cracks in rocks surrounding the cove. As rock chunks fell away, the monument was left behind. Fallen chunks were then tumbled by waves, eroding to form rounded, pumpkin-sized boulders. Like Sand Beach, Monument Cove is partially sheltered from waves and currents. But Monument Cove is more exposed to the ocean than Sand Beach, so the waves and currents here are powerful enough to wash away any sand or small cobblestones that might form, leaving only large, heavy boulders behind.

Otter Cliffs

These vertical cliffs rise 110 feet above the ocean, making them irresistible to rock climbers who scamper up the sheer walls in summer and fall. Otter Cliffs is one of the only places on the eastern seaboard where you can rock climb directly above the ocean. (If you're interested in rock climbing lessons, there are two good outfitters in Bar Harbor, p.21.) Despite Otter Cliffs' name, there are no sea otters here. In fact, there are no sea otters on the entire East Coast. Otter Cliffs and Otter Point—as well as Otter Cove and Otter Creek—were likely named after *river* otters (which are found in Acadia) or the now-extinct sea mink, which was sometimes mistaken for an otter.

Otter Point

About half a mile past Otter Cliffs is the Otter Point parking area. From the parking area, a short path crosses the road and descends to Otter Point, which at low tide is one of the best places in the park to explore tide pools. Head toward the southwestern tip of Otter Point to find the largest and most impressive tide pools. Look closely and you might find barnacles, dog whelks, sea stars, and other fascinating creatures (p.65).

Fabbri Picnic Area

This small picnic area is a good place to enjoy lunch or a quick snack. A nearby memorial commemorates a naval radio station that operated here during World War I. The absence of radio noise and clear views across the Atlantic made it the Navy's best transatlantic radio receiver site. In 1932, the radio station was relocated to Schoodic Peninsula to make way for the Park Loop Road.

Otter Cliffs

Otter Cliffs

Little Hunters Beach

This small cobblestone beach is a geological delight. The cobblestones come from rocks in Acadia's "Shatter Zone," which formed roughly 400 million years ago when a large plume of magma rose under the previously formed bedrock. Following a catastrophic eruption, which created a caldera ten miles wide, the bedrock shattered into pieces. Some of the pieces fell into the magma, and when the magma cooled into granite these shattered pieces were suspended in the granite like plums in plum pudding. These "plum pudding" rocks make up the Shatter Zone. At Little Hunters Beach you can see chunks of older, mostly darker bedrock (the "plums") embedded in granite cobblestones. The rusty coloration found on some rocks is due to iron oxide. To reach Little Hunters Beach, drive roughly two miles past Otter Point. Look for a small wooden staircase on the left side of the road, then follow the stairs down to the beach.

Wildwood Stables

Wildwood Stables offers horse-drawn carriage rides ranging from one to two hours on Acadia's famous carriage roads (p.197). They offer three rides: Day Mountain Loop, a one-hour ride that circles Day Mountain, Day Mountain Summit, a two-hour ride that offers lovely views of the coast, and the Rockefeller Bridge Tour, a two-hour ride that visits several beautiful stone bridges. (Open mid-June to mid-Oct, 877-276-3622, acadiahorses.com)

Jordan Pond Gate Lodge

John D. Rockefeller Jr. built this gate lodge in 1932 as a checkpoint to keep automobiles off the carriage roads. (Today it serves as a residence for lucky park personnel.) Rockefeller believed the architecture in many national parks was random and haphazard, and he was determined to make Acadia's buildings better. In 1929, he sent architect Grosvenor Atterbury on a tour of national parks to study their architectural successes and faults. Atterbury returned with several important guidelines, most notably: (1) buildings should not compete with the local scenery, and (2) if no local style of architecture exists for reference, a suitable foreign style should be chosen. No local style existed in Acadia, so Atterbury designed the Jordan Pond Gate Lodge based on French Romanesque design. Look closely and you'll notice several whimsical details, including birdhouses in the garage gables and shutters with the letter "A" for Atterbury.

Wildwood S

Jordan Pond House

This popular restaurant, in operation for over a century, is one of the highlights of Acadia. Located on the southern shore of Jordan Pond, it offers spectacular views of the glacially sculpted scenery. Lunch and dinner are served, but many people simply snack on the house specialty: oven-fresh popovers (p.48) and tea. The menu also includes stews, chowders, salads, sandwiches, and lots of lobster. Open mid-May to mid-October. Local tip: Make an advance reservation (you'll avoid a long wait) and arrive via the Island Explorer shuttle (nearby parking is extremely limited). For reservations call 207-276-3316. (jordanpondhouse.com)

The original Jordan Pond House opened its doors in the late 1800s. Back then, it was little more than a rambling, birchbark farmhouse. Visitors arrived on foot from Seal Harbor. Later John D. Rockefeller Jr. bought the property and donated it to the park, but a fire destroyed the original building in 1979. The new, modern restaurant opened in 1982.

At 150 feet, Jordan Pond is the deepest freshwater body on the island. Towering above its north shore are the Bubbles, two glacially sculpted mountains that appear symmetrical. But the symmetry is an optical illusion. North Bubble, on the left, is actually 100 feet taller than South Bubble. But because it's situated 2,000 feet north, North Bubble appears roughly the same height as South Bubble when viewed from Jordan Pond's southern shore. You can walk to the base of the Bubbles along the Jordan Pond Trail, a moderate 3.2-mile hike that loops around Jordan Pond.

Jordan Pond House, early 1900s

Jordan Pond from South Bubble

Bubble Rock

As the Park Loop Road rises above the eastern shore of Jordan Pond, it heads between Pemetic Mountain (on your right) and the Bubbles (on your left). Keep your eyes out for rock climbers on the cliffs of South Bubble, then shift your gaze upward for a glimpse of Bubble Rock. Perched precariously on a high ledge, this 14-ton boulder was deposited by a melting glacier roughly 15,000 years ago. Geologists refer to such rocks as *glacial erratics*, and Bubble Rock is one of the most famous glacial erratics in the world.

As massive glaciers advanced over Maine during the last glaciation, loose rocks and boulders were picked up and carried along by moving ice. Geologists believe a glacier picked up Bubble Rock somewhere near Lucerne Lake, roughly 20 miles to the northwest. The glacier carried Bubble Rock over the top of South Bubble, but then global temperatures warmed and the glacier stopped advancing. As the glacier slowly melted, Bubble Rock settled on top of South Bubble in the unlikely position you see today.

Although Bubble Rock looks like it could topple over at any moment, it's actually quite secure. You can see for yourself via the short Bubble Rock Trail, a moderate, 0.7-mile round-trip trail that starts from the Bubble Rock parking area. A close examination of Bubble Rock reveals black and white crystals distinct from the pinkish crystals found in South Bubble's bedrock. Even if you're not interested in geology, a walk to the top of South Bubble is worth it for the stunning views of Jordan Pond just past Bubble Rock.

Bubble Pond

Nestled between Cadillac Mountain and Pemetic Mountain, Bubble Pond rests in a graceful, U-shaped valley that's a tell-tale sign of a glacially carved landscape. A carriage road curves around the western shore (great for a quick stroll), but swimming is prohibited because Bubble Pond is a public water supply. The stone bridge next to the pond is the only bridge in the carriage road system made entirely of stone. Most carriage road bridges are made of reinforced concrete, which was then covered with an outer layer of cut stone.

Eagle Lake Overlook

This small overlook offers beautiful views of Eagle Lake, the second largest lake on Mount Desert Island after Long Pond. In the late 1800s, before the Park Loop Road existed, the steamship *Wauwinnet* ferried tourists across Eagle Lake to the base of Cadillac Mountain. From there a small cog railroad hauled tourists to the top of the mountain. But the venture was unprofitable, and the *Wauwinnet* was sunk in Eagle Lake, where it still rests today.

Porcupine Islands

As you drive up Cadillac Mountain, you'll enjoy sweeping northeastern views of Bar Harbor, Frenchman Bay, and the Porcupine Islands. During the French and Indian War (1754–1763), French gunboats hid behind the Porcupine Islands to ambush British vessels, which is probably how Frenchman Bay got its name. Even after the war, the islands continued to make fabulous hiding places. One of the islands, Rum Key, got its name during Prohibition when rum-runners from Canada smuggled liquor into Frenchman Bay. Today four of the Porcupine Islands belong to Acadia National Park. Burnt Island, which is privately owned, belongs to the town of Gouldsboro across Frenchman Bay.

Blue Hill Overlook

The best place to watch the sunset on Cadillac Mountain is Blue Hill Overlook. Be sure to arrive early to grab one of the limited parking spaces. From the parking area, almost everyone follows the crowds to the open area to the right, but the best views are actually to the left! Follow the sidewalk to some small steps, then continue over the granite. You'll soon come to an even higher area with stunning views of Eagle Lake and Blue Hill, plus dramatic views of the Cranberry Isles to the south.

Cadillac Mountain

Towering 1,530 feet above sea level, Cadillac Mountain is the tallest mountain in Acadia and the highest point on the U.S. East Coast. From October 7 to March 6, Cadillac's summit is the first place in the U.S. to see sunrise. (In summer Mars Hill, in northern Maine, is the first place in the U.S. to see sunrise.)

Cadillac Summit Road twists 3.5 miles to the top of Cadillac Mountain. Over the past decade, as park visitation surged, traffic jams snaked down the mountain. Today, all vehicles must have a timed-entry permit to drive Cadillac Summit Road from late May through late October. The permits reduce congestion, improving the visitor experience for everyone. Visit recreation.gov for details.

The road to Cadillac's summit is filled with hairpin turns and spectacular views. A pullout 1.5 miles from the start offers western views of Eagle Lake, Sargent Mountain, and the Bubbles. The road then twists east to reveal sweeping views of Bar Harbor, the Porcupine Islands, and Frenchman Bay. After passing a hairpin turn with southern views of the Cranberry Isles, you'll pass Blue Hill Overlook, a terrific sunset destination (see previous page).

Cadillac Summit Road ends at a large parking area. Near the entrance you'll find restrooms and a gift shop selling drinks and snacks. Cadillac Summit Trail is an easy 0.3-mile path that loops around the summit. Portions of the path are paved and wheelchair-accessible. On clear days, you'll enjoy tremendous views in all directions. As you stroll around the summit, imagine the landscape 20,000 years ago. Back then, a massive glacier buried Mount Desert Island under nearly one mile of ice and stretched 150 miles into the Gulf of Maine!

Cadillac Mountain's true peak is located near the radio tower behind the gift shop. After finding the metal USGS marker embedded in the bedrock, kick back and enjoy the tremendous southern views. On clear days you can see all the way to Isle au Haut, 26 miles southwest.

Cadillac's breathtaking panoramas are made possible by a lack of trees on the summit. Strong winds, freezing temperatures, and rapid erosion deter all but the hardiest plants. Lack of vegetation leads to poor soil development, which prevents larger plants from taking root. This is a fragile landscape. Watch your step, avoid roped-off areas, and always stay on designated trails.

In the late 1800s, a cog railroad chugged up the side of Cadillac Mountain (which went by Green Mountain back then). The half-hour ride cost $2.50 and brought visitors to the 50-room Summit Hotel, where they could spend the night. The railroad went bankrupt after a decade, and the Summit Hotel was torn down in 1896.

Sunrise, Cadillac Mountain

BEEHIVE TRAIL

SUMMARY: Short, steep, and sweet, the Beehive Trail is one of Acadia's most popular hikes. Rising to the top of a beehive-shaped dome that towers above the Park Loop Road, the trail provides unbeatable views of Sand Beach and Great Head. Although the Beehive is one of Acadia's shorter trails, it's not for the faint of heart. A few steep sections require climbing iron rungs, and several precipitous drop-offs won't sit well with anyone with a fear of heights. Many people consider the Beehive Acadia's second-most challenging hike after the Precipice. If you're afraid of heights, the route up the Beehive's steep southern face is not for you. But you can still reach the summit via the far less dramatic Bowl Trail, which wraps around the Beehive's backside. No matter which route you choose, be sure to visit the Bowl, a small pond nestled in the granite behind the Beehive. The Bowl is a perfect place to soak your feet or jump in for a refreshing swim.

TRAILHEAD: The Bowl Trail starts across the Park Loop Road from the Sand Beach parking area. Follow the Bowl Trail 0.2 miles to its intersection with the Beehive Trail, which veers to the right.

TRAIL INFO

RATING: Strenuous, Ladder

HIKING TIME: 1–2 hours

DISTANCE: 1.6 miles, round-trip

ELEVATION CHANGE: 520 feet

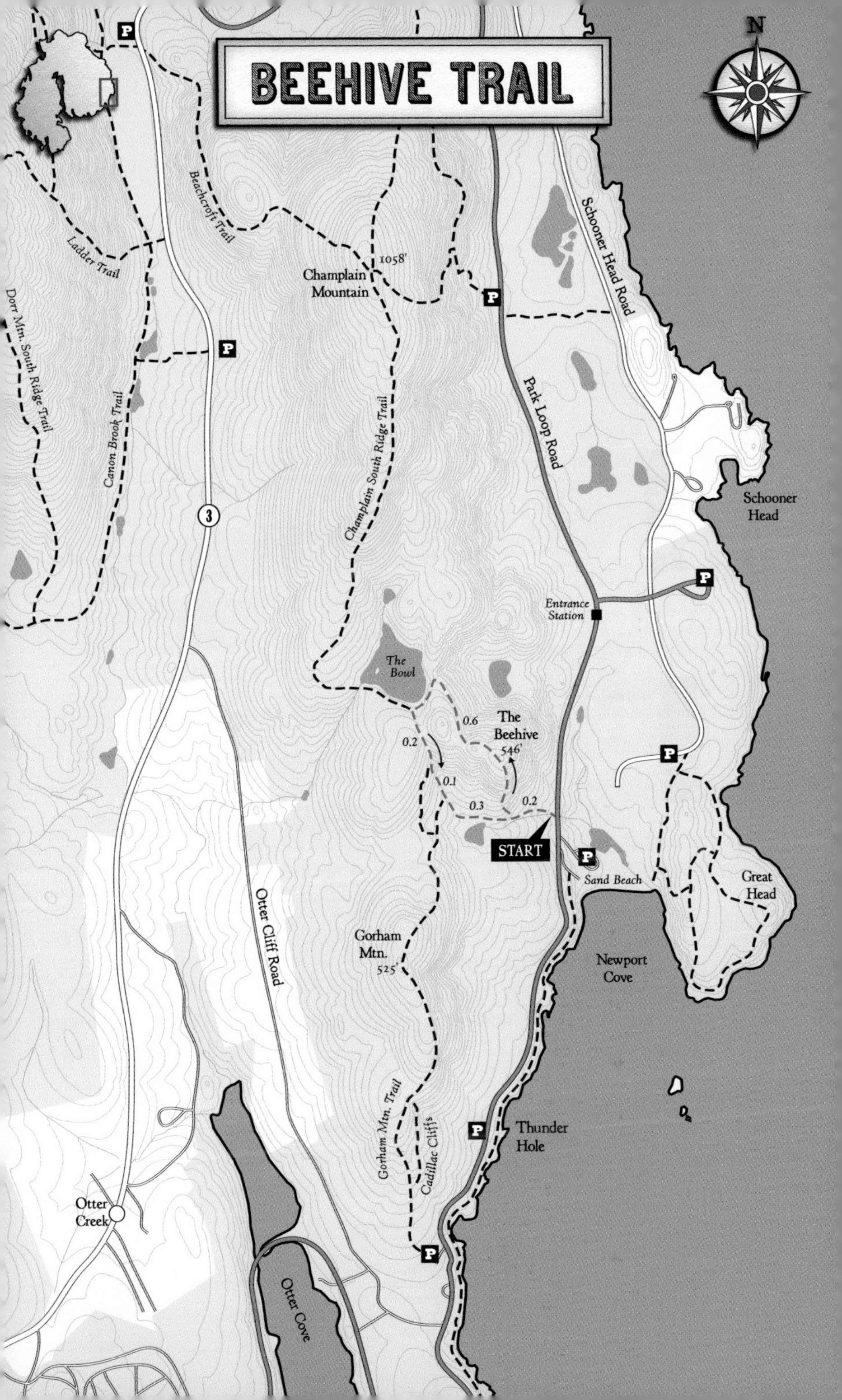
BEEHIVE TRAIL
N
Beachcroft Trail
Ladder Trail
Dorr Mtn. South Ridge Trail
Canon Brook Trail
Champlain Mountain
1058'
Champlain South Ridge Trail
Schooner Head Road
Park Loop Road
Schooner Head
Entrance Station
The Bowl
The Beehive
546'
0.6
0.2
0.1
0.3
0.2
START
Sand Beach
Great Head
Newport Cove
Gorham Mtn.
525'
Otter Cliff Road
Gorham Mtn. Trail
Cadillac Cliffs
Thunder Hole
Otter Creek
Otter Cove
3
P

THE PRECIPICE

SUMMARY: Rising nearly 1,000 feet up the sheer eastern face of Champlain Mountain, the Precipice Trail is considered the most challenging trail in the park. It's certainly the most famous. A jungle gym of stone steps and iron rungs guides hikers up the sheer cliff, which offers thrilling ascents and tremendous views of Frenchman Bay. Despite the hype, it generally takes more mental strength than physical strength to conquer the Precipice. But the trail should be avoided by small children, those with a fear of heights, and anyone during or immediately after wet weather. An alternate route to Champlain's summit is the moderate, 1.2-mile Beachcroft Path, which starts off Route 3 and ascends the mountain's western slope. From Champlain's summit, follow the North Ridge Trail and Orange and Black Path back to the Precipice parking area. Note: the Precipice Trail often closes from mid-April to late July/early August to protect nesting peregrine falcons.

TRAILHEAD: The Precipice Trail starts from the Precipice parking area off the Park Loop Road, two miles south of the Sieur de Monts entrance off Route 3.

TRAIL INFO

RATING: Strenuous, Ladder

HIKING TIME: 2–3 hours

DISTANCE: 2.5 miles, round-trip

ELEVATION CHANGE: 978 feet

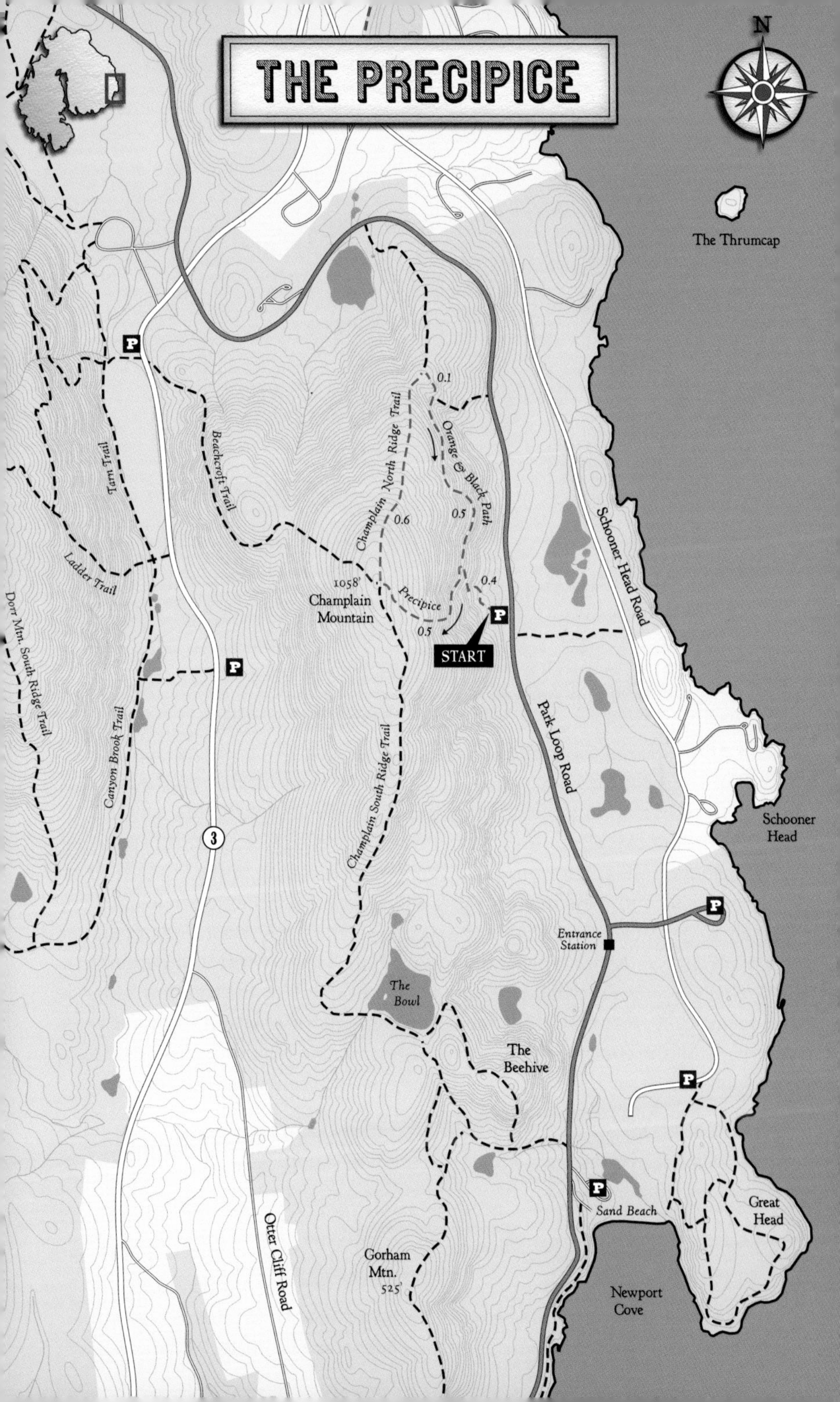

THE PRECIPICE
N
The Thrumcap
P
0.1
Orange & Black Path
Champlain North Ridge Trail
Beachcroft Trail
Tarn Trail
0.6
0.5
Schooner Head Road
Ladder Trail
1058'
Champlain Mountain
Precipice
0.4
0.5
START
Dorr Mtn. South Ridge Trail
Canyon Brook Trail
Champlain South Ridge Trail
Park Loop Road
3
Schooner Head
Entrance Station
The Bowl
The Beehive
Sand Beach
Great Head
Gorham Mtn.
525'
Newport Cove
Otter Cliff Road

GORHAM MOUNTAIN

SUMMARY: Gorham Mountain offers the best views of any moderate hike in Acadia. Great for families with young children, the trail rises to the 525-foot summit of Gorham Mountain, offering dramatic views of Otter Cliffs, Sand Beach, and the gorgeous shoreline along Ocean Drive. Cadillac Cliffs, a short spur trail that branches off the main trail, passes an ancient sea cave. (Thousands of years ago, after massive glaciers melted, the land was compressed and sea levels were relatively higher). Continue climbing towards Gorham's summit, but remember to turn around and enjoy the dramatic southern views, which are better than views from the summit. After reaching the summit, follow the trail north to the Sand Beach parking area. From there you can catch the Island Explorer back to Gorham Mountain Trailhead, or stroll roughly one mile back along the easy, beautiful Ocean Path.

TRAILHEAD: The Gorham Mountain Trail starts from the Gorham Mountain parking area, located on the right side of the Park Loop Road about half a mile past Thunder Hole.

TRAIL INFO

RATING: Moderate

HIKING TIME: 1–2 hours

DISTANCE: 2.6 miles, round-trip

ELEVATION CHANGE: 525 feet

GORHAM MTN.
N
Tarn Trail
Ladder Trail
Dorr Mtn. South Ridge Trail
A. Murray Young Path
Canon Brook Trail
Champlain Mountain
1058'
Champlain South Ridge Trail
Schooner Head Road
Park Loop Road
Schooner Head
Entrance Station
The Bowl
The Beehive
0.3
0.1
0.2
Sand Beach
Great Head
Newport Cove
Otter Cliff Road
Gorham Mtn.
525'
0.8
Gorham Mtn. Trail
0.7
Thunder Hole
Cadillac Cliffs
0.3
0.2
Cadillac South Ridge Trail
Otter Creek
START
Otter Cove
Otter Cliffs
Blackwoods Campground
3
P

CADILLAC MOUNTAIN

SUMMARY: Cadillac Mountain is the island's highest peak, offering stunning 360-degree views from its 1,530-foot summit. Hikers share those views with everyone who arrived by car, but hikers' endorphin-soaked brains enjoy them more! There are four routes up Cadillac, but I like the North Ridge Trail, which offers terrific views of Bar Harbor and the Porcupine Islands. After reaching the summit, follow the dirt path next to the gift shop to the island's true peak (look for the USGS marker embedded in the bedrock) and continue down Cadillac's South Ridge Trail. On clear days you'll be treated to spectacular views of dozens of small islands lying off MDI's southern shore. The South Ridge Trail ends at Blackwoods Campground, where you can catch the Island Explorer Shuttle (p.30) back to Bar Harbor.

TRAILHEAD: The Cadillac North Ridge trailhead is located along the Park Loop Road, 1/3 of a mile past the Y-intersection where the Park Loop Road becomes one-way. There's a small pull-out across from the trailhead. The Island Explorer stops at the Cadillac North Ridge trailhead.

TRAIL INFO

RATING: Strenuous

HIKING TIME: 3–4 hours

DISTANCE: 5.7 miles, round-trip

ELEVATION CHANGE: 1,463 feet

CADILLAC MTN.
N
START
One-way
233
Carriage Roads
Park Loop Road
Eagle Lake
2.2
Cadillac North Ridge Trail
Gorge Path
Dorr North Ridge Trail
Sieur de Mont
Visitor Center
Dorr
Mtn.
1270'
Tarn Trail
Beachcroft Trail
Ladder Trail
1530'
Cadillac
Mountain
0.5
Cadillac West Face Trail
Cadillac South Ridge Trail
A. Murray Young Path
Dorr South Ridge Trail
Canyon Brook Trail
North
Bubble
872'
Bubble Pond
0.7
South
Bubble
768'
Canon Brook Trail
3
1248'
Pemetic
Mountain
Pond Trail
Jordan Pond
Pemetic Mtn Trail
1.1
Otter Cliff Road
Jordan Cliffs Trail
Eagles Crag
0.2
Cadillac South Ridge Trail
1.0
Hunters Brook Trail
Otter
Creek
Blackwoods
Campground

PEMETIC MOUNTAIN

SUMMARY Rising 1,248 feet above sea level between Bubble Pond and Jordan Pond, Pemetic Mountain is one of my favorite hikes. From the bare granite summit you'll enjoy panoramic views of lakes, mountains, and offshore islands. There are multiple routes to the top, but my favorite starts off the western shore of Bubble Pond. After a steep one-mile hike through shady forest, you'll walk across bare granite. Views of Eagle Lake and Frenchman Bay appear to the north. Continue to the summit, where classic coastal scenery sweeps across the southwest horizon. After a well-deserved break, descend Pemetic's south ridge, which offers even better views until it drops below treeline. A wooden signpost marks a junction. Turn left to follow hiking trails and carriage roads back to Bubble Pond. Turn right to descend to Jordan Pond House, where you can catch the Island Explorer. Trail info below reflects the Jordan Pond House option.

TRAILHEAD From Bubble Pond parking area, head south along the west shore of Bubble Pond, then turn right at the wooden sign. Parking is extremely limited at Bubble Pond; it's best to ride the Island Explorer.

TRAIL INFO

RATING: Strenuous

DISTANCE: 3 miles

HIKING TIME: 2–3 Hours

ELEVATION CHANGE: 1,128 feet

PEMETIC MTN.
N
233
Eagle Lake
Carriaage Roads
Park Loop Road
Cadillac North Ridge Trial
Gorge Path
Cadillac Mtn 1,530'
Cadillac West Face
Bubble Pond
Cadillac South Face Trial
Canon Brook
North Bubble 872'
South Bubble 768'
1,373' Sargent Mtn
1.1
0.5
Pemetic Mtn 1,248'
Pemetic Mtn Trail
Pond Trail
Jordan Pond
1,194' Penobscot Mtn
Jordan Cliffs Trail
0.7
0.3
0.3
0.6
0.3
0.4
The Triad 698'
0.1
0.4
0.4
0.2
0.3
Hunters Brook Trail

PENOBSCOT MOUNTAIN

SUMMARY: Penobscot Mountain is my favorite hike above Jordan Pond. The trail to the summit is classic Acadia: a dramatic hike up a bare granite ridge with spectacular views of rounded mountains towering above the Gulf of Maine. The trail to the summit starts near the Jordan Pond House and rises through dense forest. After scrambling over a few iron rungs, you'll reach Penobscot Mountain's bare granite ridge. Hiking above treeline, you'll enjoy southern views of the Cranberry Isles and Great Duck Island and Little Duck Island. Beyond the summit, the trail dips back into the forest and descends rather steeply to Jordan Pond along Deer Brook Trail. Along the way you'll pass under magnificent Deer Brook Bridge, which boasts a graceful double arch. From the northern tip of Jordan Pond, follow the Jordan Pond Shore Trail back to Jordan Pond House, where you can feast on oven-fresh popovers and jam.

TRAILHEAD: The trail to Penobscot Mountain's summit starts behind the Jordan Pond House. Follow the Spring Trail 0.3 miles until it crosses a carriage road and connects with the Penobscot Mountain Trail.

TRAIL INFO

RATING: Strenuous

HIKING TIME: 2–3 hours

DISTANCE: 3.7 miles, round-trip

ELEVATION CHANGE: 973 feet

PENOBSCOT MTN.
N
Eagle Lake
Bubble Pond
North Bubble 872'
Sargent Mtn. North Ridge
Sargent Mountain 1373'
East Cliffs Trail
Deer Brook Bridge
0.2
0.1
South Bubble 768'
Grandgent Trail
Sargent Mtn. South Ridge
Deer Brook Trail
Maple Spring Trail
0.5
1248' Pemetic Mountain
Sargent Mtn. Pond
0.1
Jordan Cliffs Trail
Jordan Pond
Park Loop Road
Penobscot Mountain 1194'
Hadlock Brook Trail
Pemetic Mtn Trail
Penobscot Mtn. Trail
1.5
942' Cedar Swamp Mtn.
Carriage Roads
1.0
The Amphitheater
West Branch Bridge
Jordan Pond House
Spring Trail
0.3
START

SARGENT MOUNTAIN

SUMMARY: Sargent Mountain is Acadia's second-highest peak, towering 1,373 feet above sea level (just 157 feet shy of Cadillac Mountain). Like Cadillac, Sargent boasts 360-degree views from its bare granite summit. Unlike Cadillac, it's not swarming with tourists who arrived by car. In fact, because Sargent Mountain is one of Acadia's most remote and challenging hikes, you might have its summit all to yourself. There are several possible approaches, but my favorite heads up and over Parkman Mountain, then climbs the western face of Sargent Mountain via the Grandgent Trail. As you climb the steep Grandgent Trail, be sure to take frequent breaks and enjoy the wonderful western views of Somesville and Somes Sound. After reaching Sargent Mountain's summit, head down its gorgeous southern ridge and turn right on the Hadlock Brook Trail. As you return to the trailhead, you'll pass gurgling streams, shimmering cascades, and one of the carriage roads' most beautiful stone bridges.

TRAILHEAD: The Hadlock Brook Trail starts across Route 198 from the Norumbega Mountain trailhead, just north of Upper Hadlock Pond.

TRAIL INFO

RATING: Strenuous

HIKING TIME: 4–5 Hours

DISTANCE: 4.6 miles, round-trip

ELEVATION CHANGE: 1,152 feet

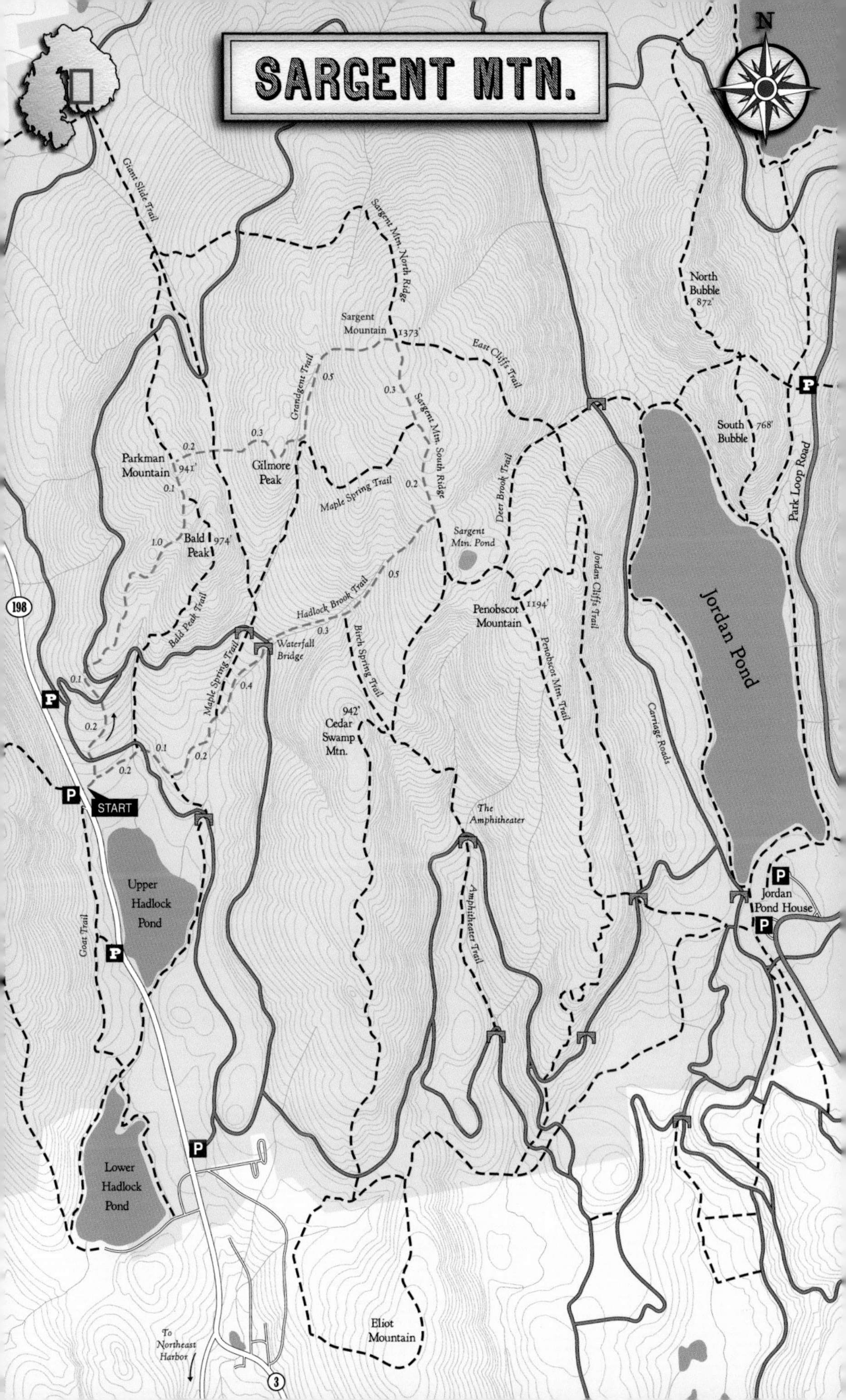
SARGENT MTN.
N
Giant Slide Trail
Sargent Mtn. North Ridge
Sargent Mountain 1373'
East Cliffs Trail
Grandgent Trail
0.5
0.3
Sargent Mtn. South Ridge
North Bubble 872'
South Bubble 768'
Park Loop Road
Parkman Mountain 941'
0.2
0.3
Gilmore Peak
0.1
Maple Spring Trail
0.2
Deer Brook Trail
Bald Peak 974'
1.0
Sargent Mtn. Pond
Jordan Cliffs Trail
0.5
Hadlock Brook Trail
Penobscot Mountain 1194'
Jordan Pond
198
Bald Peak Trail
0.3
Waterfall Bridge
Birch Spring Trail
Penobscot Mtn. Trail
Maple Spring Trail
0.4
0.1
942' Cedar Swamp Mtn.
Carriage Roads
0.2
0.1
0.2
0.2
START
The Amphitheater
Upper Hadlock Pond
Jordan Pond House
Goat Trail
Amphitheater Trail
Lower Hadlock Pond
Eliot Mountain
To Northeast Harbor
3

ACADIA MOUNTAIN

SUMMARY: Acadia Mountain is my favorite hike on the western side of Mount Desert Island. Perched above Somes Sound, it offers spectacular views of the East Coast's loveliest fjard (p.242) and the Cranberry Isles beyond. The trail starts in a shady spruce-fir forest, then scrambles over a large granite ledge en route to the top of Acadia Mountain. The view from the summit is nice, but there are even better views from the bare granite ledges a short distance beyond. Past the ledges, the trail drops roughly 600 feet in half a mile—a steep, challenging scramble. A short trail near the base of Acadia Mountain leads to Man O' War Brook Waterfall, a small cascade where 18th century ships replenished their water supply. Somes Sound is so deep that ships pulled up directly alongside the cascade. From Man O' War Brook, follow the dirt access road back to the trailhead. Local tip: After hiking Acadia Mountain, head to Echo Lake Ledges, reached via a short trail from Acadia Mountain parking area, for a refreshing swim!

TRAILHEAD: The trail starts across the street from the Acadia Mountain parking area on Route 102, about two miles north of Southwest Harbor.

TRAIL INFO

RATING: Strenuous

HIKING TIME: 2 hours

DISTANCE: 2.6-miles, round-trip

ELEVATION CHANGE: 581 feet

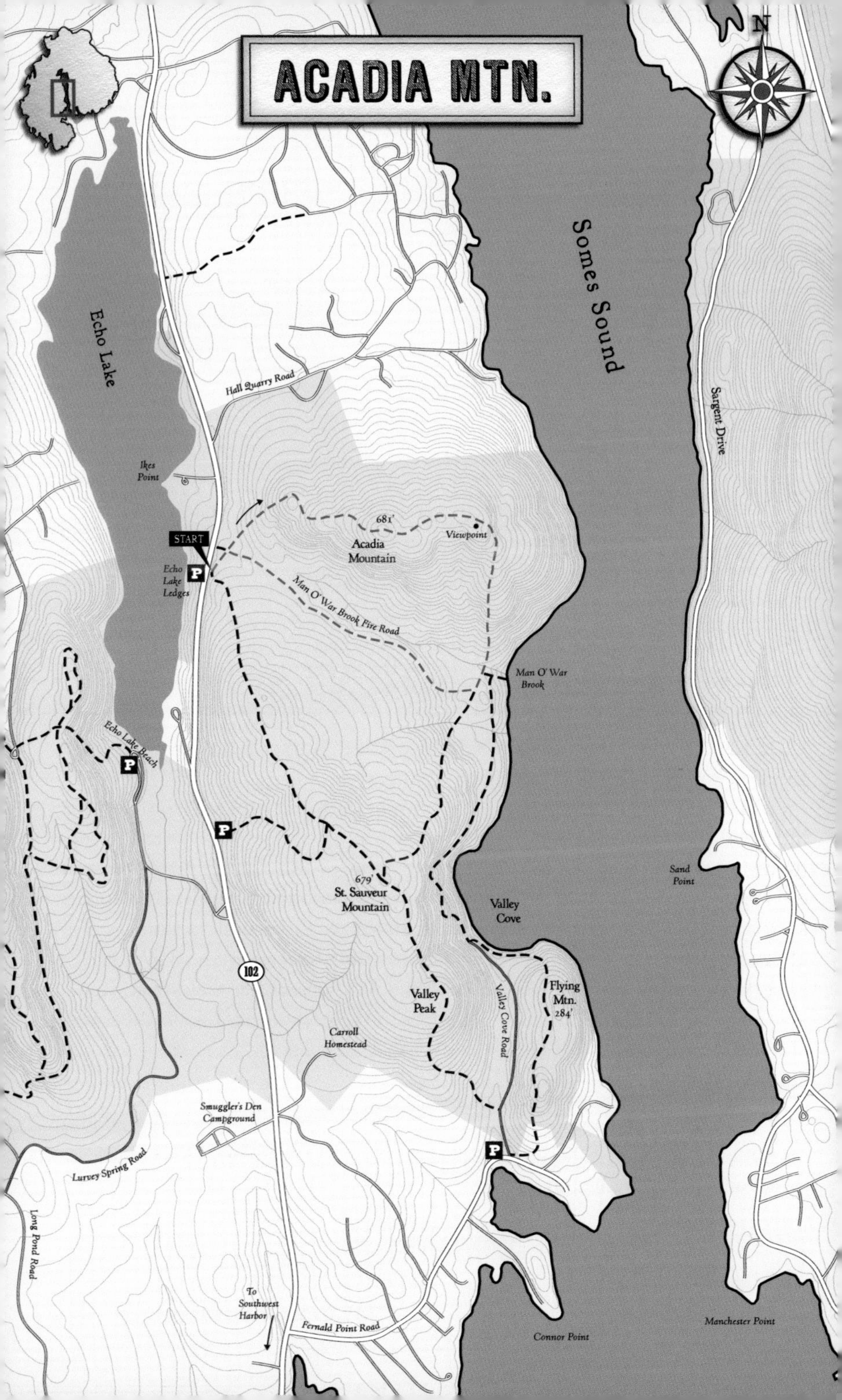
ACADIA MTN.
N
Echo Lake
Somes Sound
Hall Quarry Road
Sargent Drive
Ikes Point
START
Echo Lake Ledges
681'
Acadia Mountain
Viewpoint
Man O' War Brook Fire Road
Man O' War Brook
Echo Lake Beach
679'
St. Sauveur Mountain
Sand Point
Valley Cove
102
Valley Peak
Valley Cove Road
Flying Mtn. 284'
Carroll Homestead
Smuggler's Den Campground
Lurvey Spring Road
Long Pond Road
To Southwest Harbor
Fernald Point Road
Connor Point
Manchester Point

BEECH MOUNTAIN

SUMMARY: This rewarding hike, which starts from a hilltop parking area, gets you up high with minimal effort, showcasing some of western MDI's most dramatic scenery. From the Beech Mountain parking area, follow the Beech Mountain Trail until it forks. This is the start/finish of Beech Mountain Loop. I like hiking the loop clockwise, which means bearing left. After hiking uphill 0.4 miles through the forest, you'll arrive at Beech Mountain's summit, which offers panoramic views of western MDI's southern shore. The metal fire tower on top of Beech Mountain—last used in 1976 but occasionally open to the public (check local papers or visitor centers)—offers even better, 360-degree views that stretch all the way to the Camden Hills. To return to the parking area, follow the western branch of the Beech Mountain Trail back to the parking area. Along the way you'll enjoy spectacular views of Long Pond.

TRAILHEAD: Follow Route 102 south of Somesville, then turn right onto Pretty Marsh Road. After 0.3 miles turn left onto Beech Hill Road, which heads south for three miles before ending at the Beech Mountain parking area.

TRAIL INFO

RATING: Moderate

HIKING TIME: 1 hour

DISTANCE: 1.1 miles, round-trip

ELEVATION CHANGE: 360 feet

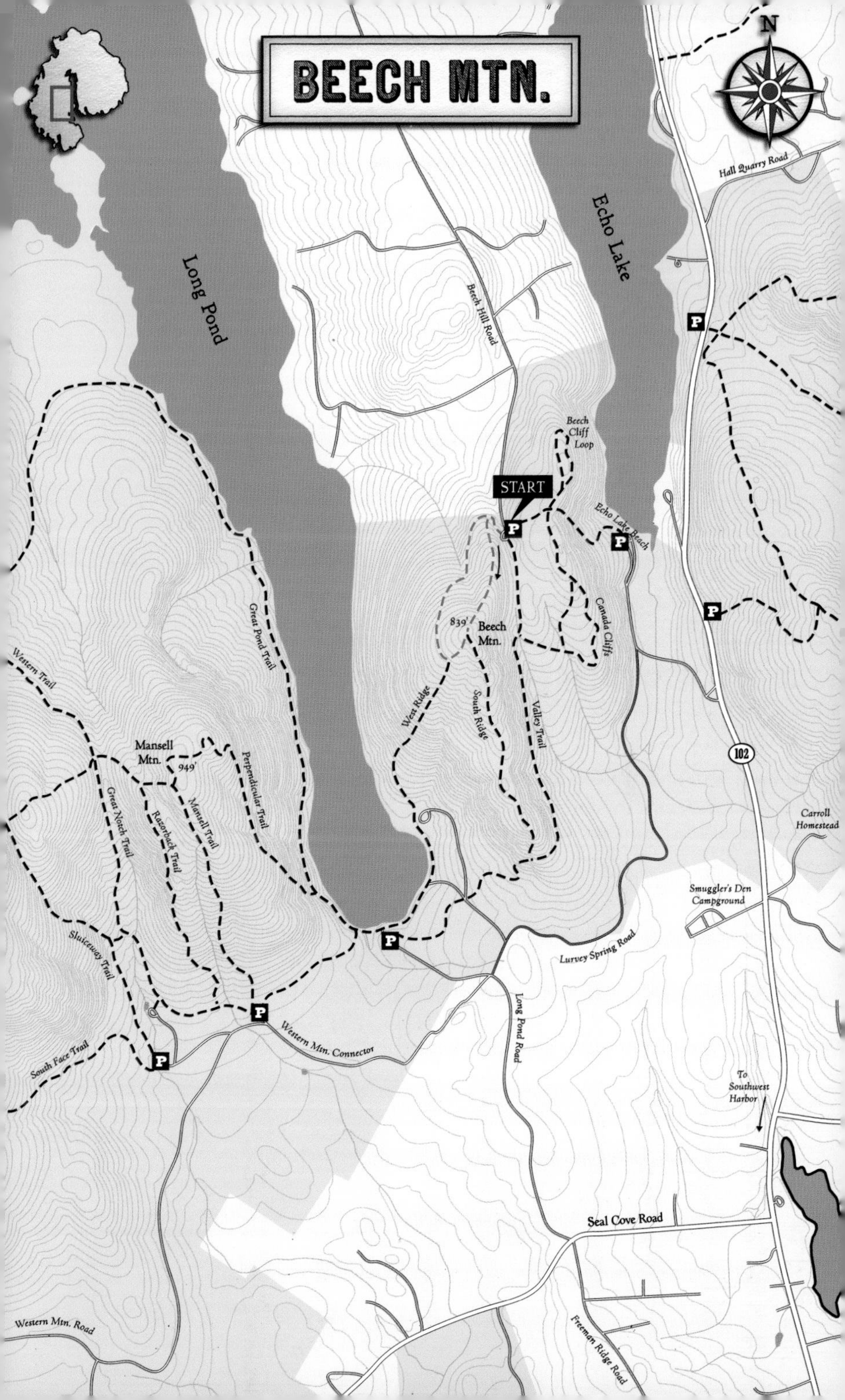
BEECH MTN.
N
Hall Quarry Road
Echo Lake
Long Pond
Beech Hill Road
Beech Cliff Loop
START
Echo Lake Beach
Canada Cliffs
839'
Beech Mtn.
West Ridge
South Ridge
Valley Trail
Great Pond Trail
Western Trail
Mansell Mtn.
949'
Perpendicular Trail
Great Notch Trail
Razorback Trail
Mansell Trail
102
Carroll Homestead
Smuggler's Den Campground
Lurvey Spring Road
Sluiceway Trail
South Face Trail
Western Mtn. Connector
Long Pond Road
To Southwest Harbor
Seal Cove Road
Western Mtn. Road
Freeman Ridge Road
P

MANSELL MOUNTAIN

SUMMARY Rising nearly 1,000 feet above the western shore of Long Pond, Mansell Mountain is the second-tallest mountain west of Somes Sound. There are no views from the forested summit, but you'll enjoy beautiful coastal views on both the ascent and descent. From the trailhead, hike 0.2 miles along the southwest shore of Long Pond, then turn left onto the Perpendicular Trail. Rising nearly 900 feet to Mansell's summit, the Perpendicular Trail boasts hundreds of impressive granite steps, a small ladder, and three iron rungs. As you approach the summit, you'll pass a clearing with nice views of Long Pond and Southwest Harbor. From the summit two good routes (Mansell Trail and Razorback Trail) descend to the southern base of the mountain. I like Mansell Trail, which boasts offshore views that stretch from the Cranberry Isles to Isle au Haut. After descending to Gilley Field, follow Cold Brook Trail back to the trailhead.

TRAILHEAD From Southwest Harbor, drive north on Route 102, turn left onto Seal Cove Road, then turn right onto Long Pond Road. Follow Long Pond Road to the southern shore of Long Pond.

TRAIL INFO

RATING: Strenuous, Ladder

DISTANCE: 2.5 miles

HIKING TIME: 2–3 Hours

ELEVATION CHANGE: 891 feet

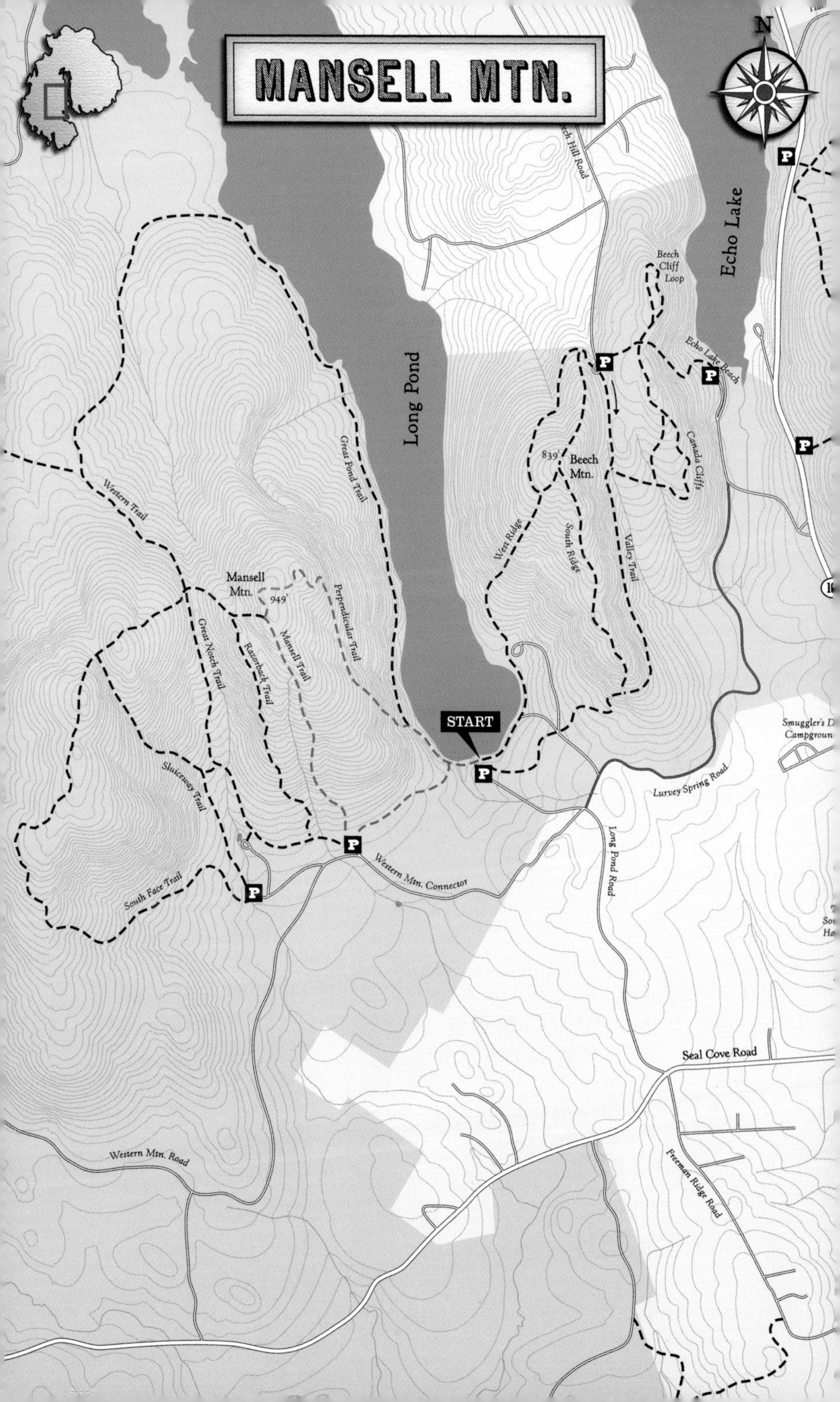

MANSELL MTN.
N
Echo Lake
Long Pond
Beech Cliff Loop
Echo Lake Beach
Canada Cliffs
839'
Beech Mtn.
West Ridge
South Ridge
Valley Trail
Great Pond Trail
Western Trail
Mansell Mtn.
949'
Perpendicular Trail
Mansell Trail
Razorback Trail
Great Notch Trail
Sluiceway Trail
South Face Trail
Western Mtn. Connector
START
Lurvey Spring Road
Long Pond Road
Smuggler's D
Campgroun
Seal Cove Road
Freeman Ridge Road
Western Mtn. Road

Duck Brook Bridge

CARRIAGE ROADS

ACADIA'S CARRIAGE ROADS are a fairy tale come to life. They were once part of the private estate of John D. Rockefeller Jr., who later donated the road network to Acadia National Park. Today 57 miles of gravel roads twist across Mount Desert Island, passing lush forests, sparkling streams, and stunning lakes. The road network also boasts 17 exquisite stone bridges hand-crafted by stonemasons out of native rock. When first constructed, Rockefeller's carriage roads provided automobile-free enjoyment for horse-drawn carriages. Today bicycles are the most popular mode of transportation. However you enjoy them, the carriage roads are one of the highlights of Acadia National Park.

The carriage roads form a network of "broken-stone" roads on the eastern half of Mount Desert Island. They extend south from Paradise Hill (near downtown Bar Harbor) to the old Rockefeller family estate in Seal Harbor. There is no official start or end to the carriage roads, just six popular entry points. Upon entering the network, you can choose your own adventure. Numbered signposts at each intersection make it hard to get lost—provided you have a good map, like the ones included at the end of this chapter.

Bicycle rentals are available in Bar Harbor (p.219) or Seal Harbor (p.227). Another great option is booking a horse-drawn carriage ride at Wildwood Stables (p.158). Or you can simply stroll the carriage roads on foot. Note: Twelve miles of carriage roads near Seal Harbor, which are managed by the Land & Garden Preserve, are open only to hikers and horseback riders—no bicycles. Keep your eyes out for "No Bicycle" signs posted at intersections.

The carriage roads' fascinating history traces its roots to the year 1837, when a wooden bridge first connected Mount Desert Island to the mainland. Before the bridge, Mount Desert Island was accessible only by sea. After the bridge, visitors could arrive by land. At the time, this produced relatively little change to island life. A few horse-drawn carriages rolled across the bridge, but ships remained the primary mode of transportation. By the late 1800s, however, the first automobiles arrived, sparking a heated culture war on Mount Desert Island.

By the time Henry Ford introduced the Model T in 1908, cars were already banned on Mount Desert Island. The ban served two purposes: it allowed rich summer visitors to take refuge from the sputtering, soot-spewing automobiles in big cities, and it allowed year-round islanders to limit the pretentious lifestyles of the rich. All that changed with the introduction of the Model T. As moderately priced autos flooded the nation, local islanders were determined not to be left out of the fun. On a practical level, the new autos offered cheap, efficient transportation for local businesses. In 1909, a group of islanders tried to repeal the ban on automobiles. Their efforts were blocked by a group of wealthy summer residents who lobbied to keep the ban in place. The islanders, vowing revenge, promised to revisit the matter as soon as possible.

Two years later, a temporary compromise was reached that limited automobiles to Bar Harbor. But when an islander died because a horse-drawn carriage did not reach the hospital in time, the automobile ban was widely denounced. By 1915, automobiles were cruising through every town on Mount Desert Island.

Among the summer residents most alarmed by this turn of events was Rockefeller, who had recently purchased a Seal Harbor estate as a summer refuge from New York City. At a time when most wealthy Manhattan businessmen commuted to work in shiny new automobiles, Rockefeller drove himself to work in a horse-drawn carriage—a habit that spoke volumes about his poor fit among the office buildings of New York. Since birth, Rockefeller had been groomed to take over his family's vast Standard Oil business, but Rockefeller and Standard Oil were hardly a match made in heaven. Happiest outdoors, Rockefeller coped with the stress of Manhattan office life by chopping wood after work. After a few years at the helm at Standard Oil, he quit the family business, devoted himself to a life of philanthropy, and purchased a 150-acre Seal Harbor estate.

When Rockefeller arrived in Seal Harbor in 1910, the Great Automobile War (as it later became known) was just beginning. Perhaps sensing the inevitable, Rockefeller began building a series of gravel roads on his sprawling Seal Harbor estate where he could enjoy the simple pleasures of a horse-drawn carriage ride. As his road network grew, Rockefeller decided to connect it in a continuous loop. But to do so required passing through land owned by the Hancock County Trustees of Public Reservations (the predecessor of Acadia National Park). Rockefeller tried to buy the land in question, but his offer was refused. He was, however, granted permission to build roads through the land with the knowledge that they might one day be shut down.

Rockefeller accepted the risk and expanded his road network. Things went smoothly until a planned road in Northeast Harbor drew heat from summer residents. Among the most upset was George Wharton Pepper, who fired off a letter to Rockefeller. "In my judgement," Pepper wrote, "it would be a serious mistake to extend your well conceived system of roads into this area." Rockefeller reluctantly agreed and halted construction of the road. But many people who were using and enjoying the previously built carriage roads openly supported

JOHN D. ROCKEFELLER JR.

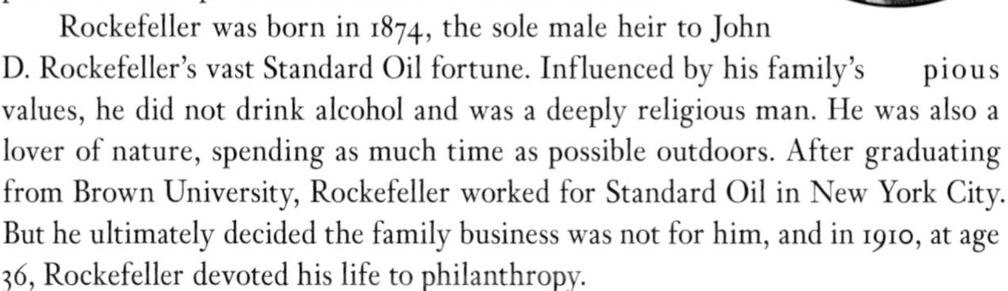

Without John D. Rockefeller, Jr.'s deep pockets and deep sense of philanthropy, Acadia National Park would not exist as we know it today. He is the park's most famous benefactor, embodying both the generosity and public-minded spirit that continues to define Acadia.

Rockefeller was born in 1874, the sole male heir to John D. Rockefeller's vast Standard Oil fortune. Influenced by his family's pious values, he did not drink alcohol and was a deeply religious man. He was also a lover of nature, spending as much time as possible outdoors. After graduating from Brown University, Rockefeller worked for Standard Oil in New York City. But he ultimately decided the family business was not for him, and in 1910, at age 36, Rockefeller devoted his life to philanthropy.

Rockefeller first visited Mount Desert Island in college, but it wasn't until he returned with his wife, Abbey, in 1908 that he truly fell in love with the island. Two years later, Rockefeller bought a hilltop estate in Seal Harbor and constructed a sprawling, 100-room mansion. Shortly after his arrival, Rockefeller was approached by local philanthropist George Dorr, who was soliciting funds to protect land on the island from private development. After hearing Dorr's vision of a national park, Rockefeller opened his enormous wallet.

Over the following decades, Rockefeller became Acadia's greatest benefactor. When he first met Dorr, the park consisted mostly of mountaintops. Rockefeller spent millions buying land between the peaks, unifying and protecting Mount Desert Island's most spectacular scenery. By the time he finished, Rockefeller had donated roughly one-third of Acadia National Park.

Rockefeller also spearheaded and financed both the Park Loop Road and the carriage roads, both of which drew strong opposition. Some conservationists felt a paved motor road would ruin the wild nature of the park. Rockefeller fervently disagreed. A firm believer that nature could make people "happier, richer, better," Rockefeller argued that roads and paths were necessary to make nature more accessible to the public.

Rockefeller's work in Acadia set the stage for decades of involvement with the National Park Service. In 1927, he donated $5 million to establish Great Smoky Mountain National Park in Tennessee. Fifteen years later, he donated 35,000 acres in Wyoming to create Grand Teton National Park.

Rockefeller died in 1960, but his family's philanthropic legacy continues on Mount Desert Island. In 2015, his youngest son, David, celebrated his 100th birthday by donating over 1,000 acres of family property in Seal Harbor to the Land and Garden Preserve (gardenpreserve.org).

Rockefeller's plans. A group of locals circulated a petition urging Rockefeller to continue construction of his roads. The *Bar Harbor Times* published an op-ed in full support of Rockefeller. Despite the outpouring of support, the ever-cautious Rockefeller stayed out of the fray, and he did not resume construction of the road in question.

The road-building controversy was particularly worrisome to George Dorr, the savvy founder and first superintendant of Acadia National Park. Dorr realized Rockefeller's wealth was essential to acquire additional land for the park, and he did not want to alienate the wealthy benefactor. Recognizing Rockefeller's obvious enthusiasm for road building, Dorr suggested that Rockefeller help build an "access" road next to Jordan Pond. Rockefeller jumped at the idea, and by 1921 the access road had expanded into a series of roads that connected with Rockefeller's previously built roads. Although the new roads were officially ordered by Dorr, it was Rockefeller who studied and planned them, simply making "suggestions" where they might be placed.

Rockefeller financed the new roads with one condition: that a new motor road also be constructed through the park. Despite his aversion to automobiles, Rockefeller was also a realist. He recognized that automobiles were inevitable, and he wanted to plan for them wisely.

Rockefeller's proposed motor road immediately drew heat from the same people that opposed his carriage roads. Again it was George Pepper, by this time a senator from Pennsylvania, who led the charge. Pepper contacted Secretary of the Interior Hubert Work and used his influence to halt construction of both the motor road and the new carriage roads. Pepper and others felt the new national park was already drawing too many people to Mount Desert Island. A motor road, they argued, would only encourage more to come. Such feelings were summed up in a 1924 article in the *Boston Evening Transcript*: "Protests were especially emphatic from the view-point of many of the summer residents, who had long enjoyed the blissful quiet and primitive beauty of the island. They freely stated their fear that the proposed development would bring in a 'peanut crowd' of the Coney Island type, and that the park would speedily be littered with egg shells, banana peels, old tin cans."

> "When I thought a thing was worth doing, I made up my mind that the annoyances, the obstacles, the embarrassments had to be borne because the ultimate goal was worthwhile."
>
> —John D. Rockefeller Jr.

Rockefeller saw things differently. As he pointed out during a similar road building incident at another national park, "What are these parks for ...? The average American can't afford to go into the secluded areas or to have private trips into the parks. He must travel on such a highway. That's the whole point of the national park system." Rockefeller believed in making parks accessible for the common man, as well as for the elderly and the handicapped.

Rockefeller had the support of year-round residents, who looked forward to the flood of money that road construction and increased tourism would bring. With the backing of local residents and Maine politicians, Rockefeller and Dorr pushed hard to continue construction of both the motor road and the carriage roads. In the face of such strong opposition, Senator Pepper backed down. Shortly thereafter, the secretary of the interior arrived to examine the situation firsthand. After viewing the roads, he concluded they were indeed a worthy improvement. He gave his full blessing to the roads already under construction—with the stipulation that any future roads be approved by his office.

Emboldened by overwhelming public support, Rockefeller charged ahead with plans for an even larger network of carriage roads and an expanded motor road. To bypass the approval demanded by Secretary Work, Rockefeller built new roads on land that was earmarked for (but not yet donated to) the park. Only when the roads were finished would he transfer the land to the park. Another round of protests erupted, but there was nothing that could be done legally to halt the construction.

By 1940, Rockefeller's grand vision was complete. A 57-mile network of carriage roads stretched from Bar Harbor to Seal Harbor, passing mountains, lakes, and ponds. Curving gracefully through the woods, the roads revealed some of the park's most beautiful, hidden scenery. Every twist and turn was personally selected by Rockefeller, whose knowledge of road building and hands-on involvement were legendary. Rockefeller also commissioned 17 exquisite stone bridges. Each bridge had a unique design, and they were handcrafted by stonemasons at extraordinary cost.

Rockefeller spent nearly three decades and several million dollars building his beloved carriage roads. When construction began in 1913, horse-drawn carriages were still popular. By 1940, however, they were a quaint pastime for the rich. Meanwhile, bicycles had grown ever more popular. Rockefeller was aware of this fact, and he was one of the first to encourage opening the carriage roads to bicycle riders.

Following Rockefeller's death in 1960, Acadia's carriage roads fell into disrepair. To remedy the situation, the nonprofit Friends of Acadia established a multi-million dollar endowment to provide ongoing upkeep. After several years of rehabilitation, Rockefeller's roads were restored to their full glory, and today they are as magnificent as ever.

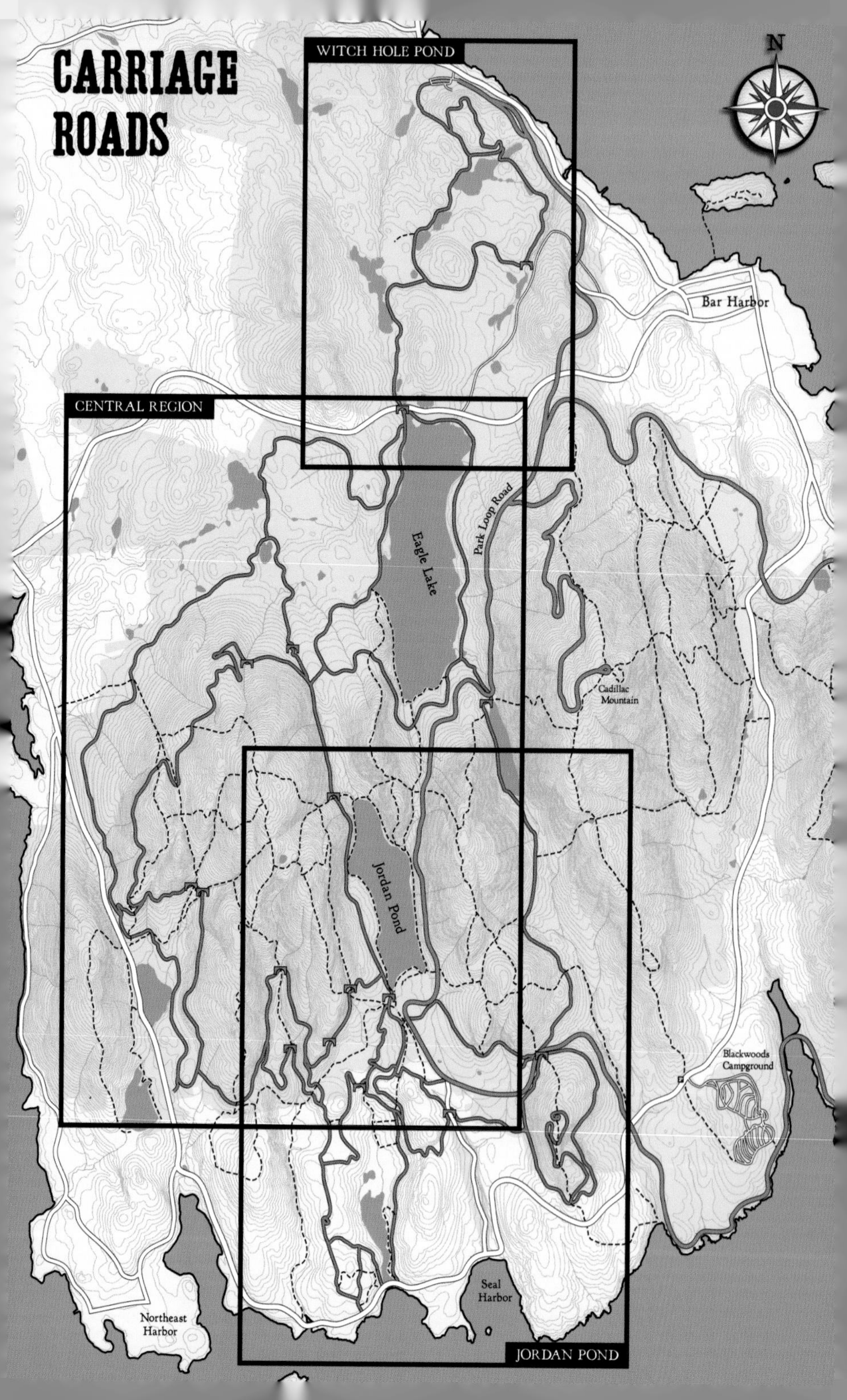

CARRIAGE ROADS
N
WITCH HOLE POND
CENTRAL REGION
JORDAN POND
Bar Harbor
Park Loop Road
Eagle Lake
Cadillac Mountain
Jordan Pond
Blackwoods Campground
Seal Harbor
Northeast Harbor

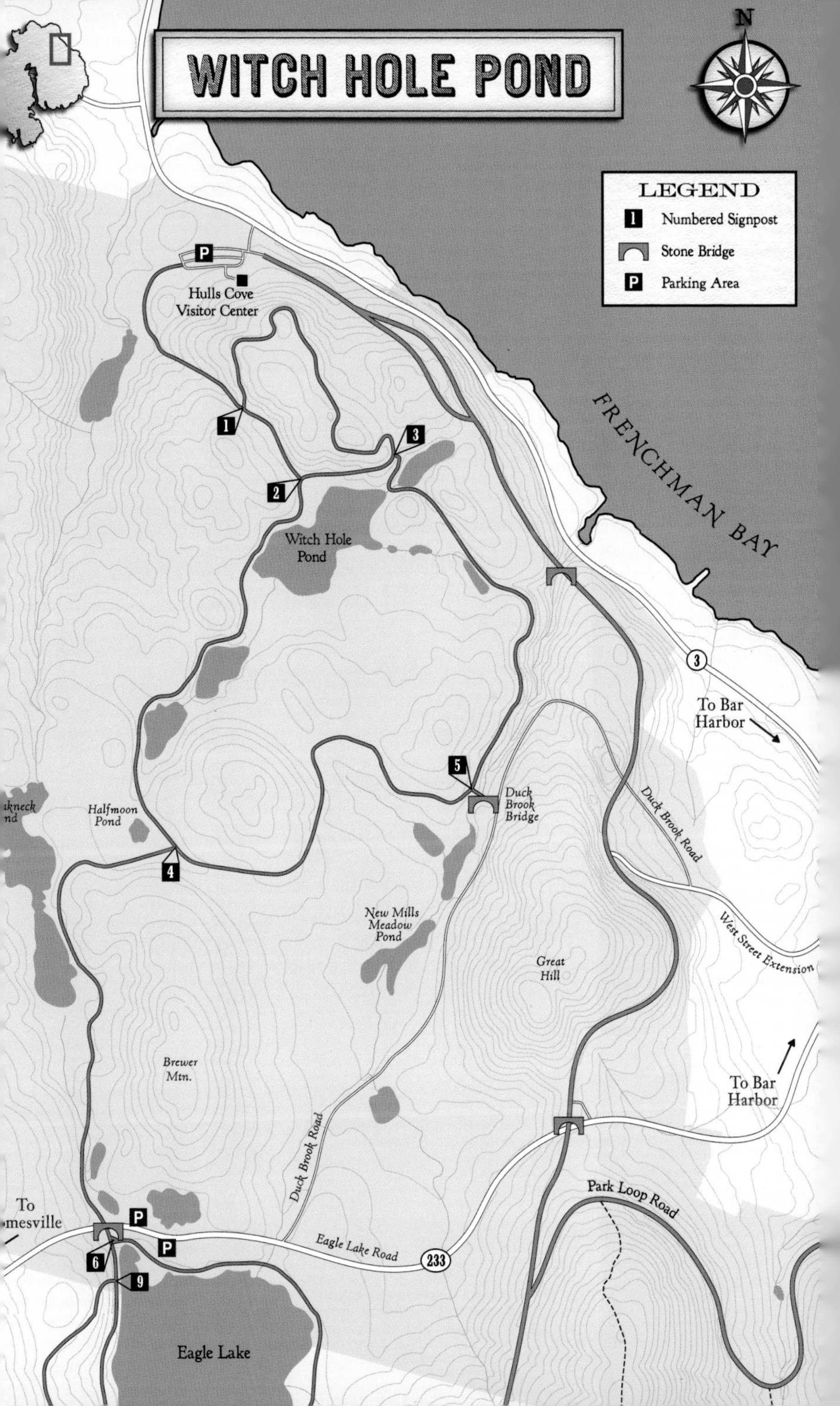

WITCH HOLE POND
N
LEGEND
Numbered Signpost
Stone Bridge
Parking Area
P
Hulls Cove
Visitor Center
1
2
3
4
5
6
9
Witch Hole
Pond
FRENCHMAN BAY
3
To Bar
Harbor
Duck
Brook
Bridge
Duck Brook Road
West Street Extension
Halfmoon
Pond
New Mills
Meadow
Pond
Great
Hill
To Bar
Harbor
Brewer
Mtn.
Duck Brook Road
Park Loop Road
To
Eagle Lake Road
233
Eagle Lake

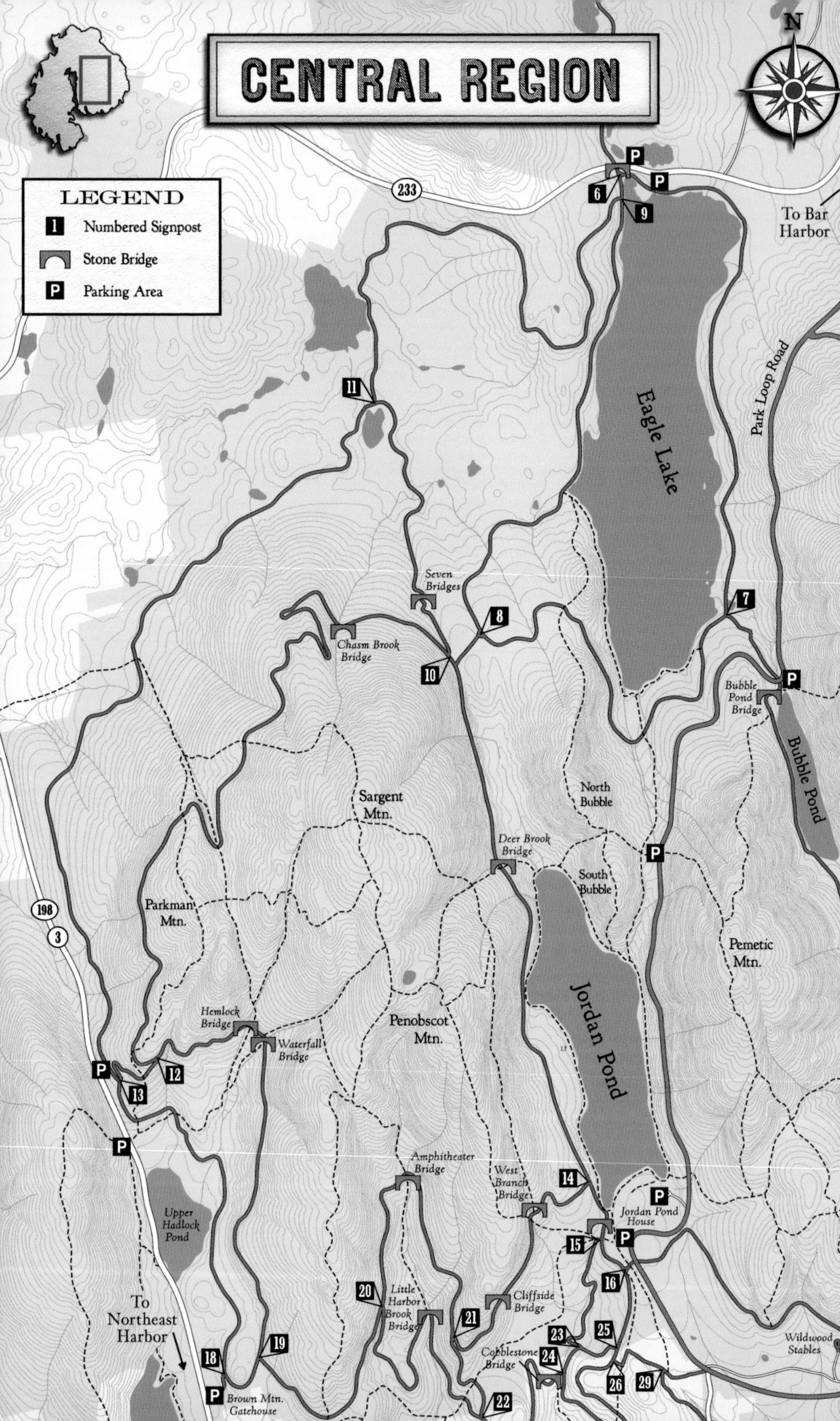

CENTRAL REGION
N
LEGEND
Numbered Signpost
Stone Bridge
Parking Area
233
To Bar Harbor
Park Loop Road
Eagle Lake
Seven Bridges
Chasm Brook Bridge
Bubble Pond Bridge
Bubble Pond
Sargent Mtn.
North Bubble
South Bubble
Deer Brook Bridge
Parkman Mtn.
198
3
Pemetic Mtn.
Jordan Pond
Hemlock Bridge
Waterfall Bridge
Penobscot Mtn.
Amphitheater Bridge
West Branch Bridge
Jordan Pond House
Upper Hadlock Pond
Little Harbor Brook Bridge
Cliffside Bridge
To Northeast Harbor
Cobblestone Bridge
Brown Mtn. Gatehouse
Wildwood Stables

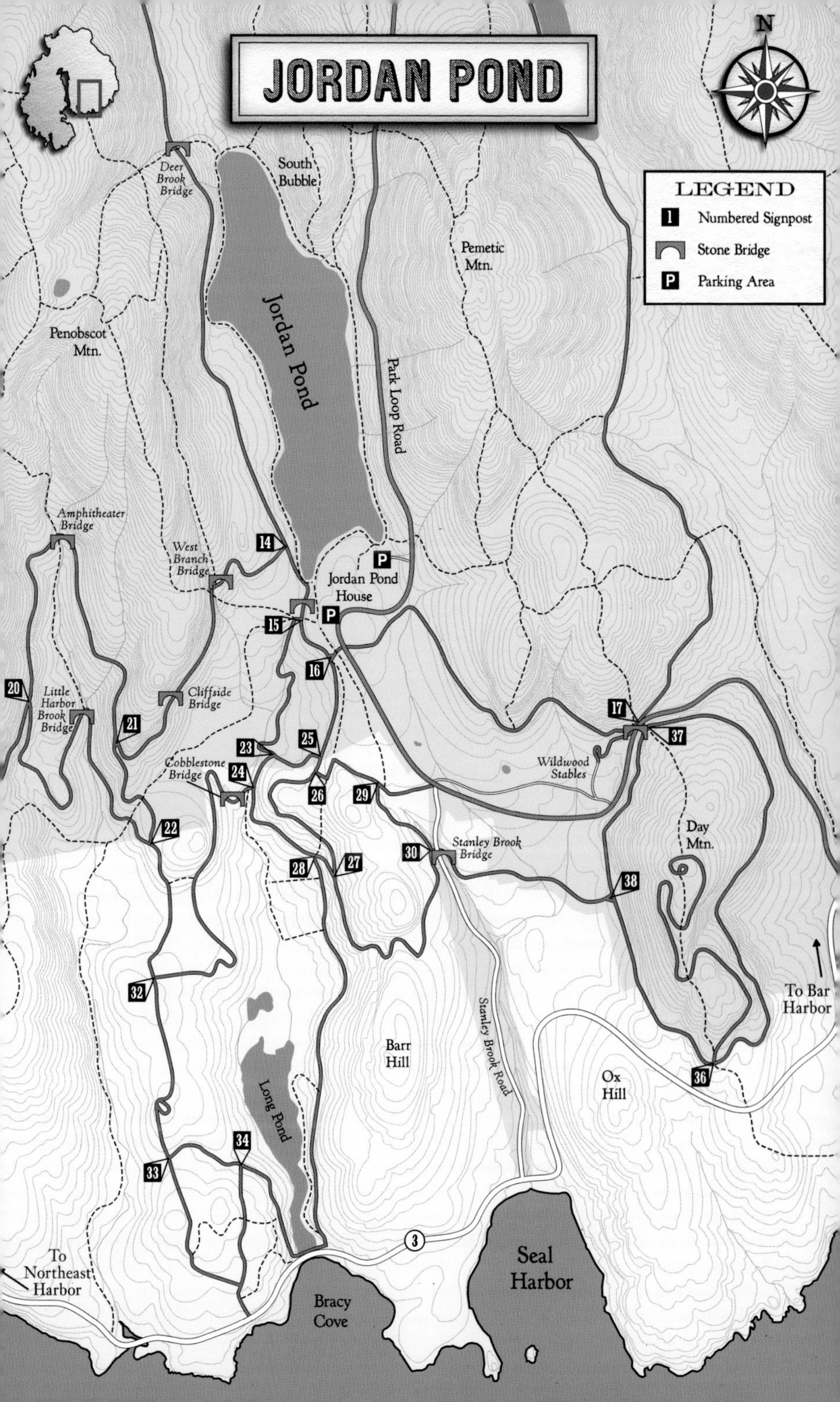

JORDAN POND
N
LEGEND
1 Numbered Signpost
Stone Bridge
P Parking Area
Deer Brook Bridge
South Bubble
Pemetic Mtn.
Penobscot Mtn.
Jordan Pond
Park Loop Road
Amphitheater Bridge
West Branch Bridge
14
Jordan Pond House
P
15
16
20
Little Harbor Brook Bridge
Cliffside Bridge
21
17
37
23
25
Cobblestone Bridge
24
26
29
Wildwood Stables
22
30
Stanley Brook Bridge
Day Mtn.
28
27
38
32
To Bar Harbor
Barr Hill
Stanley Brook Road
Long Pond
36
Ox Hill
34
33
3
To Northeast Harbor
Seal Harbor
Bracy Cove

TRENTON & NORTH ISLAND

AFTER LEAVING THE mainland at Trenton Bridge, most visitors drive through northern Mount Desert Island without stopping, rushing to more famous destinations farther south. But if you're willing to slow down, you'll discover some great restaurants and attractions.

★ MOUNT DESERT OCEANARIUM

Learn about the fascinating ecology of coastal Maine through marine exhibits, touch tanks, and an outdoor salt marsh walk. Open mid-May to late October. (207-288-5005, theoceanarium.com)

★ GREAT MAINE LUMBERJACK SHOW

This highly entertaining evening show features lumberjacks sawing, chopping, tree climbing, ax throwing, and log rolling. Open May through October. Located in Trenton off Route 3. (207-667-0067, mainelumberjack.com)

★ ATLANTIC BREWING COMPANY

The oldest and most famous craft brewer on the island offers daily tours of its facility. Their store sells beer and gifts, and the adjacent Mainely Meat BBQ serves tasty food and fresh beer on tap. (207-288-2337, atlanticbrewing.com)

HADLEY POINT BEACH

Located at the northern tip of Mount Desert Island, this pebbly beach has picnic tables and a boat launch for motorboats and sea kayaks. It's also a great place to watch the sunset. Located at the end of Hadley Point Road.

INDIAN POINT BLAGDEN PRESERVE

Protecting 110 acres near the northwest tip of Mount Desert Island, this forested preserve is a great place for birdwatching, or simply escape the crowds. Hiking trails pass through forest to 1,000 feet of shoreline. Owned and operated by the Nature Conservancy. (nature.org)

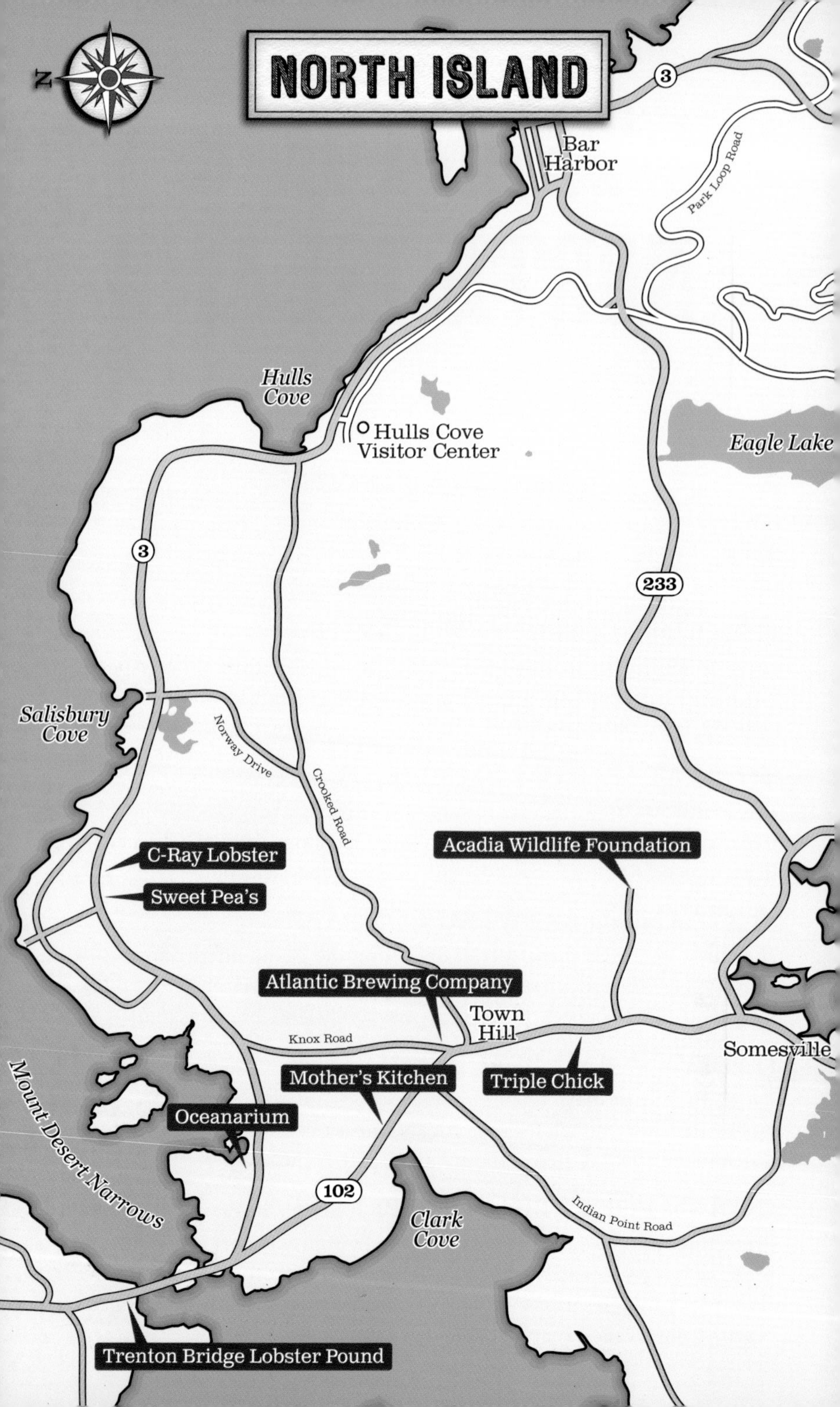
N
NORTH ISLAND
3
Bar Harbor
Park Loop Road
Hulls Cove
Hulls Cove Visitor Center
Eagle Lake
3
233
Salisbury Cove
Norway Drive
Crooked Road
C-Ray Lobster
Sweet Pea's
Acadia Wildlife Foundation
Atlantic Brewing Company
Town Hill
Knox Road
Somesville
Mother's Kitchen
Triple Chick
Oceanarium
Mount Desert Narrows
102
Clark Cove
Indian Point Road
Trenton Bridge Lobster Pound

ACADIA WILDLIFE FOUNDATION

This wonderful nonprofit treats injured wild animals with the goal of releasing them back into native habitats. Acadia Wildlife Foundation offers free educational programs on Friday and Saturday at 2pm by reservation. Other times are available by appointment. (207-288-4960, acadiawildlife.org)

BAR HARBOR CELLARS

Run by the folks behind Atlantic Brewing Company, Bar Harbor Cellars makes wine from grapes harvested in Italy and California. The tasting room, located in a 19th-century barn, offers free samples. (207-288-3907, barharborcellars.com)

TRIPLE CHICK FARM

This roadside stand offers free-range eggs and certified organic vegetables. Open Wednesday to Saturday, 10–4. (Route 102, 207-288-2888, triplechickfarm.com)

Restaurants

★TRENTON BRIDGE LOBSTER POUND $$$ (Lnch, Din)

Located next to Trenton Bridge on the mainland, this legendary lobster shack—family-owned for three generations—is famous for fresh lobster, waterfront views, and old-school devotion to wood-fired boilers. (1237 Bar Harbor Rd., 207-667-2977, trentonbridgelobster.com)

★SWEET PEA'S CAFE $$$ (Brk, Lnch, Din)

Sitting on Sweet Pea's back patio, gazing out over a lovely farm, you'll feel a world away from the traffic on Route 3. Wood-fired pizzas, farm-fresh specials, and wines from Bar Harbor Cellars. (207-801-9078, sweetpeascafemaine.com)

★MOTHER'S KITCHEN $$$ (Brk, Lnch)

This simple shack sells the best sandwiches on Mount Desert Island. Everything is delicious, including the vegan-friendly tofu and tempeh. Carnivores love the meatloaf sandwich. Baked goods and ice cream also available. Pro tip: call ahead for pickup so you don't have to wait in line. (Located next to Salisbury Hardware, 207-288-4403, motherskitchenfoods.com)

★C-RAY LOBSTER $$$ (Lnch, Din)

This laid-back restaurant, located behind a residential house, is famous for fresh, reasonably priced lobster and shellfish. Joshua, the owner, is one of three licensed clammers on the island, so his steamers are always fresh. His wife bakes tasty desserts, including blueberry pie. (207-288-4855, c-raylobster.com)

BAR HARBOR

FILLED WITH MORE shops, restaurants, and hotels than all other towns on the island combined, Bar Harbor is the unofficial capital of Mount Desert Island. Its bustling streets, perched on a hill above Frenchman Bay, lure millions of visitors each year. To some, it's a tourist trap. To others, it's a vibrant slice of Downeast Maine. No matter what your take, chances are you'll end up in Bar Harbor at some point on your trip.

The heart of Bar Harbor is the T-intersection of Main Street and Cottage Street, located one block up from the town pier. Both streets are packed with shops and restaurants catering to a wide variety of tastes. Upscale galleries sell artwork near novelty shops selling plastic lobsters. Gourmet restaurants compete with greasy spoons. It's hard to put your finger on the retail pulse of Bar Harbor, which means there's something for everyone here.

Equally incongruous is the social fabric of Bar Harbor. Fanny-packed retirees, ragged hippies, rugged outdoor adventurers, casual fleece millionaires—all find fertile ground in Bar Harbor. There are also plenty of hardworking locals, college kids on summer break, and seasonal foreign workers.

Although famous for shops and restaurants, Bar Harbor is also the jumping-off point for many of the island's most popular outdoor adventures, including sea kayaking, whale watching, and boat tours. If you want to explore Acadia's carriage roads, you can rent bikes in Bar Harbor and catch the free Island Explorer shuttle to Eagle Lake during peak season. The Bar Harbor Village Green, located in the center of town, is a transportation hub for Island Explorer shuttles, which can take you just about anywhere on Mount Desert Island. When rain puts the lid on outdoor fun, Bar Harbor's two movie theaters, multiple museums, and lively bars will keep you—and the rest of the island—entertained for hours.

During peak season in July and August, Bar Harbor is flooded with visitors—especially when cruise ships are in town. These days over 150 cruise ships visit Bar Harbor, up from just 30 in 2000. Today Bar Harbor is the most popular port of call in Maine. On days when cruise ships disgorge hundreds of passengers onto the town's streets, long lines form at popular shops and restaurants. If you happen to visit when one (or two) enormous ships are in port, consider heading elsewhere and exploring Bar Harbor another day.

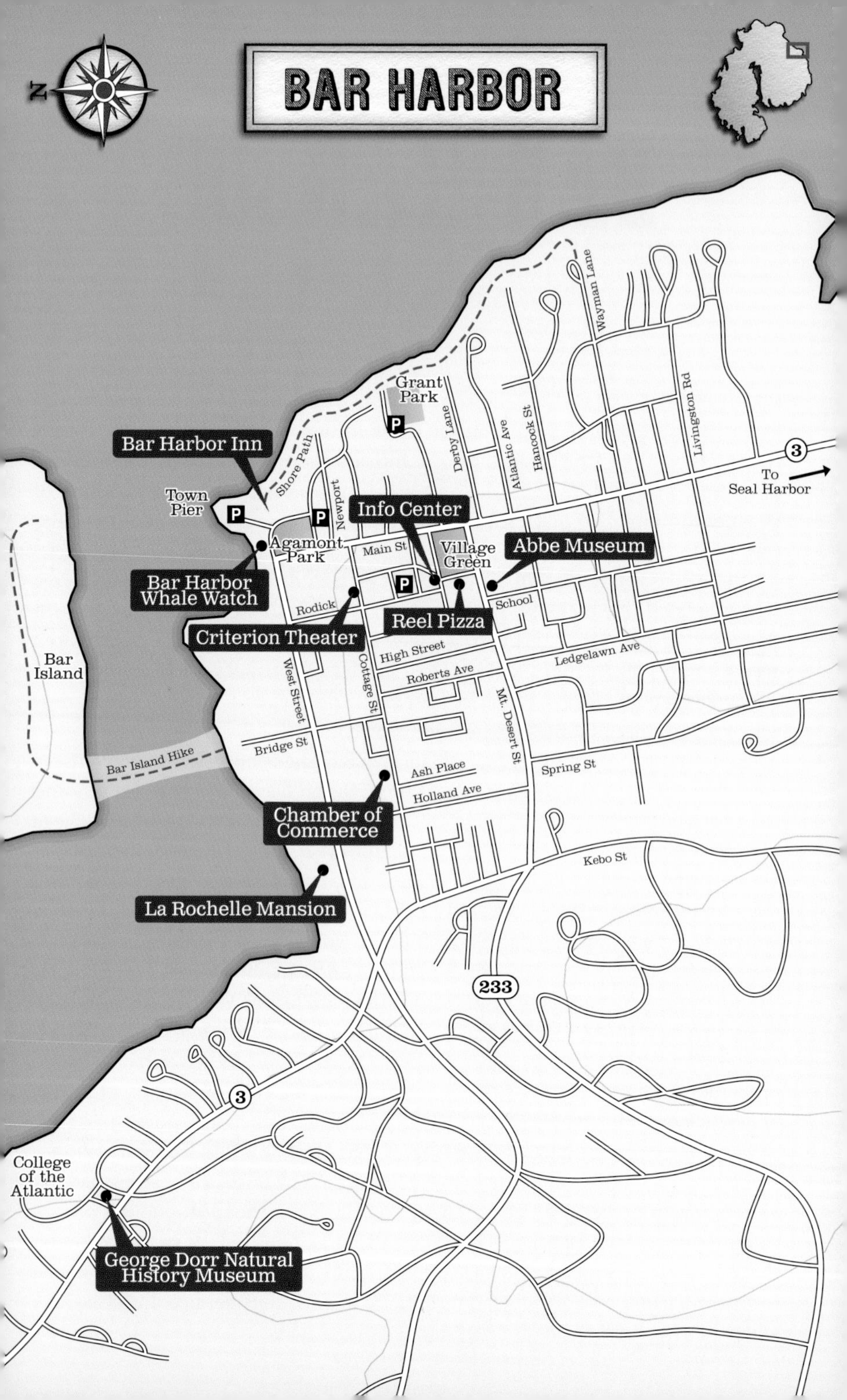

BAR HARBOR

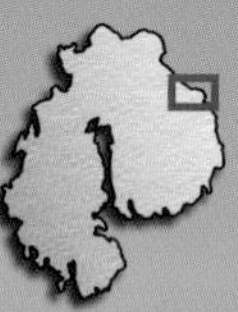

Bar Harbor Inn
Town Pier
Shore Path
Grant Park
Newport
Derby Lane
Atlantic Ave
Hancock St
Wayman Lane
Livingston Rd
3
To Seal Harbor
Info Center
Agamont Park
Main St
Village Green
Abbe Museum
Bar Harbor Whale Watch
Rodick
School
Reel Pizza
Criterion Theater
High Street
Ledgelawn Ave
Roberts Ave
West Street
Cottage St
Mt. Desert St
Bar Island
Bridge St
Bar Island Hike
Ash Place
Spring St
Holland Ave
Chamber of Commerce
Kebo St
La Rochelle Mansion
233
3
College of the Atlantic
George Dorr Natural History Museum

Bar Harbor Sights

★ BAR HARBOR SHOREPATH

This easy, three-quarter-mile path wraps around the eastern tip of Bar Harbor, offering lovely views of Frenchman Bay and the Porcupine Islands. The Shorepath was built in the late 1800s, and some sections of it pass over private property, so please be respectful. Start your stroll at the Bar Harbor town pier and follow the paved path toward the Bar Harbor Inn. To your right are two cannons that once guarded Frenchman Bay on Egg Rock Island. Past the cannons is the historic Bar Harbor Inn, which started as the Reading Room Clubhouse in 1887. At the time, the Reading Room was a private, all-male "literary club" where "most of the reading was done through the bottom of a cocktail glass." Continue down the Shorepath and you'll see Balance Rock, a large, precariously balanced boulder carried here by glaciers during the Ice Age. When the glaciers melted, Balance Rock settled into its unlikely position. Grant Park, a bit farther down on the left, is a nice place for a picnic. Near the end of the Shore Path you'll see the Bar Harbor breakwater, a stone wall that stretches into the water and shelters Bar Harbor from large waves. Local lore claims the breakwater was financed by J.P. Morgan so cocktails wouldn't spill on his yacht. At the end of the Shorepath, you have two options: turn around and retrace your steps or turn right and follow Wayman Lane up to Main Street, where Bar Harbor's famous shops and restaurants await.

Bar Island

Bar Harbor's namesake island, which lies 1,500 feet offshore, is accessible twice a day when the tide goes out, exposing an underwater sandbar that temporarily connects Bar Harbor to Bar Island. The sandbar starts at the end of Bridge Street, about a half-mile west of Bar Harbor's town pier. There's a roughly three-hour window (90 minutes before and after low tide) when you can walk across the sand bar and explore Bar Island. A half-mile path on the island heads to an overlook 120 feet above sea level that offers dramatic views of Bar Harbor. The path starts at the southern tip of Bar Island, continues past a large field, then bears left on the way toward the overlook. (Plan on a roughly 20-minute walk from the Sand Bar to the overlook). Check local papers for tide schedules before exploring Bar Island. You *do not* want to be stranded on the island when the tide comes in.

Bar Island Sand Bar

Agamont Park

AGAMONT PARK

This popular park, set on a gentle hill overlooking the shore, offers gorgeous views of Bar Harbor, the Porcupine Islands, and Frenchman Bay. The park's fountain was brought from Italy and dates to around 1600. If you're here on the Fourth of July, Agamont Park offers the town's best views of the fireworks.

VILLAGE GREEN

This large, central park hosts art and music festivals all summer. On Mondays and Thursdays in July and August, the Bar Harbor Town Band offers free concerts at 8pm. The west side of the Village Green is a hub for the Island Explorer Shuttle system (p.30).

WEST STREET

West Street is great for a short stroll if you'd like to see some of Bar Harbor's grand old mansions, many of which have been converted to inns and bed & breakfasts. Follow West Street away from the Bar Harbor Pier and soon you'll pass the century-old Bar Harbor Club. After falling into disrepair for several decades, the Bar Harbor Club was fully restored in 2008. Continue past Bridge Street—which leads down to Bar Island—and follow West Street to the La Rochelle Mansion. This elegant brick manstion was previously owned by the heirs to the Campbell Soup fortune. Today it's a beautiful museum operated by the Bar Harbor Historical Society (see following page).

Visitor Information

ACADIA NATIONAL PARK INFORMATION CENTER

This small brick building, located near the northwest corner of the Village Green, is staffed by experts who can answer questions about Acadia National Park. You can also purchase park passes and pick up free park publications.

Museums

★ ABBE MUSEUM

Learn about Maine's native cultures at this fascinating museum, which displays tools, crafts, cultural artifacts, and modern work by native artists. The museum's layout follows a reverse timeline, which starts in the present and goes backwards in time. A small shop sells native baskets, traditional crafts, and books. The Abbe also offers educational programs, craft workshops, and archaeological field schools. (26 Mount Desert Street, 207-288-3519, abbemuseum.org)

★ LA ROCHELLE MANSION

This stunning 41-room, 13,000-foot waterfront mansion, operated by the Bar Harbor Historical Society, is a great place to learn about the town's colorful history. Exhibits explore native history, Bar Harbor's opulent Cottage Era, the creation of Acadia National Park, and local legends like landscape architect Beatrix Farrand. The mansion's back porch offers fabulous views of Frenchman Bay. (127 West Street, 207-288-0000, barharborhistorical.org)

★ GEORGE B. DORR NATURAL HISTORY MUSEUM

Located at the College of the Atlantic (half a mile north of downtown Bar Harbor on Route 3), this charming museum focuses on the natural history of Mount Desert Island. There are exhibits on local wildlife and a touch tank filled with crabs, starfish, sea cucumbers, and other intertidal creatures. (105 Eden Street, Route 3, 207-288-5395, coamuseum.org)

What's That Sound?

Every day at noon and 9pm, a booming sound blasts through downtown Bar Harbor, frightening and confusing anyone near the Village Green. The sound comes from a powerful air horn located on top of the Bar Harbor Fire Station. A century ago, the noon blast helped people synchronize their clocks, and the 9 pm blast alerted minors of a citywide curfew. Today it's simply a colorful tradition, although the horn is still used to notify villagers of winter school closures due to snow.

Boat Tours

★BAR HARBOR WHALE WATCH COMPANY

Bar Harbor Whale Watch offers several exciting trips. The most popular is whale watching on the *Friendship V* (p.24). Other cruises include Nature and Sightseeing, Lobster Fishing and Seal Watching, and a Lighthouse Tour that visits five local lighthouses. (207-288-2386, barharborwhales.com)

★LULU

Climb aboard the 42-foot *Lulu* to learn about lobstering. The crew hauls traps and pulls out live lobsters for a fascinating show and tell. You'll also enjoy seal watching at Egg Rock. (207-963-2341, lululobsterboat.com)

★MISS SAMANTHA

The 56-foot *Miss Samantha* offers naturalist-guided tours of Baker Island, the most remote of the Cranberry Isles (p.285). En route you'll pass the spectacular eastern shore of Mount Desert Island, home to dramatic cliffs and beautiful mansions. The tour is five hours round-trip. (207-288-5374, barharborwhales.com)

ISLANDER

The 67-foot *Islander* offers four-hour fishing trips in Frenchman Bay. Cod, harbor pollock, and mackerel are some of the species you might catch. The crew can help with every step of the process—setting the line, landing the fish, filleting the catch. Great for kids and beginners. (207-801-2300, acadianboattours.com)

Sea Kayaking

COASTAL KAYAKING TOURS

For over three decades, Coastal Kayaking Tours has specialized in tours of Frenchman Bay and the Porcupine Islands. Half- and full-day tours, plus sunset paddles, family tours, and multi-day trips. (207-288-9605, acadiafun.com)

NATIONAL PARK SEA KAYAK

National Park Sea Kayaking specializes in paddles on the western shores of Mount Desert Island, which is quieter and less developed than Frenchman Bay. Half-day tours and sunset paddles available. (207-288-0342, mainestatekayak.com)

Bus Tours

OLI'S TROLLEY

Oli's offers several narrated trolley tours: Cadillac Mountain (1 hour), Acadia National Park (2.5 or 4 hours), Downtown Bar Harbor (30 minutes). Tickets are available in the Oli's Trolley store at 1 West Street, next to the town pier. (866-987-6553, acadiaislandtours.com)

ACADIA NATIONAL PARK TOURS

Acadia National Park Tours offers a 2.5-hour naturalist-narrated bus tour of Bar Harbor and Acadia National Park. Trips depart downtown Bar Harbor from May through October. Tickets are available at Testa's Restaurant, 53 Main Street. (207-288-0300, acadiatours.com)

Bike Rentals

BAR HARBOR BICYCLE SHOP

Since 1977, Bar Harbor Bicycle Shop has catered to both casual tourists and hardcore bike enthusiasts. Open March through December. (141 Cottage Street, 207-288-3886, barharborbike.com)

ACADIA BIKE AND CANOE

In addition to bike rentals, Acadia Bike and Canoe offers organized biking trips on Mount Desert Island, Schoodic Peninsula, and Swan's Island. Multi-day bicycle tours are also available. (48 Cottage Street, 207-288-9605, acadiabike.com)

Scenic Flights

SCENIC FLIGHTS OF ACADIA

These Cesna flights offer the best value. The office is located in a small building next to the airport runway just south of the Trenton Market on Route 1A. (207-667-6527, scenicflightsofacadia.com)

ACADIA AIR TOURS

For a truly unique experience, fly around the island in a yellow biplane (built in the late 1990s) or soar on an engine-less glider. Acadia Air Tours has two offices: one in Bar Harbor at 1 West Street, and one near the airport just north of the Trenton Market. (207-667-7627, acadiaairtours.com)

Notable Shops

SHERMAN'S BOOKSTORE

The best bookstore for miles, with a broad selection of books on Acadia and Downeast Maine. Sherman's also sells stationery, greeting cards, gifts, toys, and puzzles. (56 Main Street, 207-288-3161, shermans.com)

CADILLAC MOUNTAIN SPORTS

Locally owned and operated, Cadillac Mountain Sports has the best selection of outdoor gear on Mount Desert Island. From hiking boots to waterproof jackets to rock climbing equipment, Cadillac Mountain Sports has you covered. (26 Cottage Street, 207-288-4532, cadillacsports.com)

Entertainment

In addition to the attractions listed below, there are a number of seasonal events and festivals held throughout the summer and fall (p.41).

CRITERION THEATER

This historic art-deco theater, open since 1932, plays Hollywood movies and often features live shows. Operated as a nonprofit, the theater was renovated in 2015. Local tip: the balcony seats upstairs are definitely worth the extra price. (35 Cottage Street, 207-288-3441, criteriontheater.org)

REEL PIZZA

This two-screen theater shows a mix of Hollywood hits and small independent and foreign films. Enjoy fresh pizza and cold beer on couches and reclining chairs. (33 Kennebec Place, 207-288-3811, reelpizza.com)

IMPROVACADIA

This improv comedy troupe, founded by the former music director of Chicago's legendary Second City, performs nightly. It's improv, so performances vary, but it's almost always worth the price of admission. (15 Cottage Street, 2nd Floor, 207-288-2503, improvacadia.com)

Drinks & Nightlife

Bar Harbor has the liveliest nightlife on the island. The town is home to about half a dozen popular bars, all with a laid-back, casual vibe. The **Thirsty Whale** (40 Cottage St.) gets my vote for Bar Harbor's most classic watering hole, popular with locals and tourists alike. **The Annex** (51 Rodick St.) is consistently popular for its outdoor deck, live music, cold beer, and tasty cocktails. The best craft beer is at **Atlantic Brewing Company** (52 Cottage St.). **Dog and Pony** (4 Rodick Place) has a fun open-air porch that draws thirsty crowds on hot summer nights. **Leary's Landing** (156 Main Street) is the town's best Irish pub. On Cottage Street you'll find the tiny but popular **Cottage Street Pub** (21 Cottage St.) and the charming **Finback Alehouse** (30 Cottage St.), which boasts the most impressive bar in Bar Harbor. Craft beer lovers should check out **Blaze** (198 Main St.), where over two dozen Maine microbrews are offered on tap. Down by the waterfront, **Geddy's** (19 Main St.) has been serving adult beverages amidst kitschy nautical decor since the 1970s.

Groceries

The largest grocery store in town is **Hannaford** (86 Cottage Street, 207-288-5680). There's also the natural food store **A&B Naturals** (101 Cottage Street, 207-288-8480). For farm-fresh food visit the weekly **Bar Harbor Farmer's Market**, held every Sunday 10am–2pm in the YMCA parking lot (21 Park Street).

Bar Harbor Restaurants

★ THE BURNING TREE $$$ (Din)

Famous for exceptional seafood, the Burning Tree combines flavors from around the world with fresh, local ingredients. Many of the herbs and veggies are grown in the adjacent garden. This cozy restaurant is located five miles south of Bar Harbor on Route 3, but it's definitely worth the drive. Great wine, craft cocktails. (69 Otter Creek Drive, 207-288-9331)

★ SALT & STEEL $$$ (Din)

One of Bar Harbor's best (and priciest) restaurants, Salt & Steel specializes in seasonal Maine flavors. Abundant seafood, homemade pasta and sausage, New England cheese plate, farm-to-table vegetables. The ultimate splurge: a four -course tasting menu with wine pairings. Craft cocktails, excellent wines. (321 Main Street, 207-288-0447, saltandsteelbh.com)

★ CAFÉ THIS WAY $$$ (Brk, Din)

Café This Way offers creative cuisine in a friendly, casual atmosphere. Hearty breakfasts include eggs Benedict, expert omelets, and homemade corned beef hash. Delicious dinners range from pecan-crusted halibut to lamb kofta sliders to kung pao cauliflower. Good wine list, creative cocktails. (14 ½ Mount Desert Street, 207-288-4483, cafethisway.com)

★ MCKAY'S PUBLIC HOUSE $$$ (Din)

This upscale bistro/pub, located in a historic Victorian house, serves a wide range of hearty favorites, from steak and seafood to gourmet burgers. The cozy bar has a great selection of beer and wine. The outdoor tables are delightful on warm summer nights when live music drifts through the air. Open year-round. (231 Main Street, 207-288-2002, mckayspublichouse.com)

★ PEEKYTOE PROVISIONS $$$ (Lnch, Din)

If you love seafood and shellfish, head to Peekytoe Provisions (named after a tasty Maine crab species). Everything's fresh and local at this fish market/restaurant. Indulge in lobster rolls, crab cakes, fish tacos, oysters, chowder, bisque, local seaweed salad, plus Maine-made specialty products. (244 Main Street, 207-801-9161, peekytoeprovisions.com)

SIDE STREET CAFE $$$ (Lnch, Din)

This charming cafe is popular for its combination of delicious, reasonably priced food, creative cocktails, and cheerful ambiance. Sandwiches, wraps, salads, burgers, mac & cheese, plus great lobster dishes, including one of the island's best lobster rolls. When the weather's nice, grab a seat on the porch. Open year-round. (49 Rodick Street, 207-801-2591, sidestreetbarharbor.com)

HAVANA $$$ (Din)

Local food prepared with Latin flair. Lobster moqueca, conchinita pibil, empanadas, paella. Good wine list, plus mojitos, caiparinas, pisco sours, and other south-of-the-border cocktails. (318 Main Street, 207-288-2822, havanamaine.com)

TWO CATS $$$ (Brk)

Great breakfast in a cheerful setting. Famous for eggs Benedict served on homemade biscuits. There's almost always a wait, but reservations are accepted. Open until 1pm daily. (130 Cottage Street, 207-288-2808, twocatsbarharbor.com)

ROSALIE'S PIZZA $$$ (Din)

The best pizza on Mount Desert Island. In a town where it's easy to spend $150 on dinner for two, Rosalie's is a superb value, especially for families. Fresh ingredients and homemade dough make all the difference. There are also subs, calzones, stuffed slices, and salads. (46 Cottage Street, 207-288-5666, rosaliespizza.com)

WEST STREET CAFE $$$ (Lnch, Din)

Set back a few dozen yards from the water, West Street Cafe serves delicious, traditional New England seafood at non-waterfront prices. (76 West Street, 207-288-5242, weststreetcafe.com)

JORDAN'S $$$ (Brk, Lnch)

Eating at this classic diner feels like stepping into a Norman Rockwell painting. It's where locals go to meet friends, gossip, and fill up on blueberry pancakes. Open 5am–1pm. (80 Cottage Street, 207-288-3586, jordanswildblueberry.com)

MDI ICE CREAM $$$

Bar Harbor's best ice cream. "Fearless Flavor" handcrafted in small batches. Two locations: 7 Firefly Lane, 325 Main Street. (207-801-4007, mdiic.com)

Best of Bar Harbor

Best Breakfast: Cafe This Way, Two Cats
Best Dinner: Burning Tree, Salt & Steel
Best Lobster Roll: Peekytoe Provisions
Best Seafood: Burning Tree, Peekytoe Provisions
Best Value: Jordan's, Rosalie's

Best Lobster In Bar Harbor

Bar Harbor restaurants serve over 5 *million* pounds of lobster each year. If you’r looking for authentic lobster shacks (p.44), look elsewhere. But Bar Harbo does have some great waterfront options.

THE CHART ROOM $$$ (Lnch, Din)

Located in Hull’s Cove (5-minute drive from downtown), the Chart Room is an under-the-radar gem. Waterfront dining, old school classics (lobster Newburg baked stuffed haddock)—all delightfully removed from Bar Harbor’s touris crush. (207 288-9740, chartroombarharbor.com)

THE FISH HOUSE GRILLE $$$ (Lnch, Din)

This easygoing, waterfront seafood joint, located next to the Bar Harbor Pier serves all the classics—lobster dinners, baked seafood, homemade clam chowder—plus a raw bar with oysters and cherrystones. (1 West Street, 207-288-3070 fishhousegrillme.com)

TERRACE GRILLE $$$ (Lnch, Din)

Perched in front of the elegant, historic Bar Harbor Inn, the open-air Terrace Grille combines upscale food with fabulous waterfront views (7 Newport Drive, 207-288-3351)

STEWMAN’S LOBSTER POUND $$$ (Lnch, Din)

The largest and busiest place for lobster in Bar Harbor. Stewman’s waterfron

SEAL HARBOR

SEAL HARBOR IS a tiny village with few tourist attractions—and its ultra-wealthy residents would like to keep it that way. Ox Hill, which rises above the eastern shore of Seal Harbor, is home to some of the most expensive homes in New England. But drive along its twisty roads and all you'll see are tiny wooden signs (painted in patented "Seal Harbor Green") proclaiming the names of sumptuous mansions lying at the end of the long, long driveways—*Felsmere*, *Keewaydin*, *Glengariff*. Down on Main Street, high-priced shops and boutiques are absent from a town that boasts a greater net worth than many small countries. And such establishments are unlikely to arrive anytime soon.

Although Seal Harbor is one of the wealthiest summer colonies in America, it remains relatively unknown because its residents prefer to *escape* the spotlight. Seal Harbor is about getting back to nature—albeit from the comfort of 60-room mansions and million-dollar yachts. But despite the throngs of private servants, private gardeners, and private assistants roaming Ox Hill each summer, your average Seal Harbor "cottager" would rather talk about native plants and migratory birds than hedge funds and currency swaps. This attitude is best embodied by the Rockefellers, who remain actively involved with local charities and land conservation organizations.

But while Seal Harbor is known (or not known) for its stealth wealth, the town's otherwise low profile was thrust into the limelight with the arrival of Martha Stewart in 1997. After purchasing *Skylands*, a sprawling hilltop estate once owned by the Ford family, Martha dazzled her fans with glossy magazine spreads of her new summer hideaway. Suddenly, domestic divas everywhere knew Seal Harbor was the *real* place to be in Maine. Despite the unsolicited attention, local residents simply hunkered down and let the commotion pass, and today the tiny seaside village remains as charming and lackluster as ever.

In fact, Seal Harbor is probably one of the most under-appreciated towns on the island. Most visitors simply drive by with little more than a glimpse of the picture-perfect harbor. But Seal Harbor's tiny town green and jewel-like beach are great places to kick back and relax. And Little Long Pond, located on the Rockefellers' former estate just west of town, is a lovely place to slow down and enjoy the peaceful scenery.

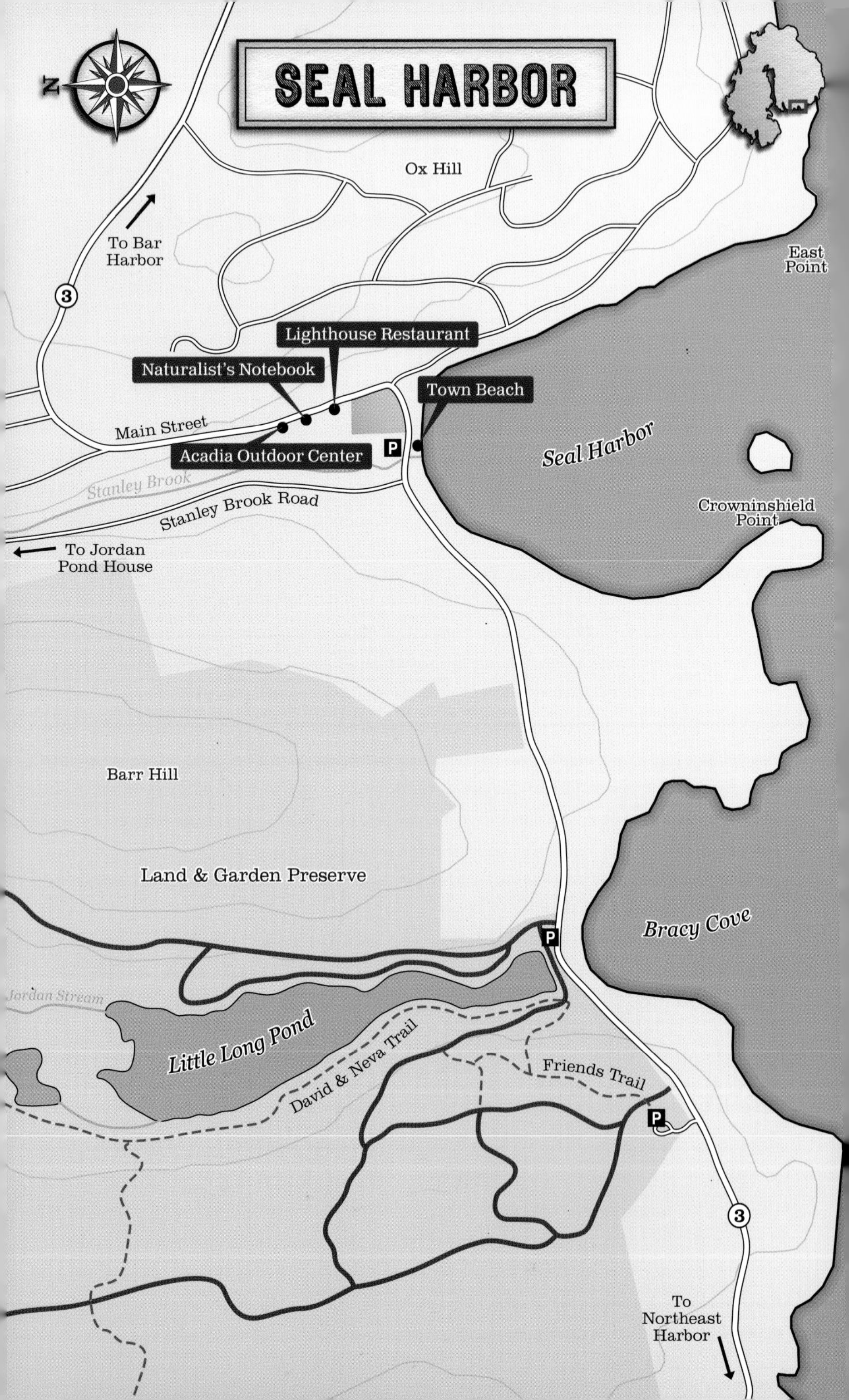
SEAL HARBOR
N
Ox Hill
To Bar Harbor
3
East Point
Lighthouse Restaurant
Naturalist's Notebook
Town Beach
Main Street
Acadia Outdoor Center
P
Seal Harbor
Stanley Brook
Stanley Brook Road
Crowninshield Point
To Jordan Pond House
Barr Hill
Land & Garden Preserve
Bracy Cove
P
Jordan Stream
Little Long Pond
David & Neva Trail
Friends Trail
P
3
To Northeast Harbor

★ SEAL HARBOR TOWN BEACH

This small public beach is one of only two natural sand beaches on the island (the other is Sand Beach on the Park Loop Road). Visit during low tide when there's plenty of space to spread out. A small parking area with restrooms is located across from the beach on Route 3.

★ NATURALIST'S NOTEBOOK

Nature and science lovers flock to this charming store/museum/exploratorium, which features one of the most thoughtfully curated bookshops anywhere. There are also kid-friendly exhibits, photos, specimens, and art displays spread across three floors. Be sure to inquire about special events. (16 Main Street, 207-801-2777, thenaturalistsnotebook.com)

ACADIA OUTDOOR CENTER

The closest bike rental shop to Jordan Pond, Acadia Outdoor Center helps visitors explore Acadia's fabulous southern carriage roads, which are just a short pedal from Seal Harbor. Acadia Outdoor Center also sells outdoor gear, coffee, and ice cream. (18 Main Street, 207-801-9343, acadiaoutdoorcenter.com)

LIGHTHOUSE RESTAURANT $$$ (Lnch, Din)

Seal Harbor's only sit-down restaurant boasts old-school nautical decor and a menu to match. Lots of seafood options. (12 Main Street, 207-276-3958)

Border Garden

Abby Aldrich Rockefeller Garden

Gardens are taken *very* seriously in Seal Harbor, and no garden is more revered than the Abby Aldrich Rockefeller Garden. Located on the former estate of John D. Rockefeller Jr. and his wife, Abby, it combines the posh perfection of an English border garden with antique Asian statues. Legendary landscape architect (and Bar Harbor summer resident) Beatrix Farrand (p.235) designed the garden in the 1920s, and in 2017 John and Abby's son David donated it to the nonprofit Land & Garden Preserve. Today the garden is open to the public between mid-July and mid-September. Reservations, which are required for entrance, are available at gardenpreserve.org.

The Abby Aldrich Rockefeller Garden is located on Barr Hill between Seal Harbor and Little Long Pond. From the parking area you'll walk through a shady spruce-fir forest carpeted with luxuriant mosses. The mosses thrive thanks to regular cleaning with leaf blowers, which remove leaves, pine needles, and forest debris. (Prior to the use of leaf blowers, the mosses were less impressive.)

Most visitors enter the three-acre walled garden through the South Entrance Gate (below). Both the gate and the red walls are modeled after Beijing's Forbidden City, and the ceramic roof tiles were actually made for the Forbidden City in the 18th century. Pass through the gate and stroll along the Spirit Path, lined with Korean funerary statues dating back to the 14th century. The Spirit Path, which runs parallel to the flower-filled Border Garden, ends at an overlook of Little Long Pond with a Buddhist Votive Stele.

Enter the central Border Garden and feast your eyes on the flourishing flowers. Concentric rectangular paths showcase exquisitely tended flower beds. Perennials form the foundation of the beds, and annuals burst with color. Even on foggy days, the flowers are radiant, particularly in August during peak blooms. The flowers are arranged around a central lawn where the Rockefellers once hosted private parties. A circular moon gate lies at the northern end of the garden. An Oval Garden at the southern end features a 5th–6th century Chinese pagoda overlooking a reflecting pool that's home to native frogs.

When you're ready to leave the garden, exit the South Gate and follow the Eyrie Path past antique granite lanterns from Korea and Japan. *The Eyrie* was the Rockefellers' sprawling 107-room summer mansion. It was razed in 1963 (upkeep was steep, even for Rockefellers), but you can still explore its stone terrace, which offers beautiful views of Seal Harbor.

Little Long Pond

This small pond (not to be confused with the much larger Long Pond on the western side of Mount Desert Island) was once part of the Rockefeller family's sprawling Seal Harbor estate. In 2015, David Rockefeller celebrated his 100th birthday by donating the pond and over 1,000 acres of surrounding forests, meadows, and marshes to the nonprofit Land & Garden Preserve (gardenpreserve.org). Today 10 miles of hiking trails and carriage roads are open to the public year-round. A free trail map is available on the Land & Garden Preserve website. Bikes are not permitted on the carriage roads, but dogs are allowed on the trails.

Little Long Pond's main entrance is located off Route 3 across from Bracy Cove. There are 10 parking spaces near the Bracy Cove entrance gate. An additional 22 parking spaces are available at Upper Lot off Peabody Drive, located

one-half mile west of Little Long Pond off Route 3. The 0.4-mile Friends Trail connects Upper Lot to Little Long Pond, passing beautiful mosses and lichens along the way.

From the Bracy Cove Entrance, follow the path that skirts Little Long Pond's eastern shore. You'll stroll past several lovely viewpoints before reaching the Rockefeller boathouse about one-quarter mile from the main gate. This is a good place to turn around if you're only interested in a short stroll.

For a longer hike, continue north on the carriage road, turn left (west) on Jordan South Spur Trail, then turn left (south) and follow the David & Neva Trail along the western shore of Little Long Pond. The trail is named after David Rockefeller, who blazed the trail in the 1940s, and his daughter Neva, who revived it 25 years later. At the pond's southern tip, a carriage road heads back to the main gate. The full loop is about two miles long.

FAR OUT

NORTHEAST HARBOR

If SEAL HARBOR is a town of stealth wealth, Northeast Harbor is becoming a town of wealth on prominent display—to the consternation of old money families that have summered here for generations. Once upon a time the Rockefellers, Astors, and Fords drove around Northeast Harbor in beat-up automobiles, wore tattered clothes, and pretended they were not, in fact, worth millions of dollars. But over the past few decades, a new breed of summer visitor has crept in, bringing bigger yachts, fancier cars, and other forms of conspicuous consumption to prove they are, in fact, worth millions of dollars.

Some old-timers worry their tranquil hideaway is becoming "trendy." The thought of Mount Desert Island ever becoming the next Martha's Vineyard or, worse, *Hamptons*, has many blue bloods clutching their pearls. But to date, the Kardashians have yet to motor into the harbor, and despite the influx of a few billionaires who earned their money, Northeast Harbor appears to be hanging on to its relatively low-key profile just fine. Summer residents still keep copies of the "Redbook"—an exclusive directory listing the winter and summer addresses of the Northeast Harbor/Seal Harbor elite—and private clubs have decades-long "waiting lists" for new members wishing to apply.

But despite the private drives, private clubs, and other private enclaves, Northeast Harbor is a fabulous place for the public to visit. And some of its top attractions are—wait for it—free! But don't leave your credit card at home. Main Street is filled with pricey art galleries and other high-end shops catering to gourmet tastes, so plan accordingly.

Oddly, Northeast Harbor was born of rather humble circumstances. In the early 1800s it was home to farmers and fishermen. The first summer visitors were artists, clergymen, and professors who arrived in the 1880s. At one point, when a wealthy New York banker offered to buy a Northeast Harbor farmer's property, the farmer responded, "We have some very fine people in Northeast Harbor, including a Bishop and three college Presidents. We don't want any Wall Street riffraff!" My, how times have changed.

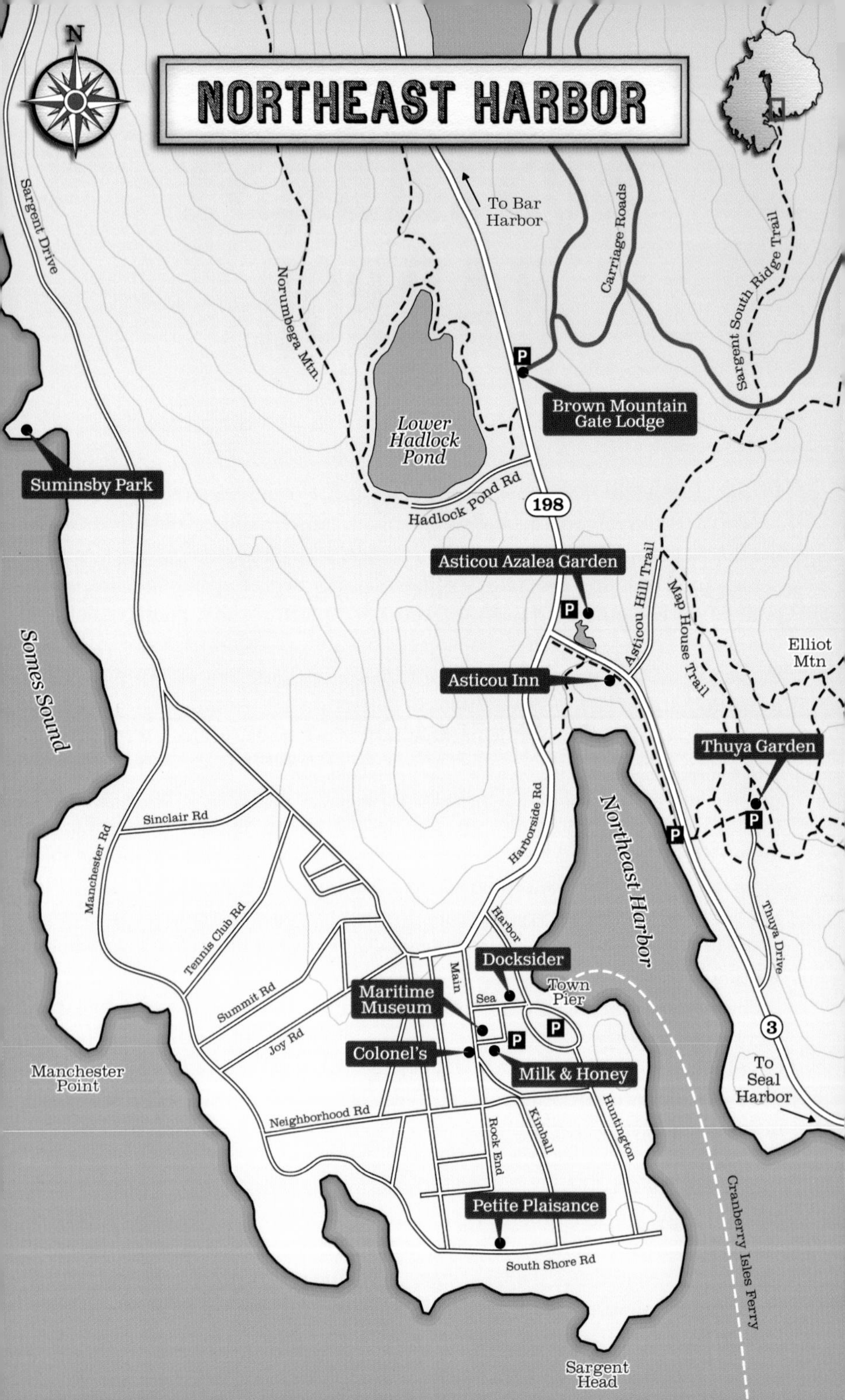

N
NORTHEAST HARBOR
To Bar Harbor
Carriage Roads
Sargent South Ridge Trail
Sargent Drive
Norumbega Mtn.
Lower Hadlock Pond
P
Brown Mountain Gate Lodge
Suminsby Park
Hadlock Pond Rd
198
Asticou Azalea Garden
Asticou Hill Trail
Map House Trail
Elliot Mtn
Asticou Inn
Sones Sound
Thuya Garden
Harborside Rd
Northeast Harbor
Sinclair Rd
Manchester Rd
Tennis Club Rd
Harbor
Thuya Drive
Main
Dockside
Town Pier
Sea
Maritime Museum
Summit Rd
Joy Rd
Colonel's
Milk & Honey
3
To Seal Harbor
Manchester Point
Neighborhood Rd
Rock End
Kimball
Huntington
Petite Plaisance
South Shore Rd
Cranberry Isles Ferry
Sargent Head

Thuya Garden

★ THUYA GARDEN & LODGE

Perched high above Northeast Harbor, this hilltop garden bursts with color in late summer. Thuya Garden is located at the end of a ¼-mile trail that starts just south of the Asticou Inn. Stone steps rise 200 feet through Asticou Terraces, where multiple lookouts offer views of the harbor below. (You can also drive to Thuya Garden, but hiking is more fun.) The trail ends at Thuya Lodge, the former summer home of landscape architect Joseph Curtis, who conceived the Asticou Terraces Trail. The rustic lodge, delightfully trapped in time, features an extensive botanical library. Following Curtis' death in 1928, Asticou Inn owner Charles K. Savage became trustee of Asticou Terraces, and in 1958 he converted Curtis' apple orchard into Thuya Garden. (Curtis planted the orchard to make hard cider in defiance of Prohibition; Savage didn't allow liquor at the Asticou Inn). A pair of magnificent hand-carved wooden gates, designed by Savage and featuring native flora and fauna, mark the entrance to Thuya Garden. The gates are made of native white cedar, *Thuja occidentalis*, from which Thuya Garden takes its name. Many of Thuya's trees and shrubs came from the Bar Harbor garden of Beatrix Farrand, who designed the East Garden at the White House and the Rose Garden at the New York Botanical Garden. Thuya Garden is open mid-June through October. A $5 per person donation is suggested. (gardenpreserve.org)

Charles K. Savage also created Asticou Azalea Garden, Thuya's sister garden near the Asticou Inn (see following page). You can hike roughly one mile from Thuya Garden to Asticou Azalea Garden by following Map House Trail to Asticou Hill Trail, a private road that allows foot traffic.

Asticou Azalea Garden

★ASTICOU AZALEA GARDEN

This Japanese-inspired garden features over 70 varieties of azaleas, laurels, and rhododendrons. A pond reflects the dramatic blooms, which generally peak in late May/early June. Summer blooms include Japanese iris, smoke bush, and waterlilies. Fiery foliage lights up the garden in autumn. Rounded mugo pines, which grow along the pond's southwest shore, pay homage to Acadia's rounded mountains. A short path twists through the soothing scenery, passing stone lanterns en route to a meticulously raked sand garden, modeled after Ryoan-ji Temple Rock Garden in Kyoto, Japan. The Zen garden suggests a Maine seascape of small, mossy islands rising above tiny sand waves. Charles K. Savage, whose grandfather founded the Asticou Inn, created the garden in 1957 using plants rescued from Beatrix Farrand's legendary Reef Point garden in Bar Harbor. John D. Rockefeller Jr., a longtime friend of Savage, helped with funding. Today the garden belongs to the Land & Garden Preserve (gardenpreserve.org). After strolling through the 2.3-acre garden, follow Asticou Stream Trail (marked by a wooden signpost on Route 3) to the northern shore of Northeast Harbor. Asticou Azalea Garden is open May to November, 10am–6pm. There's a small parking area off Route 198. A $5 per person donation is suggested.

★DOWNTOWN NORTHEAST HARBOR

Northeast Harbor's charming Main Street boasts some of the best boutiques and art galleries on the island. Among the highlights: Shaw Contemporary Jewelry, Artemis Gallery, Island Artisans, and Redfield Artisans.

Sargent Drive

★ SARGENT DRIVE

Twisting along the eastern edge of Somes Sound, Sargent Drive is one of the island's most beautiful roads. About two miles north of downtown Northeast Harbor there's a turnoff to Suminsby Park, a gorgeous waterfront park with picnic tables, grills, and fire pits overlooking Somes Sound.

NORTHEAST HARBOR TOWN DOCK

If you like boats, venture down to Northeast Harbor's town dock—one of the best places in the world to see Hinckley and Morris yachts (p.255) in their native habitat. The meticulously cared-for boats are most impressive in July and August. By late September most have been put in storage or sent to the Caribbean.

GREAT HARBOR MARITIME MUSEUM

This delightful museum, located in the old firehouse, features changing exhibits that explore the region's maritime heritage. Open Tues–Sat, 10am–5pm, late June to mid-September. (125 Main Street, 207-276-5262)

PETITE PLAISANCE

This is the former home of French novelist Marguerite Yourcenar, the first woman inducted as an "immortal" into the Academie Francaise. Yourcenar fled France during World War II, and once in Northeast Harbor she decided she could never live anywhere else. Free tours in English or French are given by appointment June 15–August 31. (207-276-3940, petiteplaisanceconservationfund.org)

Boat Tours

★SEA PRINCESS

For over 40 years *Sea Princess* has offered professionally narrated cruises past some of Acadia's most stunning offshore scenery. If you're interested in nature or history, this is the boat for you. Morning and afternoon trips include a 45-minute stop at Islesford (p.286). (207-276-5352, barharborcruises.com)

HELEN BROOKS

There are two ways to enjoy sailing out of Northeast Harbor at your leisure: inherit millions of dollars and (even more unlikely) a mooring in the harbor, or book a trip on the *Helen Brooks*. This gorgeous Friendship sloop offers afternoon and sunset sails. Private charters are also available. (207-266-5210, sailacadia.com)

Northeast Harbor Restaurants

★PEABODY'S AT THE ASTICOU $$$ (Brk, Lnch, Din)

Located in the historic Asticou Inn—the oldest hotel on the island (1883)—Peabody's serves delicious food paired with old-school Yankee elegance. Enjoy oven-fresh popovers on the outdoor deck, which has fabulous views of Northeast Harbor. (15 Peabody Drive, 207-276-3344, asticou.com)

★MILK & HONEY $$$ (Brk, Lnch)

Tucked away behind Great Harbor Maritime Museum, this laid-back cafe specializes in sophisticated flavors. Delicious sandwiches, salads, baked goods, and dessert, plus coffee, beer, and wine. Great for takeout. Dinner Thursday nights. (3 Old Firehouse Lane, 207-276-4003, milkandhoneykitchen.com)

★ABEL'S LOBSTER $$$ (Lnch, Din)

Perched above Somes Sound, this waterfront restaurant is an island classic. Since 1939 Abel's has served fresh lobster cooked in traditional wood-fired boilers. Indoor and outdoor dining. No reservations. (abelslobstermdi.com)

COLONEL'S RESTAURANT $$$ (Brk, Lnch, Din)

This local favorite serves seafood entrees, burgers, sandwiches, soups, and salads. A full bar serves beers on tap. The attached bakery sells breads and pastries. (143 Main Street, 207-276-5147, colonelsrestaurant.com)

THE DOCKSIDER $$$ (Lnch, Din)

For over four decades the Docksider has served lobster rolls overflowing with tails and claws. Burgers, sandwiches, seafood dinners, and ice cream are also available. (14 Sea Street, 207-276-3965)

Bear Island Lighthouse

This gorgeous lighthouse, located on tiny Bear Island just off Northeast Harbor, first went into operation in 1839. The 31-foot-tall brick tower sits on the island's highest point, and the beacon can be seen up to 10 miles away. In the early 1980s, the lighthouse was decommissioned and fell into disrepair. In 1987, Acadia National Park acquired the lighthouse, and in 1989 Friends of Acadia refurbished the building and relit the beacon. To help pay for upkeep, the park service leases the lighthouse to a private individual.

Somes Sound

This five-mile inlet, which nearly slices Mount Desert Island in two, is Acadia's most dramatic waterway. Surrounded by mountains, Somes Sound reaches a maximum depth of 152 feet at Valley Cove, which lies at the base of 679-foot St. Sauveur Mountain. For years people boasted Somes Sound was the only fjord on the East Coast. But true fjords, like those in Norway, have thousands of feet of elevation change above and below water. Somes Sound only has hundreds of feet of elevation change, which is more characteristic of submerged glacial valleys called fjärds.

Fjord, fjärd—however Somes Sound self-identifies, it was sculpted by a glacier nearly 18,000 years ago. After the glacier melted, the land rebounded and Somes Sound spent a few thousand years as a freshwater lake. Then, around 7,000 years ago, sea levels rose and connected it to the sea.

Today the best way to experience Somes Sound is by boat. The Sea Princess (p.239) offers motor boat cruises of Somes Sound departing from Northeast Harbor. Sail Acadia (p.252) offers both sailing and motorboat cruises on Somes Sound that depart from Southwest Harbor. Sea kayakers should use extra caution on Somes Sound, which can experience strong winds and choppy waves.

SOMESVILLE

SOMESVILLE IS SO quaint it hurts. The white clapboard houses, leafy sidewalks, and well-tended flower beds feel like a Norman Rockwell painting. But this small village is the real deal, complete with a Strawberry Festival in July, a Blueberry Festival in August, and weekly pie sales at the Somesville Union Meeting House.

Drive down Route 102, traveling at the posted speed limit of 25 mph, and you'll pass through Somesville in under a minute. Blink and you might miss it. But you'll know you're there when you see an arched white footbridge on the right side of the road—one of the island's most famous landmarks. Officially called the Thaddeus Shepley Somes Memorial Bridge, it was built in 1981 and lies next to the tiny Selectmen's Building, which dates to the 1780s. The footbridge crosses a stream in front of the Somesville Museum and Gardens, which are maintained by the Mount Desert Island Historical Society.

Somesville was the first permanent town on Mount Desert Island. In 1761, 22-year-old Abraham Somes sailed north from Gloucester, Massachusetts, and built a log cabin on the shore of this well-protected harbor. The location offered plenty of oak trees (perfect for lumber), nearby streams (perfect for hydropower), and a saltwater marsh (perfect for hay). The following year, Somes returned with his wife and three daughters and named the town "Betwixt the Hills." Before long, several other families joined them. According to an early report, by the 1830s Somesville had "one small store, one blacksmith shop, one shoemaker's shop, one tan-yard, two shipyards, one bark mill, one saw mill, one lath mill, one shingle mill, one grist mill, and one schoolhouse."

In the summer of 1855, Somesville hosted a group of visitors who spent one month at a local tavern. One of the visitors was Frederic Church, a landscape artist whose paintings of Mount Desert Island would catapult the island to fame. Church's paintings lured thousands of visitors, but the new arrivals preferred staying in Bar Harbor and Southwest Harbor, which lay closer to coastal shipping routes. Before long, Somesville was no longer the most important town on the island and development ground to a halt, pickling this picture-perfect place in a colonial time warp that continues to the present day.

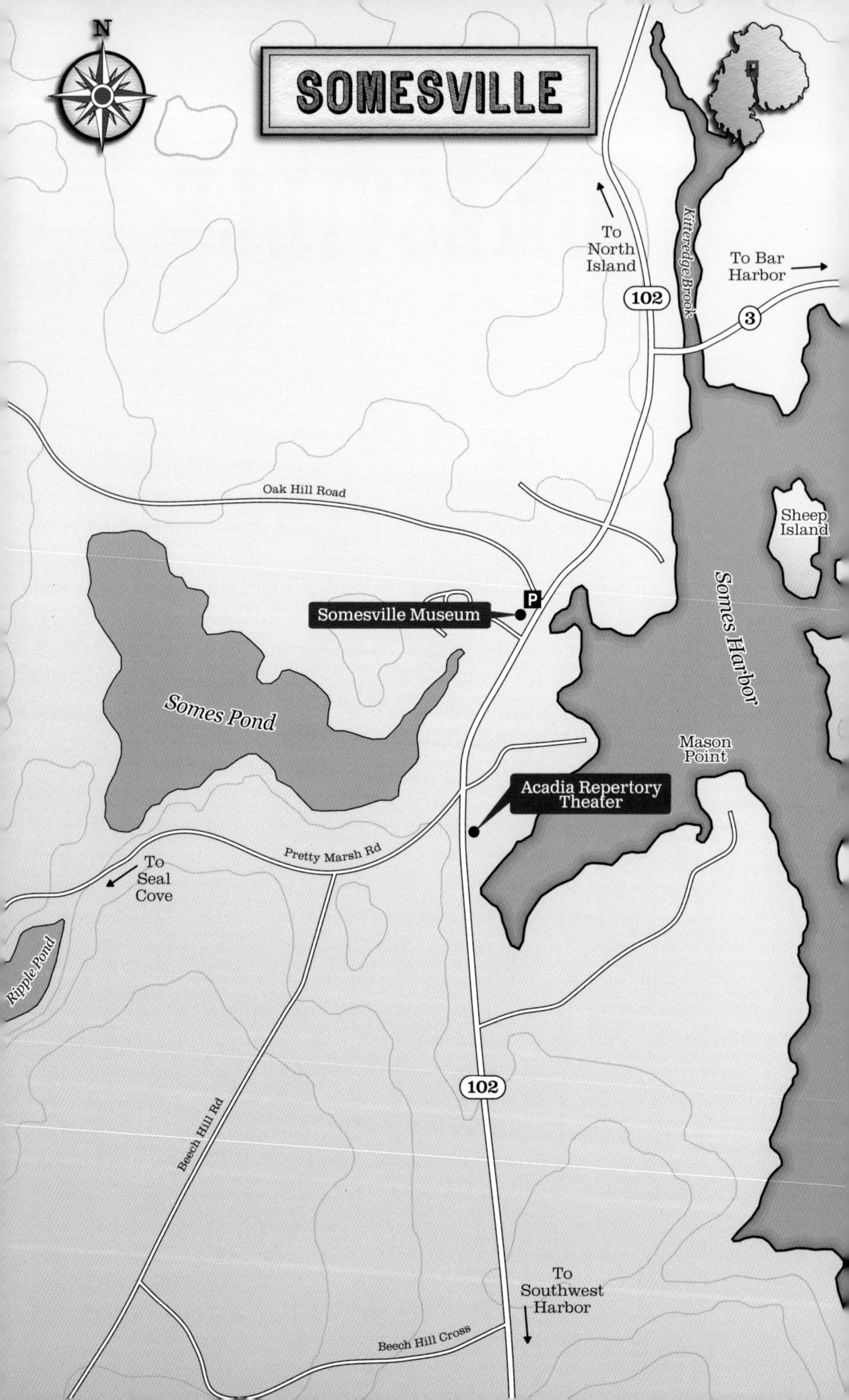
N
SOMESVILLE
To North Island
102
Kitteredge Brook
To Bar Harbor
3
Oak Hill Road
Sheep Island
P
Somesville Museum
Somes Harbor
Somes Pond
Mason Point
Acadia Repertory Theater
To Seal Cove
Pretty Marsh Rd
Ripple Pond
102
Beech Hill Rd
To Southwest Harbor
Beech Hill Cross

★SEAL COVE AUTO MUSEUM

This out-of-the-way museum preserves the stunning antique car collection of Richard Paine, who inherited a fortune and spent much of it on Brass Era (1895–1917) autos. There are Model Ts, Stanley Steamers, and dozens of other classics. (1414 Tremont Road, 207-244-9242, sealcoveautomuseum.org)

SOMESVILLE MUSEUM AND GARDENS

Located across from Somesville's famous footbridge, this small museum features changing exhibits and an heirloom garden. Open late June through Labor Day. (207-276-9323, mdihistory.org)

LONG POND

The largest lake on Mount Desert Island, Long Pond has a small, popular beach near its northern tip, just off Pretty Marsh Road. You can rent canoes, kayaks, and stand-up paddle boards across the street at National Park Canoe and Kayak Rental (207-244-5854, nationalparkcanoerental.com).

ACADIA REPERTORY THEATER

Between July and September this local theater company performs a mix of comedies, dramas, children's plays, and Agatha Christie murder mysteries in Somesville's historic Masonic Hall. (207-244-7260, acadiarep.com)

BEECH HILL FARM STAND

This organic farm sells produce and artisanal local goods such as honey, preserves, meat, eggs, dairy products, baked goods, juice, and specialty foods. Open 9am–4pm, Tues–Sat, June –October. (207-244-5204, 171 Beech Hill Road)

FREEDOM II
Southwest Harbor

SOUTHWEST HARBOR

SOUTHWEST HARBOR IS the largest town on the western side of Mount Desert Island. Centered around a beautiful working harbor, it's a delightful mix of fishermen, summer residents, and tourists. Unlike Bar Harbor, which revolves around tourism, Southwest Harbor is a genuine island town that just happens to have some great attractions.

Much of daily life in Southwest Harbor revolves around boats. The island's largest marina, best maritime supply shops, and most famous boatbuilders are all located here. In addition, several great boat tours depart from the harbor. Visitors can enjoy sailing trips, nature tours, lobster cruises, and deep-sea fishing.

Southwest Harbor is also a great jumping-off point for land-based adventures. Some of the island's best hikes are just a short drive away. And because Southwest Harbor is home to some of the island's best hotels and restaurants, you'll never lack for creature comforts. If you don't mind being 30 minutes away from the island's famous eastern side—or you aren't thrilled about the crowds you'll encounter there—Southwest Harbor is a terrific alternative.

Due to its physical separation from the rest of the island, Southwest Harbor has always been a bit different. It was the first town to lift the famous automobile ban imposed by wealthy summer residents in the early 1900s, and today it revels in being more laid back than its exclusive neighbors across Somes Sound. Southwest Harbor's popular Oktoberfest features over 20 Maine breweries, while the town's annual Flamingo Parade revels in lowbrow absurdity. For years the parade was presided over by Don Featherstone, the real-life inventor of pink plastic flamingos. The post-parade cocktail party is sponsored by the town's fictional "Yacht and Polo Club."

But as more and more "summer folks" buy pricey homes on the west side of the island, the idea of a Southwest Harbor "Yacht and Polo Club" is becoming more and more plausible. Rising property taxes are pressuring many locals and small businesses. Hinckley Yachts moved its boatbuilding operations to the mainland years ago, and boatbuilding legend Ralph Stanley was forced to close his waterfront workshop. Whether gentrification permanently changes Southwest Harbor remains to be seen. For the moment, however, it's one of the island's most enjoyable towns.

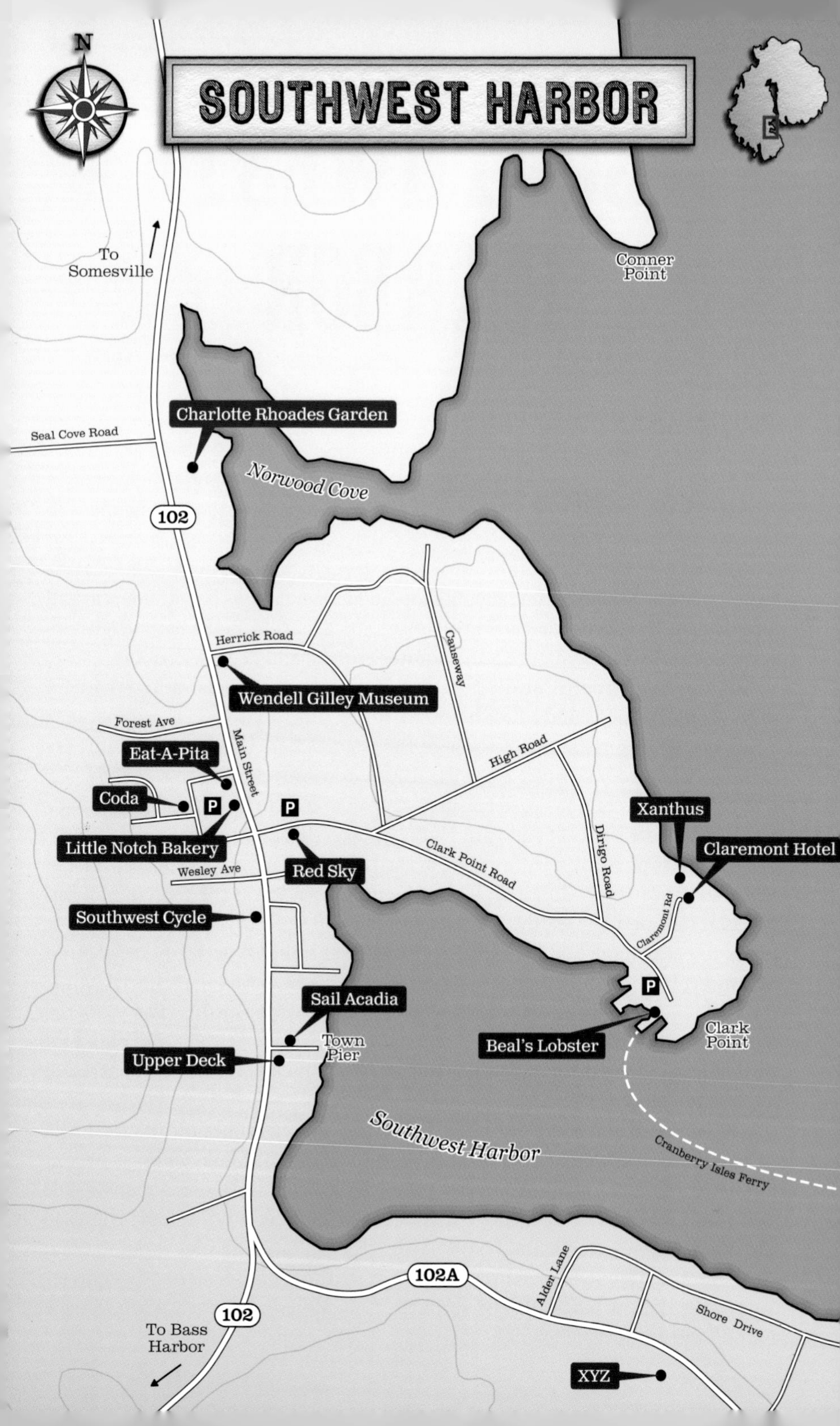

N
SOUTHWEST HARBOR
To Somesville
Conner Point
Charlotte Rhoades Garden
Seal Cove Road
Norwood Cove
102
Herrick Road
Causeway
Wendell Gilley Museum
Forest Ave
Main Street
Eat-A-Pita
High Road
Coda
P
Little Notch Bakery
Red Sky
Wesley Ave
Clark Point Road
Dirigo Road
Xanthus
Claremont Hotel
Claremont Rd
Southwest Cycle
Sail Acadia
Town Pier
Upper Deck
Beal's Lobster
Clark Point
Southwest Harbor
Cranberry Isles Ferry
102A
Alder Lane
Shore Drive
102
To Bass Harbor
XYZ

★ CLAREMONT HOTEL

This historic hotel, established in 1884, boasts spectacular views of Somes Sound and the island's tallest peaks. And you don't have to be a guest to enjoy the scenery. The Claremont's restaurant, Little Fern, is open to the public, and its waterfront boathouse offers cocktails and small plates. There's also the annual Croquet Classic in August, which is held on the Claremont's waterfront lawn. (22 Claremont Road, 800-244-5036, theclaremonthotel.com)

★ ECHO LAKE

Located three miles north of Southwest Harbor, this is the island's most popular swimming area. At the southern end is Echo Lake Beach, popular with families and young children. To get there, look for the "Acadia National Park, Echo Lake Entrance" sign on Route 102, just north of Smuggler's Den Campground. More adventurous swimmers enjoy Echo Lake Ledges, where you can jump off the not-too-high rocks. To get to the ledges, head to the Acadia Mountain parking area and follow the stairs down to a wooded path that ends at the shore.

★ MAINE GRANITE HISTORICAL SOCIETY

You probably didn't come here to learn about the history of Maine granite, but this quaint museum, filled with historic tools and photos, is one of the island's true gems. Owner/curator Steve Haynes' passion for granite is infectious. Be prepared for a whirlwind, hands-on romp through geologic and American history. (62 Beech Hill Crossroad, 207-244-0175, mainegraniteindustry.org)

WENDELL GILLEY MUSEUM

Birders love this small museum, which displays the wooden bird carvings of local legend Wendell Gilley. The museum also has special exhibits, bird carving demonstrations, and bird carving workshops. (4 Herrick Road, 207-244-7555, wendellgilleymuseum.org)

CHARLOTTE RHOADES PARK BUTTERFLY GARDEN

This waterfront flower garden is a great place to escape the crowds. A handful of shaded picnic tables overlook Norwood Cove.

CARROLL HOMESTEAD

Built in 1825, this historic farmhouse offers an interesting glimpse into the hard-scrabble lives of early settlers. Check local publications for open house hours. Located off Route 102, just south of Echo Lake.

SOUTHWEST CYCLE

A great place to rent bikes, especially if you're heading to the Cranberry Isles or Swan's Island (p.295). (370 Main Street, 207-244-5856, southwestcycle.com)

Boats, Boating & Sea Kayaking

★ACADIA LOBSTER CRUISE

"The only thing better than lobster fresh off the boat ... is lobster fresh *on* the boat!" says Jason Clark, who hauls lobster and cooks a traditional Downeast feast onboard. See page 25 for more info. (207-370-7663, acadialobstercruise.com)

★ SAIL ACADIA

Delightful sailing trips on the beautiful 42-foot Friendship sloop *Alice E.* (p.25) and motorboat lobster tours on the 33-foot *Elizabeth T.* See page 25 for more info. (11 Apple Lane, 207-266-5210, sailacadia.com)

★MAINE STATE SEA KAYAKING

Southwest Harbor's premier sea kayak outfitter offers tours of Blue Hill Bay, Western Bay, and Somes Sound. Four-hour trips are limited to a maximum of 12 people. (254 Main Street, 207-244-9500, mainestatekayak.com)

ACADIA DEEP-SEA FISHING

The 43-foot *Vagabond* offers half-day and full-day fishing trips in search of cod, mackerel, bluefish, and more. (207-244-5385, acadiafishingtours.com)

MANSELL BOAT RENTAL

Sailboat and motorboat rentals. Daily and weekly rates are available on boats from 14 to 31 feet. (207-244-5625, mansellboatrentals.com)

Restaurants

★ RED SKY $$$ (Din)

Southwest Harbor's most acclaimed restaurant serves exquisite meals in a casual, elegant atmosphere. Maine-raised meats, house-made sausage, and plenty of fresh, local seafood. Great wine, craft cocktails, decadent desserts. (14 Clark Point Road, 207-244-0476, redskyrestaurant.com)

★ CAPTAIN'S GALLEY AT BEAL'S $$$ (Lnch, Din)

Beal's has everything you want from a lobster shack: pick-your-lobster saltwater tanks, picnic tables, paper plates, and beautiful waterfront views. One of MDI's top lobster experiences. (182 Clark Point Road, 207-244-3202, bealslobster.com)

★ XYZ $$$ (Din)

Authentic Mexican flavors from Xalapa, Yucatán, and Zacatecas. Despite the out-of-the-way location, it's always packed. Excellent meals, great margaritas, legendary XYZ pie. (80 Seawall Road, 207-244-5221, xyzmaine.com)

★ CODA $$$ (Din)

Farm-to-table dining with nearly everything—soups, stocks, pasta—made in-house. Regular live music makes Coda one of the liveliest restaurants in town. (18 Village Green Way, 207-244-8133, codasouthwestharbor.com)

EAT-A-PITA/CAFE 2 $$$/$$$ (Brk, Lnch, Din)

By day Eat-A-Pita sells tasty breakfasts and healthy pita sandwiches stuffed with veggies. At night Cafe 2 offers seafood, steak, and pasta in a charming, casual atmosphere. (326 Main Street, 207-244-4344, eatapitasouthwestharbor.com)

LITTLE FERN $$$ (Din)

Located in the historic Claremont Hotel, Little Fern serves delicious food in a classic setting with gorgeous views of Somes Sound. (22 Claremont Road, 207-244-5036, theclaremonthotel.com)

SIPS $$$ (Brk, Lnch, Din)

From crepes to risottos to falafels, this casual wine bar offers a tasty array of Mediterranean-influenced cuisine. Abundant seafood, great cocktails. (4 Clark Point Road, 207-244-4550, sipsmdi.com).

UPPER DECK $$$ (Lnch, Din)

Perched above Dysart's marina, this bar/restaurant offers terrific views of the boat-filled harbor below. (433 Main Street, 207-244-8113, upperdeckdining.com)

LITTLE NOTCH BAKERY $$$ (Lnch, Din)

This local bakery is a great place for fresh bread and takeout sandwiches, plus soups, salads, pizza and paninis. (340 Main Street, 207-244-4043)

Hinckley Yachts

BOATBUILDING ON MOUNT DESERT ISLAND

BOATS AND BOATBUILDING have played a vital role on Mount Desert Island for centuries. From the Wabanaki, who plied the waters in birchbark canoes, to the first settlers, who came in search of raw sailboat materials, islanders have always depended on the sea. Not surprisingly, local boatbuilding knowledge is second to none.

The most renowned local boatbuilder is Hinckley (hinckleyyachts.com), famous for its high-tech luxury yachts. Want advanced soundproofing materials built into the Kevlar/carbon hull? Comes standard. Need a wine rack for slightly wider bottles from Burgundy? They do that. What started in 1928 as a boatyard for local fishermen morphed into a sailboat company devoted to pleasure craft. In the 1950s, Hinckley was an early adopter of fiberglass, thrusting them to the forefront of the high-tech, luxury sailing world. In 1994, the company introduced the elegant, jet-propelled "picnic" boat, which reimagined classic Maine lobster boats as stylish luxury cruisers. Picnic boats, which start around $500,000 and go into the millions, now make up the majority of Hinckley's sales.

Morris Yachts (morrisyachts.com) started making high-end sailboats in 1972, and sailing remains their primary focus. Morris yachts are the first choice of many sailors. What's the difference between a Hinckley and a Morris? Martha Stewart bought a Hinckley, Jimmy Buffett bought a Morris.

Want a smaller sailboat? The Classic Boat Shop (classicboatshop.com) custom-builds elegant, 21-foot daysailers. Still can't find the Mount Desert Island boat of your dreams? Ellis Boat Company (ellisboat.com) and John Williams (jwboatco.com) offer customized boats based on traditional Downeast designs. Wilbur Yachts (wilburyachts.com) specializes in highly customized designs. Want a jacuzzi or a baby grand piano on your boat? Wilbur Yachts does that.

Starting in the 1950s, most boatbuilders switched from wood to fiberglass, but one Southwest Harbor resident proudly bucked the trend. Ralph Stanley (1929–2021) learned the boatbuilding craft at a time when all boats were made of wood. Despite the time and money savings fiberglass offered, Stanley never abandoned wood. As he once told a group of local schoolchildren, "If God wanted fiberglass boats, he'd have made fiberglass trees." In 1999, Stanley was chosen as one of 12 National Heritage Fellows, and he has been named "Boatbuilder Laureate of the Maine Coast."

BASS HARBOR

PERHAPS THE BEST way to describe Bass Harbor is to describe what it's not. Located near the southwestern tip of Mount Desert Island, Bass Harbor is about as far away from Bar Harbor—physically and metaphorically—as you can get. There are no cruise ships, T-shirt shops, or tourist swarms. Instead, Bass Harbor is a traditional Downeast fishing village with a lobster boat-filled harbor surrounded by wooden piers. Pickup trucks outnumber SUVs, and local lawns are piled high with lobster traps and colorful buoys. On an inherently touristy island, Bass Harbor can be a breath of fresh air.

Best of all, there's still plenty to do. Nearby attractions include Mount Desert Island's only lighthouse, two easy hiking trails, a delightful boat tour, and one of the island's best lobster shacks. If Bass Harbor still doesn't feel remote enough, you can catch a ferry to Swan's Island (p.295) or Frenchboro (p.293), two offshore islands that make Bass Harbor look hectic.

Bass Harbor's unpretentious spirit was perhaps best captured by its most memorable summer resident: Julia Child. Around the time Martha Stewart purchased her sprawling Seal Harbor estate, *The French Chef* host made her final visit to the log cabin she hand-built with her husband on Lopaus Point. For six decades, Child visited the cabin in summer, spending her days fishing, relaxing and—of course—cooking fresh meals in her simple, functional kitchen.

Back when Julia arrived, sardines were the economic engine of Bass Harbor. Underwood Wharf, the large brick building on the eastern side of the harbor, was once Maine's largest sardine cannery. In the 1950s, there were roughly 50 sardine canneries along the coast, employing more people than any other industry. Spotter planes located schools of herring (sardines) offshore and alerted local fishermen. When herring populations dwindled in the 1960s, Underwood Wharf switched to canning blueberries, then closed for good in 1977. Lobster eventually became the most important catch, and today Bass Harbor is home to roughly 80 lobster boats—one of the largest fleets in Maine.

Technically, the village of Bass Harbor lies on the eastern side of Bass Harbor, the village of Bernard lies on the western side of Bass Harbor, and both are part of the town of Tremont. Continue north on Route 102 and you'll pass the tiny communities of Goose Cove and Seal Cove before reaching Pretty Marsh.

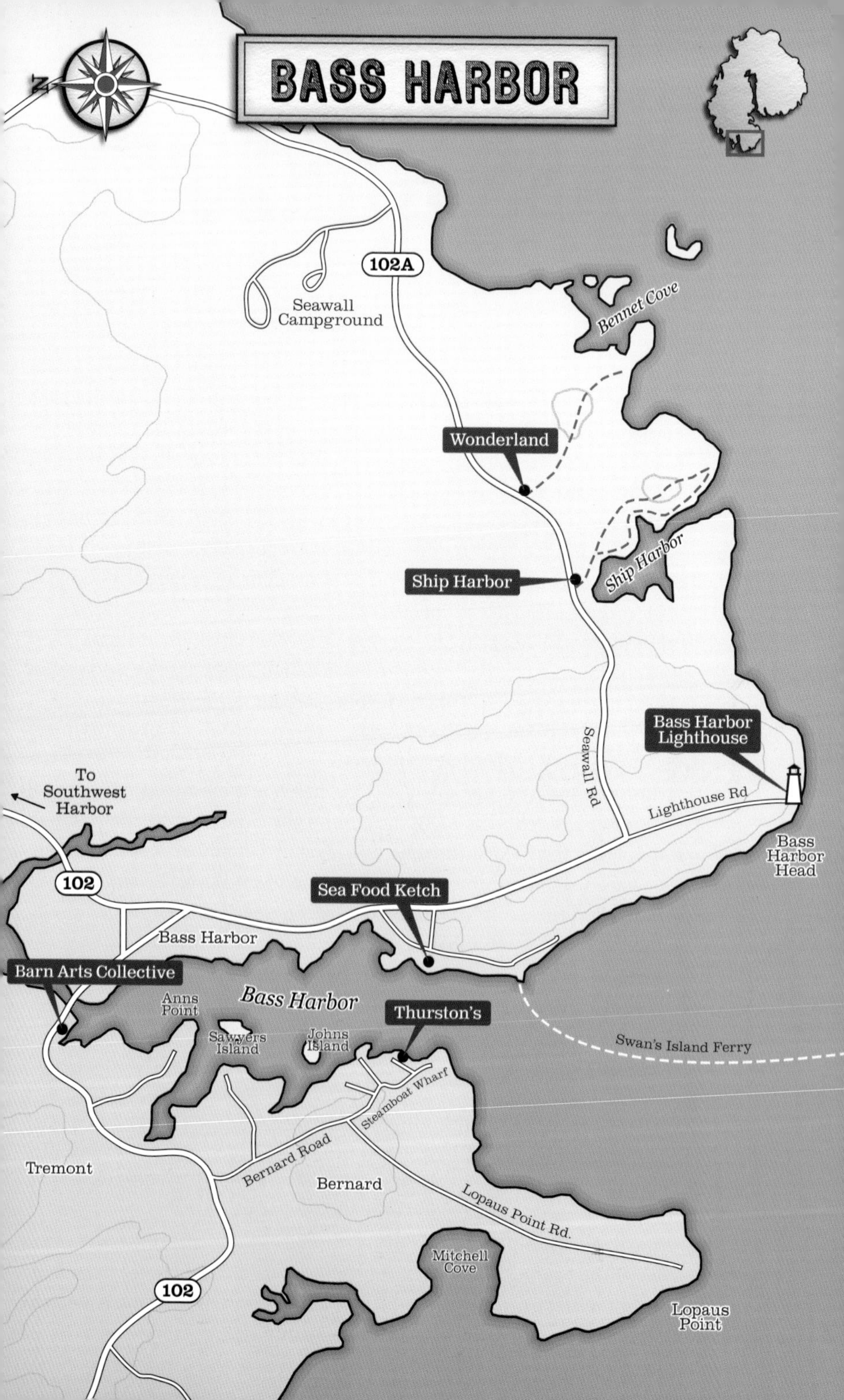

BASS HARBOR
N
102A
Seawall Campground
Bennet Cove
Wonderland
Ship Harbor
Ship Harbor
Seawall Rd
Bass Harbor Lighthouse
Lighthouse Rd
Bass Harbor Head
To Southwest Harbor
102
Sea Food Ketch
Bass Harbor
Barn Arts Collective
Bass Harbor
Anns Point
Sawyers Island
Johns Island
Thurston's
Swan's Island Ferry
Steamboat Wharf
Bernard Road
Tremont
Bernard
Lopaus Point Rd.
Mitchell Cove
102
Lopaus Point

★ BASS HARBOR LIGHTHOUSE

The only lighthouse on Mount Desert Island is Bass Harbor's must-see destination (p.260). Wooden steps lead from the parking area to the rocky shore below. Open sunrise to sunset.

★ ISLAND CRUISES

Fascinating cruises aboard the *R.L. Gott* (p.25) pass through the gorgeous islands south of Bass Harbor. (207-244-5785, bassharborcruises.com)

BARN ARTS COLLECTIVE

This lively theater troupe puts on creative performances for all ages. Productions run the gamut from puppet shows to original works of theater to *The Rocky Horror Picture Show*. (barnarts.me)

SHIP HARBOR NATURE TRAIL

My favorite hike near Bass Harbor is the 1.3-mile round-trip Ship Harbor trail, which wanders through the woods and along the peaceful shores of Ship Harbor. Try to arrive during low tide, when you can explore the tide pools.

WONDERLAND

An easy 1.4-mile trail heads through the woods to a nice cobblestone beach, then loops around the tip of a small, rocky peninsula. Try to visit at low tide, when several large tide pools are exposed at the edge of the peninsula.

BERNARD ROAD

This quiet road is home to a handful of eclectic antique shops and art galleries. Drive down the road, keep your eyes open for signs, and stop wherever strikes your fancy.

Restaurants

★ THURSTON'S $$$ (Lnch, Din)

The most famous lobster shack on Mount Desert Island. Pick your live lobster from a tank in the counter, grab a table on the waterfront porch, then watch lobstermen motor in and out of the harbor while you eat. The adjacent post-and-beam bar offers upscale ambiance with impressive views. In addition to lobster and shellfish, Thurston's offers burgers, sandwiches, and tasty chowders. (Steamboat Wharf Road, 207-244-7600, thurstonslobster.com)

SEA FOOD KETCH $$$ (Lnch, Din)

Beautiful waterfront views paired with seafood classics. The menu is filled with surf and turf—including one of the best lobster rolls on the island—plus beer, wine, and cocktails. When the weather's nice, the outdoor patio is hard to beat. (47 Shore Road, 207-244-7463, seafoodketch.com)

Bass Harbor Lighthouse

Since 1858, the Bass Harbor Lighthouse has faithfully guarded the entrance to Bass Harbor and Blue Hill Bay. The beacon, originally lit by whale oil, is now automated and powered by electricity. All lighthouse beacons have a specific flash pattern, called a signature, listed on maritime charts. The red Bass Harbor beacon flashes every four seconds, and on clear days it can be seen up to 13 miles at sea. In 1897, a 4,000-pound bronze bell was installed near the 26-foot tower, but the bell was later replaced by offshore bell buoys. Listen closely and you'll notice that each bell buoy has a distinct pitch, which aides navigation on foggy days. In 2020, the U.S. Coast Guard transferred possession of Bass Harbor Head Light Station to Acadia National Park. Today it's the most visited destination on western Mount Desert Island, which often means limited parking and big sunset crowds.

SCHOODIC PENINSULA

THIS RUGGED PENINSULA juts four miles into the Gulf of Maine just east of Mount Desert Island. Acadia National Park protects over 3,400 acres on Schoodic Peninsula, the only part of the park connected to the mainland. While not as dramatic as MDI—there are no towering mountains or sparkling lakes—Schoodic offers a gorgeous glimpse of Maine's bold, rocky coast. And its remote location keeps visitation relatively low, even in summer. If traffic jams and trinket stores are fraying your nerves, Schoodic Peninsula is a breath of fresh air.

The six-mile Schoodic Loop Road circumnavigates the peninsula, offering waterfront views that, in places, rival the Park Loop Road. Near the southern tip of the peninsula lies Schoodic Point, a rocky promontory with panoramic ocean views. The nearby Schoodic Institute, a nonprofit environmental research center, hosts free programs and public events throughout the year. Schoodic visitors also enjoy over seven miles of hiking trails and eight miles of dedicated bike paths modeled after MDI's famous carriage roads.

The word "Schoodic" is likely derived from the Mi'kmaq word *Eskowdek* ("The End"). Following European colonization, the peninsula's thin, rocky soils deterred all but the hardiest settlers. In the late 1800s, John G. Moore, a Downeast native who made a fortune on Wall Street, purchased the peninsula to develop as a private resort. But Moore died before realizing his grand dream. In 1927, his Anglophile heirs donated Schoodic Peninsula to the National Park Service on the condition that Lafayette National Park (Acadia's original name) be changed to something less French. George Dorr (p.123) suggested the name "Acadia," which was derived from *L'Acadie*—a name given to the region by the French!

In 2016, the park's Schoodic holdings expanded when an anonymous benefactor donated over 1,400 acres at the north end of the peninsula to Acadia. The donation, which thwarted plans for another private resort, added a new visitor center, Schoodic Woods Campground, and the dedicated bike paths.

Although Schoodic Peninsula lies just five miles east of Mount Desert Island, it's a one-hour drive from Bar Harbor. Another option is the 45-minute Bar Harbor/Winter Harbor ferry (207-288-4585, downeastwindjammer.com) that transports people and bikes across Frenchman Bay. From late May to mid-October the free Island Explorer Shuttle (exploreacadia.com) offers a Schoodic route that loops through Winter Harbor, Schoodic Peninsula, and Prospect Harbor.

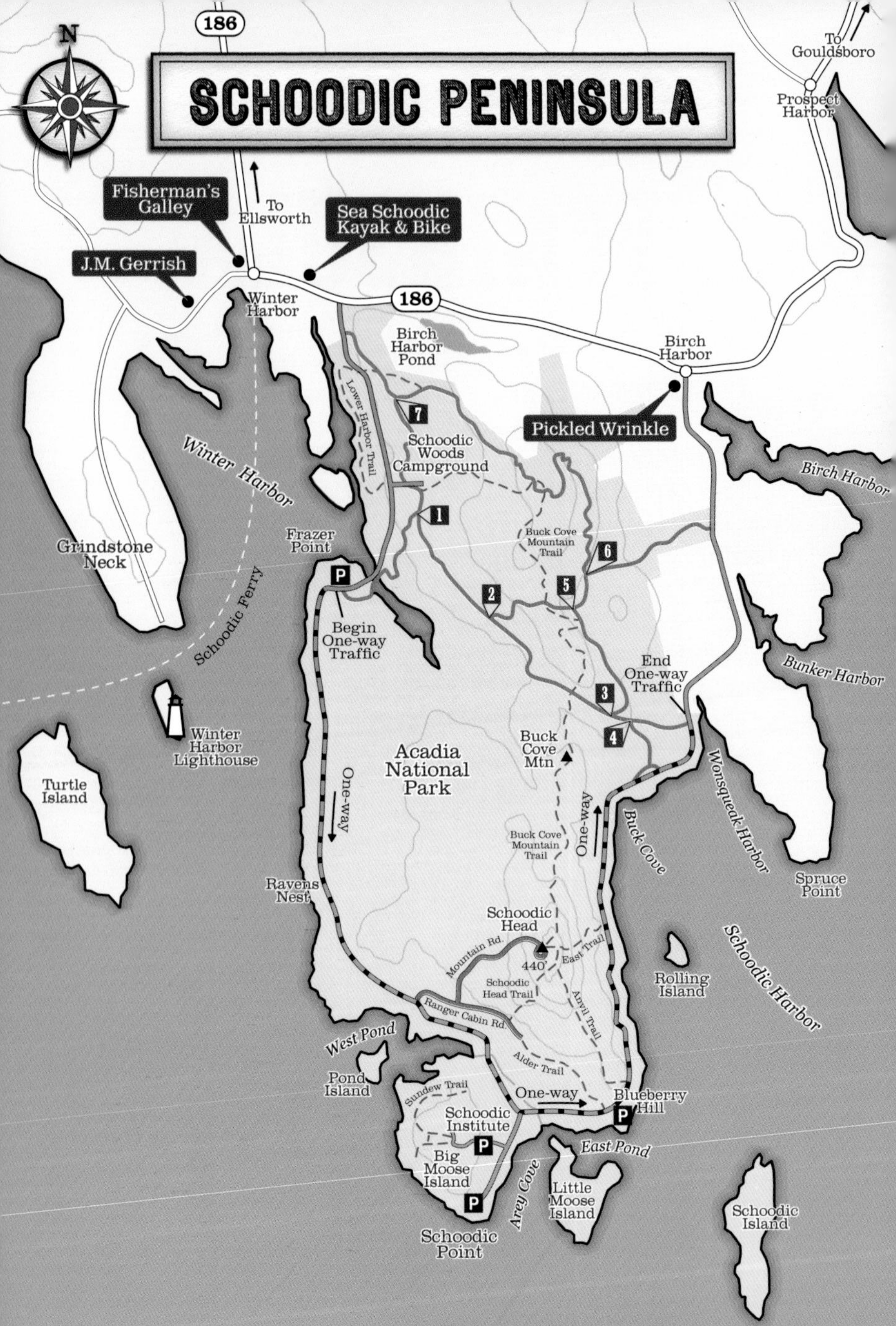

SCHOODIC PENINSULA
N
186
To Gouldsboro
Prospect Harbor
Fisherman's Galley
To Ellsworth
Sea Schoodic Kayak & Bike
J.M. Gerrish
Winter Harbor
186
Birch Harbor Pond
Birch Harbor
Pickled Wrinkle
Lower Harbor Trail
7
Schoodic Woods Campground
Winter Harbor
Birch Harbor
1
Frazer Point
Grindstone Neck
Buck Cove Mountain Trail
6
5
2
P
Begin One-way Traffic
Schoodic Ferry
End One-way Traffic
Bunker Harbor
3
4
Winter Harbor Lighthouse
Buck Cove Mtn
Acadia National Park
Turtle Island
One-way
Wonsqueak Harbor
One-way
Buck Cove
Buck Cove Mountain Trail
Ravens Nest
Spruce Point
Schoodic Head
Mountain Rd.
440'
East Trail
Schoodic Harbor
Schoodic Head Trail
Rolling Island
Ranger Cabin Rd.
Anvil Trail
West Pond
Alder Trail
Pond Island
Sundew Trail
One-way
Blueberry Hill
Schoodic Institute
P
P
East Pond
Big Moose Island
Arey Cove
Little Moose Island
P
Schoodic Island
Schoodic Point
Gulf of Maine

Winter Harbor

Named for its well-protected harbor, which offers shelter during fierce winter storms, this small fishing village (population 300) is a classic slice of Downeast Maine. It's home to lobstermen, artists, and wealthy summer residents whose giant mansions dot the shores of Grindstone Neck, a dramatic peninsula east of town. At the tip of Grindstone Neck there's a granite bench with beautiful views and a short hiking trail along the shore. Summer events include the Schoodic Arts for All Festival in late July/early August (schoodicartsforall.org), the Winter Harbor Lobster Festival on the second Saturday in August, and the week-long Winter Harbor Music Festival (winterharbormusicfestival.com) in late August. Visit jameskaiser.com for lodging and camping info.

Restaurants

★ WHARF GALLERY & GRILL $$$ (Lnch)

Perched on a wharf overlooking Corea Harbor (10-minute drive east of Birch Harbor), Wharf Gallery & Grill is one of the most scenic lobster shacks in Maine. (13 Gibbs Lane, 207-963-9077, corealunch.com)

★ J.M. GERRISH $$$ (Brk, Lnch)

This retro cafe/ice cream parlor offers tasty breakfasts (eggs, baked goods) and lunches (sandwiches, burgers, chowder). Best coffee in Winter Harbor. (352 Main Street, 207-963-7000)

THE FISHERMAN'S GALLEY $$$ (Lnch, Din)

Family-owned since 1947, the Fisherman's Galley serves lobster, shellfish, and classic Maine seafood. There's also beer, wine, and a special lobster Bloody Mary. (7 Newman Street, 207-963-5585, fishermansgalleymaine.com)

THE PICKLED WRINKLE $$$ (Lnch, Din)

Burgers, pizza, wings, and fried cheese curds are on the menu at this popular bar/restaurant. (9 East Schoodic Drive, 207-963-7916, thepickledwrinkle.com)

Adventures

SEA SCHOODIC KAYAK & BIKE

Conveniently located between downtown Winter Harbor and Acadia's Schoodic entrance, Sea Schoodic rents bikes for all ages plus kayaks for use on nearby Jones Pond. (8 Duck Pond Road, 833-724-6634, seaschoodic.com)

ACADIA PUFFIN CRUISE

This 2.5-hour cruise departs Winter Harbor and heads to Petit Manan Island, home to a small puffin colony and the second-tallest lighthouse in Maine. (147 Backshore Road, 207-598-7900, acadiapuffincruise.com)

Frazer Point

Schoodic Peninsula

Schoodic Loop Road turns south off Route 186 just east of Winter Harbor. Roughly one mile down the road there's a turnoff to the ranger-staffed Schoodic Woods Campground Welcome Center. This is a good place to ditch your car and ride the free Island Explorer Shuttle.

FRAZER POINT PICNIC AREA

You'll find picnic tables, fire rings, restrooms, and drinking water at this water-font picnic area. A 40-foot wooden pier juts into Mosquito Harbor just north of Frazer Point. Bicyclists arriving by car can park at Frazer Point and ride Schoodic Loop Road to Wonsqueak Harbor, then cut back to Frazer Point on dedicated bike paths. Frazer point is named for Thomas Frazer, a black man who settled here with his wife and seven children in the late 1700s, becoming the region's first non-native settler. Beyond Frazer Point, Schoodic Loop Road is one-way only, and parking is only permitted in designated pull-outs and parking areas.

WINTER HARBOR LIGHTHOUSE

Continue south along Schoodic Loop Road, enjoying terrific views of Winter Harbor to the right. Across the harbor is Mark Island, home to Winter Harbor Lighthouse. Built in 1856, the 19-foot tower was faithfully lit by a series of nine lighthouse keepers until 1933, when the light was discontinued and replaced by a lighted buoy offshore. Now privately owned, the lighthouse has been occupied by no fewer than five writers since 1933.

Schoodic Institute

SCHOODIC HEAD

The remnant of a 420-million-year-old volcano, Schoodic Head is the highest point on Schoodic Peninsula. Hiking is my favorite way to reach the 440-foot summit (p.272), but driving is also an option. About 2.5 miles south of Frazer Point, turn left onto unpaved Mountain Road (4WD recommended) and follow it to a small parking area located a short stroll from the summit.

BIG MOOSE ISLAND

As Schoodic Loop Road approaches its southern limit it crosses a large tidal marsh that separates Schoodic Peninsula from Big Moose Island. Turn right onto two-way Arey Cove Road, which heads south across Big Moose Island's eastern shore to Schoodic Point.

SCHOODIC INSTITUTE

This environmental research center, located on a former top-secret U.S. Navy base, partners with Acadia National Park to study the region's ecology and natural history. Open to the public, the Schoodic Institute (schoodicinstitute.org) hosts year-round programs, lectures, and outdoor activities. The visitor center, located in Rockefeller Hall—a gorgeous brick-and-beam building loosely based on John D. Rockefeller Jr.'s sprawling Seal Harbor mansion—has fascinating exhibits about Schoodic Peninsula's ecology and military history. Visitors can also hike the 1.8-mile Sundew Trail, which explores the forest and shoreline behind the Schoodic Institute.

Schoodic Point

Perched at the southern tip of Big Moose Island, this rocky promontory offers sweeping views of the Gulf of Maine. To the west, dominating the horizon, are the graceful peaks of Mount Desert Island. To the east, Maine's rugged "Bold Coast" marches northeast to Canada.

Unlike Mount Desert Island, which is sheltered by offshore islands, Schoodic Point is fully exposed to the Atlantic Ocean. During big swells, the rocks here are bombarded by powerful waves. Hurricanes sometimes kick up monstrous waves that pound Schoodic Point with unrelenting fury. No wonder early French mapmakers supposedly labeled this point "Cape Furious." As one writer remarked in the 1890s, "Nowhere can one get a better idea of the tremendous force of the waves than here on this great stretch of bare ledge."

Always be careful when visiting Schoodic Point. On September 20, 1999, when the remnants of Hurricane Floyd kicked up 10-foot swells, a rogue wave smashed into a couple posing for a dramatic picture near the water. The wave likely killed them on impact before sweeping their bodies into the ocean. During all but the calmest swells, it's best to enjoy the power and beauty of Schoodic's rugged shore from a distance. During the biggest swells, never venture from the parking area. Note: if Schoodic Point's parking area is full, which sometimes happens on summer weekends, consider parking at the Schoodic Institute, a half-mile walk down the road.

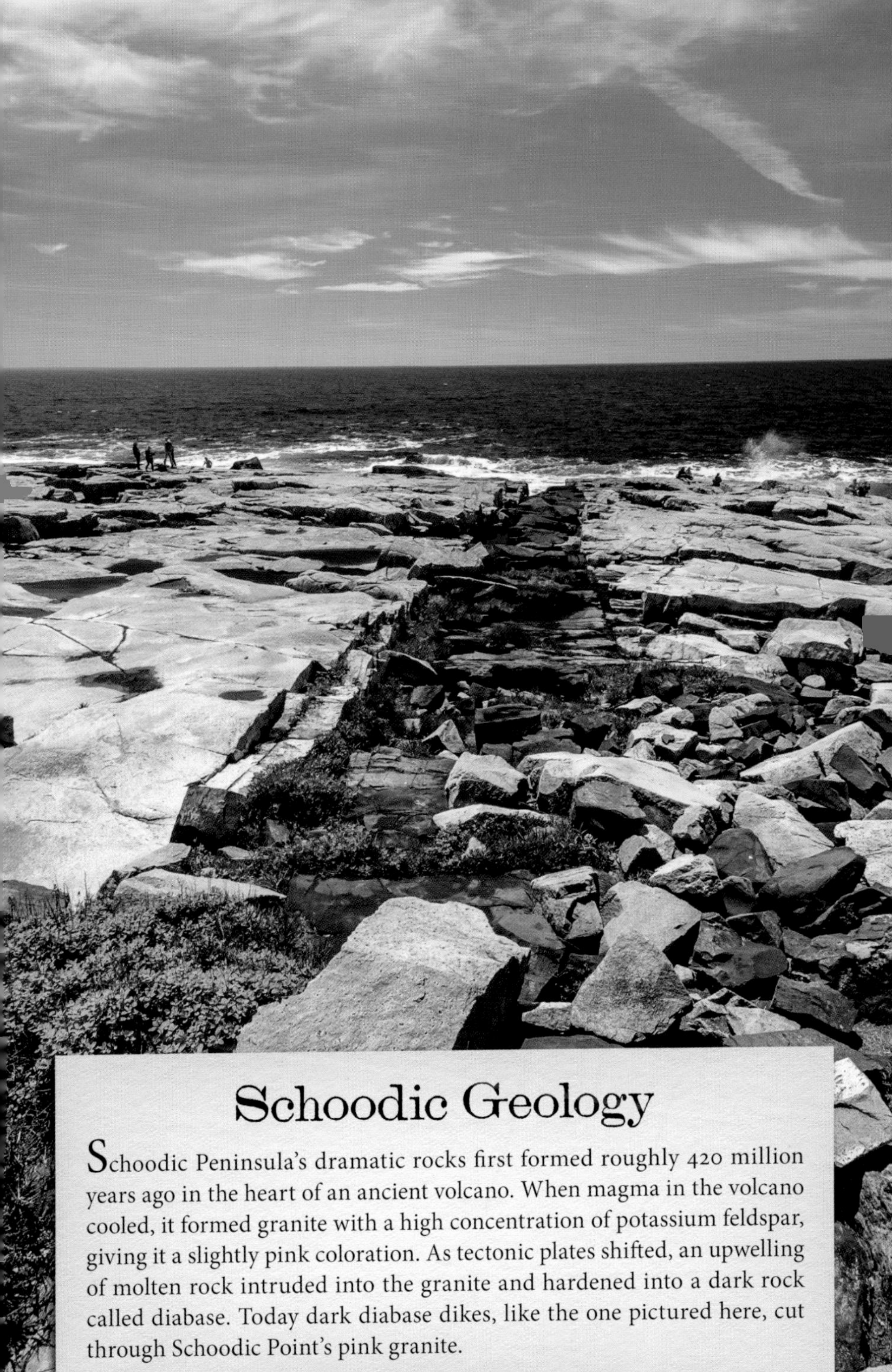

Schoodic Geology

Schoodic Peninsula's dramatic rocks first formed roughly 420 million years ago in the heart of an ancient volcano. When magma in the volcano cooled, it formed granite with a high concentration of potassium feldspar, giving it a slightly pink coloration. As tectonic plates shifted, an upwelling of molten rock intruded into the granite and hardened into a dark rock called diabase. Today dark diabase dikes, like the one pictured here, cut through Schoodic Point's pink granite.

Wonsqueak Harbor

BLUEBERRY HILL & SCHOODIC HARBOR

After passing the turnoff to Schoodic Point, Schoodic Loop Road continues one-way along the peninsula's eastern shore. Blueberry Hill Parking Area is a great place to enjoy views of Little Moose Island, which connects to the mainland at low tide, and Schoodic Island, where you can sometimes see bald eagles. Past Blueberry Hill Parking Area you'll enjoy pretty views of Schoodic Harbor, with tiny Rolling Island just offshore. After exiting Acadia National Park at Wonsqueak Harbor, Schoodic Loop Road becomes two-way. At the intersection with Route 186, turn right to return to Winter Harbor. Turn left to explore the charming coastal towns of Prospect Harbor, Corea, Stuben, and Millbridge.

Beyond Schoodic Peninsula

PROSPECT HARBOR & COREA

Follow Route 186 northeast of Schoodic Peninsula and you'll soon arrive at Prospect Harbor (population 183). It's worth a quick stop to enjoy the classic Maine scenery, including the harbor filled with lobster boats and Prospect Harbor Lighthouse, located on the eastern shore. Continue along Route 186, then turn right onto Route 195 to visit Corea (population 196), another charming harbor where you can enjoy a fresh lobster lunch at the waterfront Wharf Gallery & Grill (p.265). Nature lovers can also visit nearby Corea Heath, which protects 600 acres of forest and wetlands managed by the Frenchman Bay Conservancy (frenchmanbay.org).

Schoodic Mountain

DONNELL POND PUBLIC RESERVED LAND

This 15,000-acre protected area is one of the region's hidden treasures. In addition to Donnel Pond—great for swimming, paddling, and fishing—there are several mountains with great hiking trails. My favorite trail heads to the top of Schoodic Mountain, which rises 1,069 feet above sea level. From the peak you'll enjoy stunning panoramas of Downeast Maine, including dramatic views of Mount Desert Island. The 2.8-mile loop up Schoodic Mountain starts at the Schoodic Beach parking area. After reaching the summit, hike down to Schoodic Beach for a refreshing swim, then walk a half-mile back to the parking area.

To get to Donnell Pond Public Reserve, follow Route 1 to the town of Sullivan, then turn northeast onto Route 183. Drive about 4.5 miles, then turn left at the dark Donnell Pond sign (which can be a bit hard to see). Follow Schoodic Beach Road about five minutes to the trailhead.

PETIT MANAN POINT

Located in Steuben (pronounced "Stew-BEN"), Petit Manan Point is part of Maine Coastal Islands National Wildlife Refuge, which protects nearly 10,000 acres and over 60 offshore islands. The Petit Manan Point Division, which protects over 2,000 acres, is one of Downeast Maine's premier birdwatching destinations. Over 300 bird species have been spotted here. Several miles of hiking trails twist through the refuge, including the Hollingsworth Trail (1.8 miles roundtrip), which offers distant views of Petit Manan Island, home to a breeding puffin colony and 123-foot tall Petit Manan Lighthouse (p.111).

SCHOODIC HEAD

SUMMARY Rising 440 feet above sea level, Schoodic Head is the highest point on Schoodic Peninsula. Near the summit you'll enjoy panoramic views of Downeast Maine, including multiple lighthouses on clear days. My favorite route to Schoodic Head follows the rugged Anvil Trail, which starts just north of Blueberry Hill Parking Area. Not far from the trailhead you'll scramble up The Anvil, a steep, rocky promontory that constitutes the most challenging part of the trail. After passing through lovely spruce-fir forest, you'll reach a signed intersection. The summit, marked by a wooden sign, lies just north of the intersection, but the best views are from a rocky clearing a bit farther north. After enjoying the views head back to the intersection, then follow Schoodic Head Trail as it descends through a shady forest to Ranger Cabin Road. The east end of Ranger Cabin Road connects with the Alder Trail, an easy path (popular with birders) that heads back to Blueberry Hill parking area.

TRAILHEAD A wooden sign marks the start of the Anvil Trail, located 700 feet north of Blueberry Hill Parking Area off Schoodic Loop Road.

TRAIL INFO

RATING: Moderate

DISTANCE: 2.3 miles, round-trip

HIKING TIME: 2 hours

ELEVATION CHANGE: 440 feet

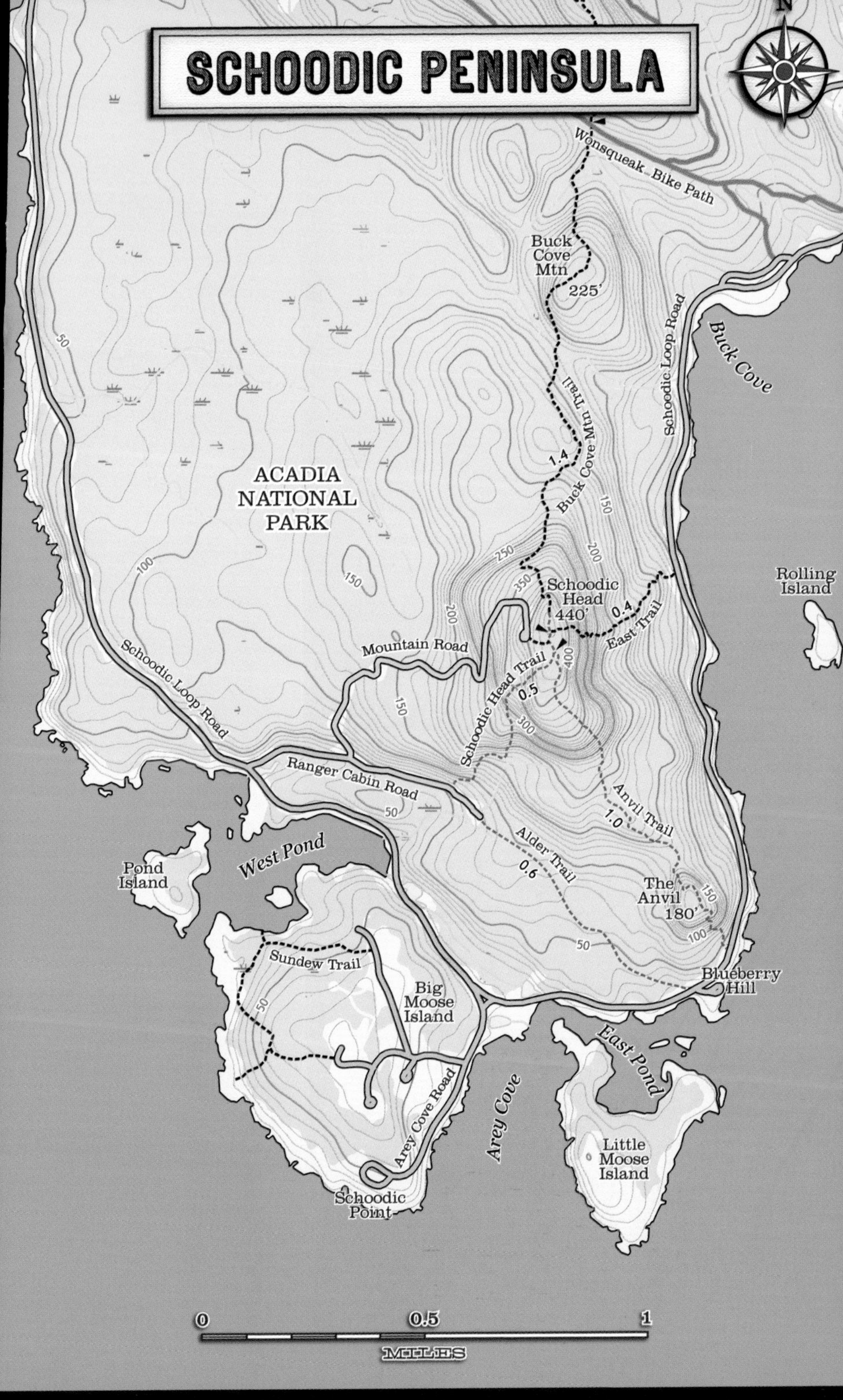
SCHOODIC PENINSULA
N
Wonsqueak Bike Path
Buck Cove Mtn
225'
Schoodic Loop Road
Buck Cove
Buck Cove Mtn Trail
1.4
ACADIA NATIONAL PARK
Rolling Island
Schoodic Head
440'
0.4
East Trail
Mountain Road
Schoodic Head Trail
0.5
Schoodic Loop Road
Ranger Cabin Road
Anvil Trail
1.0
Alder Trail
0.6
West Pond
Pond Island
The Anvil
180'
Sundew Trail
Big Moose Island
Blueberry Hill
East Pond
Arey Cove Road
Arey Cove
Little Moose Island
Schoodic Point
0
0.5
1
MILES

ISLE AU HAUT

LOCATED 15 MILES southwest of Mount Desert Island, Isle au Haut is Acadia's most far-flung parcel of property. While Mount Desert Island is defined by tourism, Isle au Haut (pronounced "I'll-a-HO") is a working Maine island where fishing has been the primary occupation for over two centuries. Only a few dozen people live year-round on the six-mile long, two-mile wide island, roughly half of which belongs to Acadia National Park. This is arguably the most pristine coastal landscape in Maine. If "rugged," "remote," and "rock-bound" are some of your favorite words, it's time to add "Isle au Haut" to your vocabulary.

Isle au Haut ("High Island") was named by the French explorer Samuel Champlain in 1604. Although Champlain voyaged up and down the Maine coast, he named very few places. But Isle au Haut, with its tallest peak rising 543 feet above the water, was too obvious to remain anonymous. Not surprisingly, Isle au Haut is great for hiking. Over 18 miles of hiking trails crisscross the park. But other than hiking, relaxing, and soaking in the bold scenery, there's not much else to do on Isle au Haut, which is exactly why some people love it.

Isle au Haut is situated farther into the Atlantic than any other large island in Maine. Getting there definitely requires some extra effort, but the logistics are surprisingly easy. First, drive to the small, beautiful town of Stonington (population 1,000) on Deer Isle, six miles north of Isle au Haut. (Bar Harbor to Stonington is a roughly two-hour drive.) From Stonington, catch the mail boat ferry to Isle au Haut (207-367-5193, isleauhaut.com). From June to mid-October, the ferry stops at Duck Harbor near Acadia's best hiking trails. Off-season you'll need to hike five miles to Duck Harbor from Town Landing.

For thousands of years, native tribes paddled to Isle au Haut to gather sweetgrass and hunt ducks by driving them into the island's narrow harbor (now named Duck Harbor). The first white settler arrived in 1772. Fifty years later, roughly 200 people lived on Isle au Haut, most of them fishermen who enjoyed the island's close proximity to rich, offshore fishing grounds. In 1860, a lobster cannery opened on Isle au Haut, and the population swelled to a peak of nearly 300. But when gas-powered engines became available in the early 1900s, fishermen could commute from the mainland, and Isle au Haut's population plummeted. Electricity didn't arrive until 1970, and phone service arrived in 1988! Today the island boasts roughly 70 year-round residents, including author Linda Greenlaw, the female swordfish captain chronicled in *The Perfect Storm*.

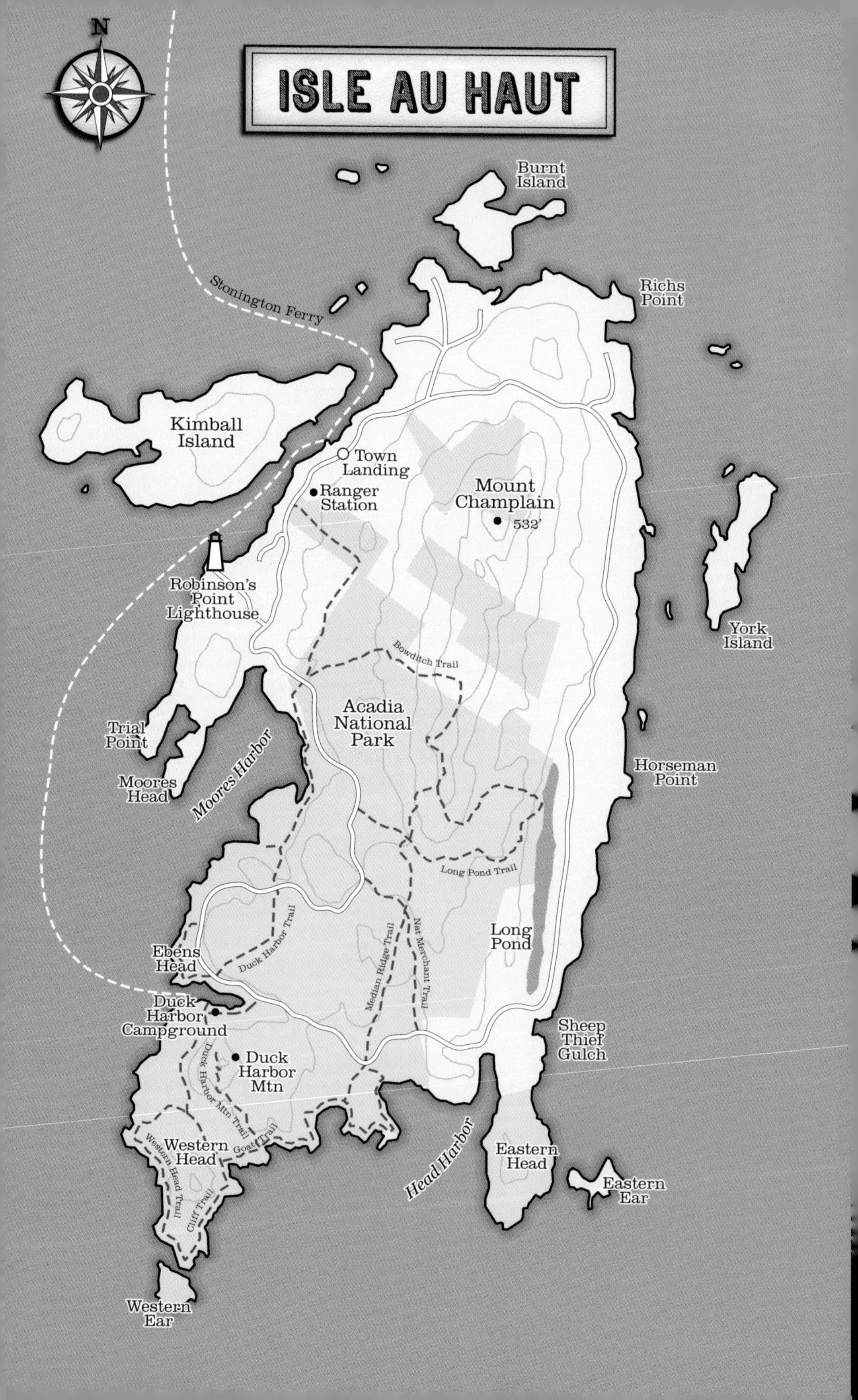

ISLE AU HAUT

Burnt Island
Stonington Ferry
Richs Point
Kimball Island
Town Landing
Ranger Station
Mount Champlain
532'
Robinson's Point Lighthouse
York Island
Bowditch Trail
Acadia National Park
Trial Point
Moores Harbor
Moores Head
Horseman Point
Long Pond Trail
Duck Harbor Trail
Median Ridge Trail
Nat Merchant Trail
Long Pond
Ebens Head
Duck Harbor Campground
Sheep Thief Gulch
Duck Harbor Mtn
Duck Harbor Mtn Trail
Goat Trail
Western Head
Western Head Trail
Cliff Trail
Head Harbor
Eastern Head
Eastern Ear
Western Ear

Lodging

Located at historic Robinson Point Lighthouse, **The Keepers House** offers the only lodging on Isle au Haut. Breakfast, lunch, and candle-lit dinners are included. Bicycles and a rowboat are available to guests. (207-335-2990, keepershouse.com)

Camping

Acadia's **Duck Harbor Campground**, perched on a hill above Duck Harbor, has five 8 x 12-foot lean-to shelters that sleep up to six people each. Facilities include fire rings, picnic tables, a fresh water pump, and a composting toilet. Open May 15 to October 15. Reservations (required) become available April 1 on recreation.gov. Summer dates are often booked within minutes of becoming available.

Town Landing

Isle au Haut's tiny "downtown" centers around the **Isle au Haut Cooperative Store** (207-335-5211, theislandstore.net), a community-owned general store near the town pier that sells groceries and basic supplies. Nearby **The Maine Lobster Lady** (207-335-5141, mainelobsterlady.com) sells delicious lobster rolls, seafood, and breakfast sandwiches from June through October. Just up the road is **Shore Shop Gifts** (207-335-2244, shoreshopgifts.com), which features local Maine artisans. Just down the road is Acadia's Isle au Haut **Ranger Station** (207-335-5551), which caps day-use visitors to just 128 per day.

Duck Harbor Mountain

Hiking

Isle au Haut's best hiking trails are concentrated at the southern tip of the island near Duck Harbor. My favorite hike is **Duck Harbor Mountain Trail** (strenuous, 1.2 miles), which rises 300 feet to the summit of Duck Harbor Mountain, where you'll enjoy sweeping views of southern Isle au Haut. A great loop hike from Duck Harbor follows the Duck Harbor Mountain Trail, then loops back to Duck Harbor along the moderate **Goat Trail**, **Cliff Trail, Western Head Trail,** and **Western Head Road Trail** (strenuous, 3.5 miles). Another good option is the **Bowditch Trail** (moderate, 2 miles), which heads to the 405-foot summit of Bowditch Mountain. If you're looking for something less challenging, **Ebens Head Trail** (easy, 0.8 miles) explores the beautiful shoreline just north of Duck Harbor. It's also possible to hike to the forested top of 543-foot Mount Champlain, the highest point on the island. An unmarked trail to Champlain's summit starts near the north end of Isle au Haut. Note: hiking trails on Isle au Haut are often rugged and overgrown. Watch your step!

Biking

There are five miles of paved roads and seven miles of unpaved roads on Isle au Haut. If you'd like to explore the entire island, a mountain bike is your best bet. But the island's roads aren't nearly as interesting or picturesque as its hiking trails, where bikes are prohibited. You can rent bikes from the Isle au Haut Ferry Service or bring your own for an additional fee.

ISLE AU HAUT
N
Moores Head
Stonington Ferry
Sharks Point
Ebens Head Trail
0.8
Ebens Head
Duck Harbor
Duck Harbor Trail
0.8
0.3
Wentworth Mtn
ACADIA NATIONAL PARK
Long Pond Trail
0.4
0.5
0.4
Median Ridge Trail
1.1
Nat Merchant Trail
0.7
Duck Harbor Campground
0.3
Duck Harbor Mtn
Duck Harbor Mtn Trail
1.2
Western Head Road
0.6
0.3
Goat Trail
0.9
0.3
Goat Trail
0.8
Merchants Cove
Merchants Point
Barred Harbor
Squeaker Cove
Western Head Trail
1.3
Western Head
Cliff Trail
0.7
Western Ear
Gulf of Maine
0
0.5
1
MILES

Isle au Haut & Kimball Island

OFFSHORE ISLANDS

OVER 3,000 ISLANDS dot the coast of Maine—one of the highest concentrations of islands anywhere in the world. Yet just 15 Maine islands are inhabited year-round. These islands, home to rugged individuals who mostly make their living from the sea, are some of the most interesting places in America. And four of them are accessible by boat from Mount Desert Island.

Just south of MDI lie the Cranberry Isles (p.285), a beautiful archipelago of five small islands. The two largest, Islesford and Great Cranberry, have year-round communities, and you can visit both on ferries that depart from Northeast Harbor and Southwest Harbor. A few miles southwest lie the even more remote islands of Frenchboro (p.293) and Swan's Island (p.295), both accessible by ferry from Bass Harbor. A fifth year-round island, Isle au Haut (p.275), is accessible by ferry from Stonington on Deer Isle.

Though largely forgotten today, Maine's offshore islands played an important role in early American history. Long before colonists landed at Jamestown, thousands of Europeans fished the rich Gulf of Maine. Arriving each spring, they hauled massive amounts of cod, which provided cheap, nutritious protein for Europe's rapidly growing populations. When settlers arrived in Maine in the late 1700s, offshore islands were some of the most sought-after real estate due to their close proximity to fishing grounds and shipping routes. They were also terrific places to raise livestock because animals couldn't escape. By the late 1800s, over 300 Maine islands were populated year-round.

Within a few decades, however, railroads and trucks displaced ships as the most important forms of transportation. Suddenly, islanders found themselves isolated from the modern world. Over the past century, most offshore islands were abandoned. Greater job opportunities lured many islanders away, and those that remained faced higher prices for just about everything. In recent years, however, the internet has opened up new economic possibilities. Technology may have robbed islands of their lifeblood a century ago, but it might lure a new generation of digital nomads seeking out the slow, easygoing rhythms that have always characterized Maine island life.

CRANBERRY ISLES

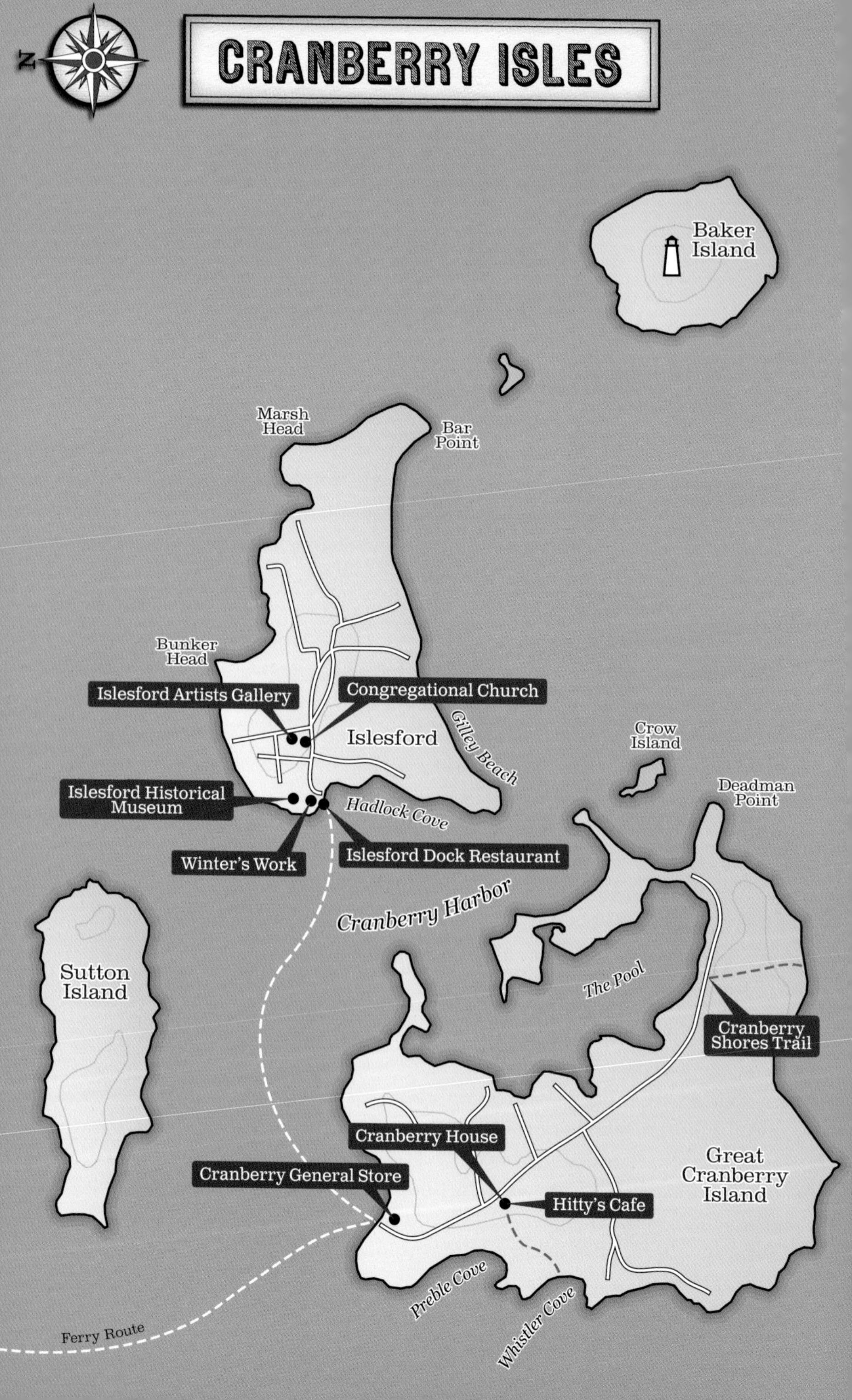

Baker Island
Marsh Head
Bar Point
Bunker Head
Islesford Artists Gallery
Congregational Church
Islesford
Gilley Beach
Crow Island
Islesford Historical Museum
Hadlock Cove
Deadman Point
Winter's Work
Islesford Dock Restaurant
Cranberry Harbor
Sutton Island
The Pool
Cranberry Shores Trail
Cranberry House
Cranberry General Store
Hitty's Cafe
Great Cranberry Island
Preble Cove
Whistler Cove
Ferry Route

CRANBERRY ISLES

THESE FIVE ISLANDS—Great Cranberry, Islesford, Sutton, Baker, and Bear—lie just south of Mount Desert Island. First settled in the late 1700s, the Cranberries acquired their name from wild low-bush cranberries that grow there. A century ago, all five islands were occupied year-round. Today only Great Cranberry and Islesford have year-round populations. Sutton Island has only summer residents, while Baker Island and Bear Island are owned by Acadia National Park. Today the combined year-round population of Islesford and Great Cranberry is roughly 100 people.

Great Cranberry and Islesford are both worth a visit. Their intriguing mix of lobstermen, artists, and wealthy summer folks—combined with spectacular views of Mount Desert Island—makes for a great day trip. Far removed from traffic and crowds, the pace of life is distinctly relaxed on the Cranberries. Don't be surprised if strangers wave as you walk past.

Passenger ferries make round-trip journeys among the Cranberry Isles, so you can visit Great Cranberry and Islesford on a single ticket. I personally like visiting Great Cranberry in the morning, then cruising to Islesford in the afternoon. Both can be explored on foot, but biking is also an option.

At their peak nearly 100 years ago, Great Cranberry and Islesford had booming shipyards, multiple schools, and vibrant fishing fleets. Over the past century, however, year-round populations have dwindled. But the economic pulse of these islands still revolves around the sea, with lobstering and boatbuilding as the primary occupations.

Getting to the Cranberry Isles

Beal & Bunker The official mailboat to the Cranberry Isles, in service since 1950, departs year-round from Northeast Harbor. (207-244-3575)

Cranberry Cove Ferry From Memorial Day through September, Cranberry Cove Ferry offers daily shuttles between Southwest Harbor and the Cranberry Isles. (207-244-5882, cranberrycoveferry.com)

Sea Princess Departing daily from Northeast Harbor, *Sea Princess* offers park ranger-narrated nature cruises through the Cranberry Isles, including a visit to Islesford. (207-276-5352, barharborcruises.com)

Water Taxis Several boats offer on-demand service to the Cranberry Isles. Cadillac Water Taxi (207-801-1898) is the most popular. Other good options include *The Delight* (207-244-5724) and *Elizabeth T.* (sailacadia.com)

Islesford

Islesford, aka "Little Cranberry Island," is the most populated of the Cranberry Isles, with roughly 70 year-round residents and 200 summer residents. It's also the most popular island to visit thanks to its dockside restaurant, historical museum, and numerous art galleries. You can bring a bike, but it's just as easy to walk around the roughly 200-acre island, which has a handful of paved roads. Gilley Beach, on the island's southern shore, makes a nice destination. The economic heart of the island is the Islesford Lobster Co-op, located next to the town pier, where lobstermen unload their catch throughout the day.

★ ISLESFORD HISTORICAL MUSEUM

This small museum, open since 1928, features exhibits and artifacts pertaining to the history, people, and culture of Islesford. The permanent collection has a strong maritime emphasis, and temporary exhibits change each year. The museum, operated by Acadia National Park since 1948, is open daily mid-June through September. (207-288-3338)

★ ISLESFORD DOCK RESTAURANT $$$ (Lnch, Din)

Perched on a 200-year-old coal dock overlooking the harbor, this waterfront restaurant offers great food and stunning views of Mount Desert Island. The menu offers plenty of fresh seafood and creative entrees, plus burgers, salads, and sandwiches. Open Wednesday through Sunday, June through September. (207-244-7494, islesforddock.com)

★ ART GALLERIES

Islesford Dock is home to Winter's Work (207-244-3500, winterswork.com), Islesford Pottery (207-244-9108), and the Islesford Dock Gallery. Just up the road is Islesford Artists (Mosswood Road, islesfordartists.com), a charming gallery founded by lobsterman/artist Dan Fernald that showcases the work of local artists. A bit further up the road you'll find signs pointing you to Island Girl Seaglass, which features folksy seaglass jewelry.

Art lovers should also visit the Islesford Congregational Church, which has beautiful seaglass windows by Ashley Bryan, Islesford's most famous artist. Bryan, who wrote and illustrated award-winning childrens books about the African-American experience, lived on Islesford for three decades before passing away in 2022. Learn more at ashleybryancenter.org.

LITTLE CRANBERRY LOBSTER

This small, tidy shack near the pier sells fresh seafood, snacks, cold drinks, and branded gifts. They also ship live lobster anywhere in the country. (844-494-2529, littlecranberrylobster.com)

LOBSTER BOAT TOUR

Islesford resident Stefanie Alley offers 90-minute tours on her lobster boat. During the tour she hauls traps and explains the lobstering process. (207-244-7466)

Great Cranberry Island

At 1,000 acres, Great Cranberry is by far the largest of the Cranberry Isles. Although its year-round population is just 40 people, its summer population swells to roughly 400. In addition to lobstering and boatbuilding, entrepreneurial locals now grow and harvest oysters in The Pool, a shallow inlet on the north side of the island. Delicious Cranberry Oysters (cranberryoysters.com) are available for preorder at the Cranberry General Store.

A two-mile road heads from the town dock to the eastern tip of the island. It's possible to explore the island on foot or bike, but another great option is the Great Cranberry Explorer, an 8-person golf cart that makes regular runs up and down the road. The narrated Explorer, driven by volunteers from the local Historical Society, is free to ride (donations are appreciated). I personally enjoy riding the Explorer to the tip of the island, hiking the Cranberry Shores Trail, then flagging down the Explorer for a ride to Cranberry House.

★CRANBERRY HOUSE

Located a half-mile from the town pier (about a 15-minute walk), Cranberry House is home to the Preble-Marr Museum, which explores the history of Great Cranberry Island. In addition to island artifacts and changing exhibits, the museum celebrates the book *Hitty, Her First Hundred Years* (winner of the 1930 Newbery Medal), written by former Great Cranberry summer resident Rachel Field. Above the museum is the Art Center, a gathering place for classes, movies, and lectures. Open Memorial Day to Columbus Day (207-244-7800, gcihs.org)

★ HITTY'S CAFE $$$ (Lnch)

Great Cranberry Island's best restaurant, located in Cranberry House, offers a delicious menu designed by Brazilian chef Cezar Ferreira. Choose from sandwiches, paninis, lobster rolls, soups, salads, and baked goods. The outdoor deck is a great place to enjoy coffee or a quick snack. Open 10am–4pm, Memorial Day to Columbus Day (207-244-7845)

CRANBERRY GENERAL STORE (Brk, Lnch)

Located next to the town dock, the Cranberry General Store sells basic food and supplies. The adjacent Seawich Café serves takeout burgers, sandwiches, and lobster rolls. (207-244-0622)

WHISTLER COVE TRAIL

This easy, one-mile trail starts behind Cranberry House, passes through a shady forest (bring insect repellent), and ends at Whistler Cove, where a cobblestone beach offers nice views of Mount Desert Island from Great Cranberry's eastern shore. The Whistler Cove Trail takes about 30 minutes round-trip.

CRANBERRY SHORES

Located near the eastern tip of the island, this 19-acre preserve is managed by Maine Coast Heritage Trust. A half-mile trail, which starts 1.6 miles down the road from the town dock, passes through spruce-fir forest en route to the rocky shore—a great place to observe seabirds and marine wildlife. (mcht.org)

Baker Island Lighthouse

Built in 1828, Baker Island Lighthouse is one of the oldest lighthouses in the region. President John Quincy Adams authorized its construction to protect mariners from nearby shoals, which have caused at least nine shipwrecks. The lighthouse is located at the highest point on Baker Island, 72 feet above sea level. William Gilley became the lighthouse's first keeper, earning an annual salary of $350 and all the sperm whale oil his family could use. Gilley used his earnings to buy Great Duck Island, five miles south, to raise sheep. In 1849, the Whig political party came to power, and Gilley was offered a choice: join the Whigs or lose his lucrative job as lighthouse keeper. Gilley defiantly boasted he would not change his political affiliation "for all the lighthouses in the United States." After he was replaced, Gilley moved to Great Duck Island and stayed there, virtually alone, for nearly two decades. His sons, meanwhile, made life as difficult as possible for the new lighthouse keepers. When Gilley was nearly 80 he returned to Baker Island to live with his married son, ultimately passing away at the age of 92. Baker Island Lighthouse's original 26-foot tall tower was replaced with the current 43-foot tower in 1855. Rising 105 feet above sea level, it's one of the highest lights in the region. In 1966, Baker Island light was fully automated.

Baker Island

This 162-acre island—the easternmost of the Cranberry Isles— was last inhabited in 1927. Today nearly all of the island belongs to Acadia National Park. Only two small houses and a rocky stretch of shore called The Dancefloor are privately owned. From mid-June to mid-September, you can explore Baker Island on a five-hour, ranger-guided cruise aboard the *Miss Samantha* (barharborwhales.com), which departs from Bar Harbor. En route to Baker Island you'll enjoy dramatic views of eastern Mount Desert Island. A small launch shuttles visitors from *Miss Samantha* to Baker Island. Once ashore, you'll enjoy fabulous views, visit the historic lighthouse, and learn about the island's history.

In the early 1800s, MDI residents William and Hannah Gilley rowed their three young children across Great Harbor to become Baker Island's first permanent settlers. (Where the name Baker came from remains a mystery.) The Gilleys, who eventually had 12 children, paid no money for the unoccupied island, which has no good harbor. They cut trees, planted crops, and raised cows, chickens, sheep, and hogs. Fish, lobster, and seabirds provided additional food. Hannah and her daughters spun wool to make homemade clothes, and the children went barefoot most of the year. Willliam and Hannah's youngest son, John, became the subject of the 1899 biography *John Gilley of Baker's Island*, written by former Harvard President Charles Eliot. The book, still in print today, chronicles the rugged, self-sufficient lifestyle of 19th-century Maine islanders. Descendants of William and Hannah lived on Baker Island for over 120 years.

Frenchboro

ISLANDS SOUTH OF BASS HARBOR

Frenchboro

This 1,500-acre island, home to a year-round population of roughly 40 people, is officially called Long Island. But there are several Long Islands in Maine, so locals call this one Frenchboro, which is the name of the island's single tiny village. The island was first settled in 1813, and in 1910 the population peaked at 197. Since then a steady stream of islanders have left for the mainland. Today the local economy revolves around lobstering. Despite the island's small population, nearly a dozen children attend K-7 in the island's one-room schoolhouse. The Frenchboro Library and Historical Society (207-334-2924) is a great place to learn about the island's history.

Frenchboro is famous for its annual Lobster Festival, held the second Saturday of August. The festival is the biggest party of the year, attracting over 500 people who arrive by lobster boat, private yacht, or a special ferry that departs from Bass Harbor in the morning. If you miss the festival, you can still enjoy fresh lobster at Lunt's Dockside Deli (207-334-2922, luntsdeli.com) in July and August. Unless you have your own boat, the best way to visit Frenchboro is with Island Cruises (p.259), which offers day trips to Frenchboro from Bass Harbor.

Placentia

Located halfway between Mount Desert Island and Swan's Island, Placentia has one of the region's most intriguing histories. In 1948, two 36-year-olds, Arthur and Nancy Kellam, purchased this 552-acre island for $7,500. For the next 35 years, the couple lived on Placentia in near total seclusion. There was no running water or electricity. They chopped their own wood and grew their own vegetables. And when the Kellams needed supplies such as kerosene or batteries, they rowed two miles to Bass Harbor in a wooden dory.

Art Kellam was a Cornell-educated engineer who worked on military aircraft for the Lockheed Corporation. Nan graduated from the University of Wisconsin. During WWII the couple lived in Southern California, and following the war they made the fateful decision to abandon modern life. After a nationwide search for a remote island, the Kellams bought Placentia. According to Nan's journal: "At 3 o' clock on the 23rd of May, Art cashed his last salary check, then we made a little round of calls, paying respects to civilization before turning our backs on it ... we hoped to build a simple house and a simple life, to learn to appreciate fundamental things."

Art died in 1985, and his ashes were spread on Placentia. Nan spent three summers and one winter by herself on the island, then moved to Bass Harbor. Following her death in 2001, the Nature Conservancy gained possession of Placentia. The Kellams' story is chronicled in the book *We Were An Island*.

Swan's Island

Lying six miles southwest of Mount Desert Island, Swan's Island boasts 7,000 acres of classic coastal scenery and one of the prettiest harbors in Maine. Home to roughly 350 year-round residents, Swan's Island feels like stepping back in time. Other than satellite TV and internet, little has changed over the past several decades, and the island's tight-knit community continues to live a life that revolves almost entirely around the sea. If you're looking for the salt of the earth, it doesn't get much saltier than Swan's Island.

When French explorer Samuel Champlain first set eyes on the island in 1604, he named it *Brûlé Côté*, "Burnt Coast"—presumably because wildfires had recently burned the island. Over the years, Brule Cote's pronunciation and spelling was twisted and mangled to "Burnt Coat," which is now the official name of Swan's Island's most famous harbor. Even today, Swan's Island continues to engage in linguistic lawlessness. Since 1986, island residents have made a deliberate attempt to restore the historically accurate apostrophe to Swan's Island—in defiance of nautical charts and the U.S. Postal Service.

Swan's Island's first white settler was Thomas Kench, who fled here after going AWOL during the Revolutionary War. For over a decade, Kench lived on the island as a hermit. He awoke one morning to find settlers arriving by boat, who told him the island had been purchased by his former Revolutionary War commander, Colonel James Swan. Tensions between Swan and Kench must have eased considerably by then. Kench lived on the island for an additional decade before moving to the mainland.

To populate his new island, Colonel Swan offered 100 acres to any homesteader who promised to stay at least seven years. The first man to accept this offer was David Smith, who arrived from New Hampshire in 1791. Over the course of his life, Smith fathered 27 children by three wives, earning him the local nickname "King David." (Today many Swan's Island residents can trace their family lineage back to King David.)

At its peak in the late 1800s, Swan's Island's population swelled to over 700 citizens. Its hardworking fishermen were consistently ranked first or second in Maine in terms of annual catch. But during the 1900s, when gas-powered engines made offshore fishing from the mainland possible, Swan's Island lost over half of its year-round population.

GETTING TO SWAN'S ISLAND

Swan's Island is accessible via a 30-minute ferry that departs Bass Harbor several times daily (schedules posted at maine.gov/mdot/ferry/swansisland). Tickets are available at the ferry terminal in Bass Harbor (207-244-3254). Be careful taking your car during the busy summer months, when space on return trips is limited. Better to rent bikes in Southwest Harbor (p.252) and enjoy them on Swan's Island's 20 miles of paved, uncrowded roads.

SWAN'S ISLAND

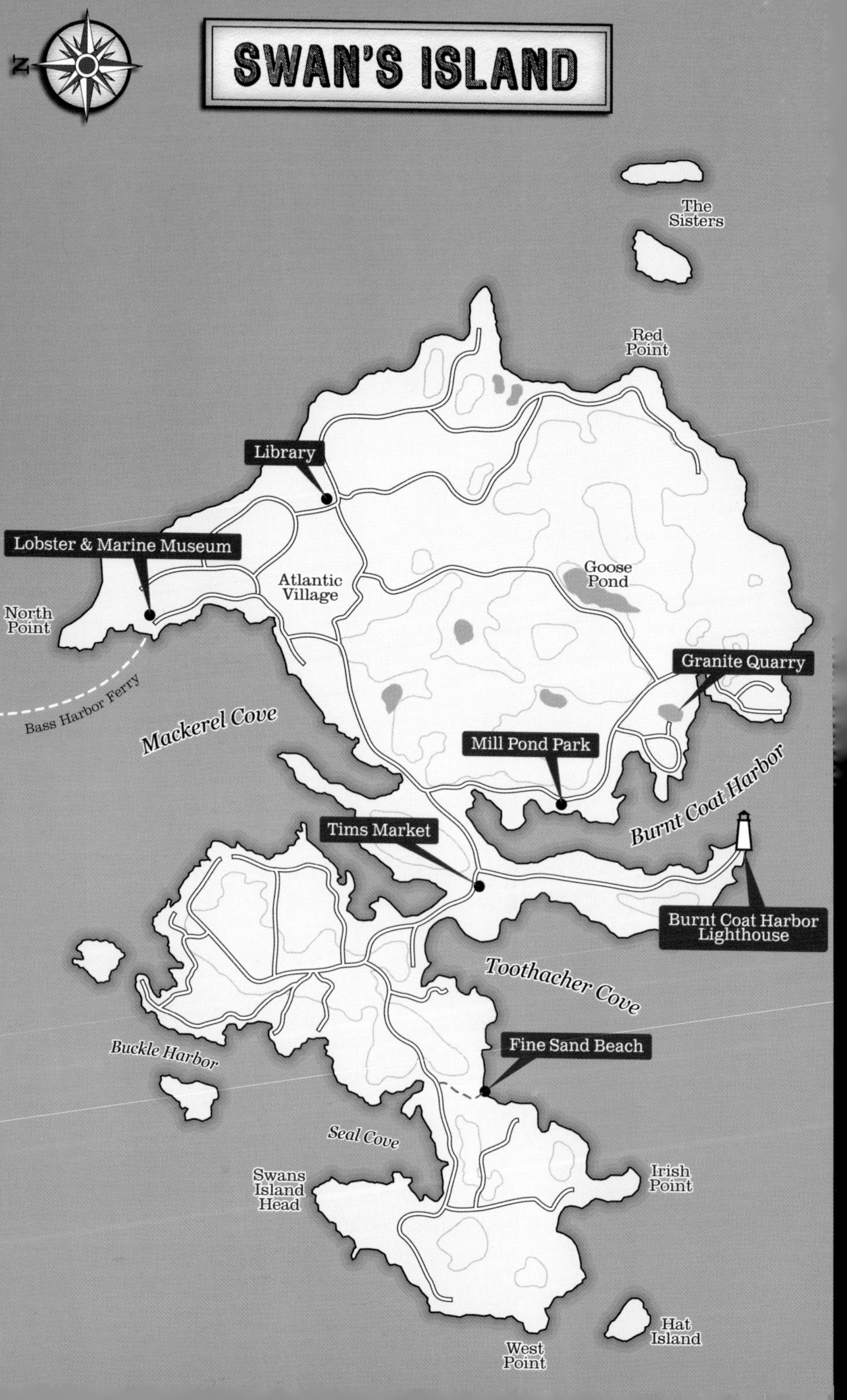

The Sisters
Red Point
Library
Lobster & Marine Museum
Atlantic Village
Goose Pond
North Point
Granite Quarry
Bass Harbor Ferry
Mackerel Cove
Mill Pond Park
Burnt Coat Harbor
Tims Market
Burnt Coat Harbor Lighthouse
Toothacher Cove
Buckle Harbor
Fine Sand Beach
Seal Cove
Swans Island Head
Irish Point
Hat Island
West Point

★ BURNT COAT HARBOR LIGHTHOUSE

Built in 1872, automated in 1975, and fully restored in 2022, this gorgeous lighthouse is the top destination on Swan's Island. Located at the tip of Hockamock Head, the lighthouse is roughly four miles from the ferry terminal. The first floor of the keeper's house has history and art exhibits. The second floor is available as a weekly rental. Guided tours take visitors to the top of the 35-foot tower, which offers tremendous views of Burnt Coat Harbor from its square iron platform. Visitors can also enjoy 1.8 miles of hiking trails on Hockamock Head. The Long Point Beach Trail twists through spruce forest along the ocean shore and passes a cobble beach. The Burying Point Trail twists through spruce forest on the harbor shore and passes a sandy beach. (burntcoatharborlight.com)

★ FINE SAND BEACH

One of the most beautiful beaches in Maine. On a hot summer day, there's no better place to swim in the icy water and soak in the sun. The beach is accessible via a short hiking trail through the woods.

★ LOBSTER & MARINE MUSEUM

Located near the ferry terminal, this small museum offers a fascinating glimpse into the human history of Swan's Island, from native times to the present day. There are several rooms of fishing and nautical artifacts, plus a display on natural history. (207-526-4423, swansislandlobsterandmarinemuseum.org)

TIMS ISLAND MARKET & TAKEOUT

This tiny market and food trailer is the social hub of Swan's Island. Check out flyers by the door to find out what's happening on the island. Basic food and supplies are available in the market, and the adjacent trailer serves seafood rolls, burgers, sandwiches, and pizza. (207-526-4410, tims-swans-island.com)

SWAN'S ISLAND LIBRARY

Books, wifi, and rotating historical exhibits. (451 Atlantic Road, 207-526-4330)

MILL POND PARK

Located just down the hill from the Mill Pond Health Center, this lovely park has picnic tables, grills, and terrific views of Burnt Coat Harbor.

GRANITE QUARRY

The island's old granite quarry is now a swimming hole. Even if you don't go swimming, the road to the quarry offers some of the best views on the island.

SWEET CHARIOT MUSIC FESTIVAL

In early August, Swan's Island hosts a three-night music festival, which is very popular with boaters. (sweetchariotmusicfestival.com)

JAMES SWAN

The remarkable story of James Swan, the first owner of Swan's Island, makes him one of coastal Maine's most colorful characters. In 1765, when Swan was just 11 years old, he arrived in America from Scotland. By age 17 the ambitious self-taught youngster had written a book arguing against slavery, making him one of America's earliest abolitionists. He later joined the Sons of Liberty, participated in the Boston Tea Party, and fought at Bunker Hill. Following the war, he was elected to the Massachusetts State Legislature. Shortly thereafter, Swan inherited a large fortune from a wealthy Scotsman who, though not related to Swan, admired the young man's ambition. Swan used the money to purchase and sell confiscated Tory property, multiplying his inheritance several times over.

Swan used his newfound wealth to lead an increasingly flamboyant lifestyle. He speculated in risky investments, fought and won a duel, and boasted of owning the most luxurious horse-drawn carriage in America. In 1786, Swan purchased Swan's Island and most of the small islands surrounding it. He referred to this property as his "Island Empire" and built a grand mansion on Swan's Island where he entertained guests in lavish style. But just one year after purchasing Swan's Island, many of his investments turned sour. To make up for the losses, Swan invested in riskier ventures. When trace amounts of gold were discovered on Swan's Island, Swan spent huge sums of money establishing a large mining operation. Three years later, the mining operation produced enough gold to make "one good sized wedding ring."

As Swan's debts compounded, he fled to Paris to escape his creditors and attempt to rebuild his fortune. Using aristocratic connections, Swan landed lucrative contracts with the French Army. But those contracts fell apart with the onset of the French Revolution. Although Swan escaped the guillotine, he was arrested for an alleged debt of 2 million francs. Although Swan had the money, he insisted that he did not owe it and refused to pay—a noble stance that landed him in prison for the next 22 years. While incarcerated, Swan paid the debts of many of his fellow inmates, but he refused to even speak with the man who claimed Swan owed him 2 million francs.

By the time Swan was released from prison, he was 76 years old. His wife and most of his friends had passed away. With nowhere to go, Swan returned to prison and pleaded to become an inmate again—but the prison refused. Three years later, James Swan died alone on a Paris street.

Fine Sand Beach